AMBIENT TELEVISION

Console-ing Passions: Television and Cultural Power *Edited by Lynn Spigel*

TV

AMBIENT

ANNA McCARTHY

TELEVISION

VISUAL CULTURE AND PUBLIC SPACE

DUKE UNIVERSITY PRESS DURHAM AND LONDON 2001

©2001 Duke University Press

All rights reserved

Printed in the United States of America on acid-free paper ∞

Text and photographs, except figs. 1, 2, 3, 4, 5, 7, and 28, © Anna McCarthy, 2000.

Fig. 28 and all drawings except fig. 25, © Rachel Harrison, 2000.

Designed by Amy Ruth Buchanan

Typeset in Minion by Tseng Information Systems, Inc.

Library of Congress Cataloging-in-Publication Data appear on the last printed page of this book.

FOR GUS

CONTENTS

ACKNOWLEDGMENTS

Many individuals and a variety of institutions provided invaluable assistance to this project as it developed from its inception in 1993. I must first thank six mentors. Mimi White taught me how to think about television and gave me support, encouragement, and friendship besides. I am indebted to Jim Schwoch for his many careful readings and for his intellectual generosity as a historian and theorist of electronic media. Tom Gunning and Laura Kipnis both taught me how to write and how to enjoy writing; I thank Tom for inspiring a love of the archive and for kindling my visual and historical curiosity. I thank Laura for her friendship and discernment and for demonstrating the creative, and political, work of cultural criticism. I am also particularly grateful to Mark Williams, who inspired the dissertation that became this book, and to Jeanine Basinger, my first teacher, who remains a model in the classroom and in the movie theater.

This project was supported at different stages by a number of institutions. Several research trips were funded by a dissertation year grant from the Graduate School of Northwestern University and by a research grant from the University Film and Video Association. Some research was also completed over the course of two fellowships, one from the Alumnae of Northwestern and one from the Smithsonian Institution. The College of Arts and Sciences and the department of Communications Studies at the University of North Carolina at Chapel Hill provided valuable support in the form of a research-and-study leave. I also thank the department of Cinema Studies in NYU's Tisch School of the Arts for crucial research support in the final stages.

Many curators and librarians generously shared their knowledge and time during the research process. I wish to thank the staff of the Louisiana

Collections in the New Orleans Public Library, the staff of the Louisville Public Library, Ron Simon at the Museum of Television and Radio, and Holly Paxon at the Marshall Fields archives. I particularly wish to thank the following archivists and librarians at the National Museum of American History for all their assistance: Fath Ruffins, John Fleckner, Reuben Jackson, Wendy Shay, Vanessa Broussard-Simmons, Amy Lynch, Deborra Richardson, Jim Roan, and Martin Kalfatovic. William L. Bird and Charles McGovern provided immensely valuable feedback on an early version of chapter 2. My thanks for their valuable advice and suggestions. I am also very grateful to Larry for his ombudsmanship in locating the tavern illustrations in chapter one. I am also particularly indebted to five people for their insightful research assistance and manuscript management over the course of this project: Sarah Fain, Peggy Anderson, Tony Perucci, Sudhir Mahadevan, and Charles Leary.

Several people read versions and parts of this manuscript at important times over the course of its preparation. They helped me through difficult moments in the process of writing and thinking, and I want to single them out with my thanks particularly: Rachel Adams, William Boddy, Jennifer Doyle, Laurel George, Heather Hendershot, Henry Jenkins and Ken Wissoker. I want to thank Rachel Harrison here also, for making the drawings in this book and for sharing ideas and inspiration over the duration of this project.

Numerous other scholars and friends provided all kinds of assistance in this project as well. For discussions, support, source material, and always helpful criticisms I thank Tim Anderson, Bill Balthrop, Annette Barbier, Victor Braitburg, Israel Burshatin, Rich Cante, Amanda Claybaugh, Mary Morley Cohen, Nick Couldry, Andy Cox, Ann Cvetkovich, Joe Danno, Cori Dauber, Cathy Davidson, Chad Dell, Mary DesJardins, Andrew Douglas, Spencer Downing, erik doxtader, Judith Farquhar, Mia Fineman, Magnus Fiskesjo, Ed Flounder, Adam Frank, Kati Franz, Joseba Gabilondo, David Galinsky, William Galperin, Lisa Graham, Nitin Govil, Alison Griffiths, Lawrence Grossberg, John Hanhardt, Ann Harris, Keith Harris, John Hartigan Jr., John Hartley, Amelie Hastie, Joanne Hershfield, Dave Hesmondhalgh, Brad High, Ken Hillis, Michelle Hilmes, Jonathan Horowitz, Elizabeth Hutchinson, Eithne Johnson, Victoria Johnson, Hap Kindem, Chuck Kleinhans, Arthur Knight, Antonia Lant, Sanjoy Majumder, Amy Marver, Rick Maxwell, Gerard McCarthy, Gwen McCarthy, Terence McCarthy, Molly McGarry, Meg McLagan, John McMurria, Tara McPherson, Christine Meyer, Toby Miller, José Muñoz, Jeff Montez de

Oca, Mark Olson, Katherine Ott, Marvette Perez, Della Pollock, Julie Pomerleau, Joe Probus, Lauren Rabinovitz, Chad Rafael, Nic Sammond, Cynthia Schneider, Ulrich Schoenherr, Britta Sjogren, Lynn Spigel, Evalyn Stadler, Priscilla Stadler, Tuck Stadler, Robert Stam, Theresa Tensuan, Matthew Tinkcom, Sean Uyehara, Amy Villarejo, Cary Walker, Eric Weissman, Patty White, Barbara Wilinsky, Karen Williams, Rick Wojcik, Zhang Zhen, Sophie Ziencek, Tina Zwarg.

My greatest debt, however, is to Gustavus Stadler. Not only did you read everything, even when you were really busy, but you shared your amazing insights — on television, on expressive writing, on finding peace in the world. This book is dedicated to you, Gus, with all my love.

THE PUBLIC LIVES OF TV

We tend to think of the location of the TV screen as the home, or even the living room, but this book is about television's presence in the routine locations we move through when we *leave* the house—the store, the waiting room, the bar, the train station, the airport. These sites of commerce, bureaucracy, and community, constituting the landscape of public life today, are also arenas in which we commonly encounter the television screen. TV enters the everyday built environment under numerous guises, from art to advertising, from entertainment to information. Sometimes it is in the form of a commercial TV system especially dedicated to one type of location, like CNN's Airport Network. At other times, particularly in retail stores, it is in the form of "point-of-purchase video," designed by marketers to motivate acts of consumption on the sales floor. And in other locations still, a monitor sits where it can fit, on an overhead shelf or on top of a refrigeration unit, placed there for the viewing pleasures of the space's users and employees. We don't always pay much attention to these various forms of ambient television, although, as I will suggest, they can teach us a great deal about the power politics of spectatorship and commerce in contemporary public space. What the TV set *does* outside the home—what social acts it performs, or is roped into, what struggles it embodies and intervenes in, what agencies speak through it, and which subjects it silences or alternately gives a voice—are the questions that drive this book.

The quotidian geography of TV in public is composed of sites where commerce and bureaucracy, purpose and drift, routine and event interweave, places in which television's presence remains largely unexamined by scholars and critics. In these places, as at home, the screen serves site-specific purposes, its placement and use carrying out local tasks and channeling larger socioeconomic forces into the environment—perhaps the most egregious example of the latter phenomenon is the traffic in audiences set in motion when networks like the Airport Channel or the Commuter Channel enter a place. The term *site-specific* is generally used to describe a certain genre of installation art—work designed solely for a particular place or institution, work that cannot be transplanted elsewhere.[1] But it is also a useful term for thinking about the social and spatial operations of the TV set because it focuses attention on the ways in which the audiovisual and material forms of TV blend with the social conventions and power structures of its locale. This property of the TV screen, and the micropolitics it enacts within a site, is extensively documented in historical and ethnographic studies of the domestic TV set, such as Lynn Spigel's *Make Room for TV* and David Morley's *Family Television*. As these studies show, when the TV set becomes part of the family living room, it not only adapts to the conventional spatial or sensorial arrangements of its location, but it also enters into, and takes up a position within, the immaterial networks of power that characterize family life. Such studies, scrutinizing how domestic conflicts play out in both representations and acts of TV viewing, forcefully demonstrate how TV activates, and embodies, the gendered struggles that lie beneath the surface of domestic space. Moreover, in addition to uncovering a small-scale politics of viewing—revolving around seating arrangements, lighting, authority over program choice, etc.—they show how television images play out a broader cultural ideology of space as well. By appearing to make "elsewhere" present in the home, the screen serves as a discursive and material figure for the ways in which family life is integrated into macrolevel issues of the nation, international politics, and the global marketplace.[2]

Ambient Television traces analogous processes of adapting and integrating TV, and media power, into the social rhythms and material life of spaces outside the home. The TV screen, whether it offers a private view for individuals or addresses large collectivities en masse, always manages to interweave its images, sounds, and commercial appeals into the institutional and not-so-institutional practices that define its public locations. Indeed, although we might complain about the medium's pervasive presence, writing letters to the editor or nodding vigorously when we read journalistic jeremiads against the omnipresent screen, the fact is that TV integrates into everyday environments so well that we barely notice its presence in "our taverns and our metropolitan streets"—and to update Walter Benjamin's famous litany, our shopping malls, delis, laundromats, airports, and other places besides. As several theorists building on Benjamin's figure of the *flaneur* have noted, spectatorship — visual culture's discursive positioning of subjects — is part and parcel of modern life, activated in the succession of consumer spectacles that punctuate the everyday itineraries of the shopper, the customer, the tourist, the commuter.[3]

Television's pervasive presence in public space not only makes this visual positioning of the mobile modern subject a very material and literal social fact; it also allows us to explore the variability of this process from site to site, for the ways in which the screen inhabits the local power structures and sedimentary habits associated with various public environments changes greatly from one place to another. As I will suggest over the course of this book, the site-specific nature of many institutional and personal uses of TV means that it is impossible to single out one mode of spectatorship to define the relationship between screen and environment, regardless of the latter's particular features. Rather, the diffuse network of gazes and institutions, subjects and bodies, screens and physical structures that constitutes the televisual place sustains quite particular effects in each place. There are of course continuities among these effects, as the chapters in this book make clear, but they still arise from the flexibility and adaptability of TV technology. Diverse site-specific practices of television convey the spatial complexity of the medium, its ability both to position people in physical locations and to render visible the entwined domains of contest, control, and consumption that define such places within broader cultural logics of space.

A preliminary hint of the challenges involved in seeing television as a site-specific form, and in discerning its roles in particular places accordingly, emerges in the awkward and uncertain terminology that categorizes the nondomestic TV spaces that form the basis of this study. Although we commonly call locales like shopping malls or restaurants "public" places, many of them are also, in one way or another, private too. They may be privately owned, they may restrict access to certain populations or individuals, or they may limit the kinds of speech and actions that take place within them. It would thus be far more accurate to say that such sites are neither public nor private but that they embody, in one way or another, a particular sense of the relationship between public and private. A desire to speak in vernacular terms, even ones that designate problematic and unstable categories, led me to use the term *public space* in my title, although the awkward (and problematically negative) term *nondomestic space* would be more accurate. The significance of this terminological point goes beyond mere semantic precision when we attempt to diagram the tasks television screens carry out in the diverse places where they are installed. For just as social space cannot be fixed, conceptually, as one unvarying way of experiencing relations between public and private (or for that matter as a consistent understanding of consumer activity, of work and leisure, a singular way of gendering or racializing power relations in the everyday built environment), neither can we hope to come up with a general set of social operations that television *always* performs, regardless of its place. If categories like public and private are variable and ambiguous, changing their meaning and expression from site to site, then so too, surely, are the ways in which television screens and images materialize these abstract categories as particular lived and experienced elements of a place.

Television shapes the way we experience a place as public or private, in other words, but not always in identical ways, producing identical meanings. The architectural construction of a private viewing experience in public is a convention of television outside the home, but it means one thing when it takes place via a miniature monitor attached to a recumbent bike in the gym and quite another thing when it happens via the use of concrete barriers that shield disturbing video images from children's eyes at the United States Holocaust Memorial Museum. The concept of site-specificity allows us to explore these differences, tracing not only how different spaces and institutions incorporate television as an environmental media technology but also the very different social and affective meanings that arise from its presence therein.

This point would almost be too obvious to mention were it not for the fact that a pervasive strain of cultural criticism offers an opposing view. Television, in different ways, is very frequently characterized by journalists and academics alike in singular terms: as the privatization of public space, as a contaminant polluting the polis, bombarding us with images, destroying the pristine space of the public sphere.[4] I argue in this book that we have more interpretive options for analyzing TV's presence outside the home than this. A lot gets obscured when we move quickly to demonize television as an agent of the cultural decline of public life. Too often such attitudes seem like reflexive gestures, reminiscent of the anti-TV hysteria that serves as the bread and butter of Hollywood's middle-of-the-road social conscience.[5] The option I advocate here, an increased awareness of site-specificity, is not automatically a "celebration" of television's presence in public space, despite frequent assumptions that this is the only alternative to condemnation. But it is a rather more finely tuned diagnostic tool than the "either/or" logic of much journalistic TV criticism in that it focuses analysis on what social and institutional tasks TV is asked to carry out in different environments. Similarly, a site-specific approach retards the rampant proliferation of a metaphor prevalent among contemporary critics of public space, urbanists and architects in particular: the frequent observation that the new American city is, in Michael Sorkin's words, "just like television."[6] For surely, if this is the case, then mourning and nostalgia for the mythic architectural ideals of the eighteenth century are not very useful responses. If architecture and television are indeed getting closer to each other, then perhaps architects need to take some classes in TV studies. Through its in-depth examination of TV's role in the architectural forms that such critics condemn—theme restaurants, shopping malls, "Urban Entertainment Destinations"—this book advocates a critical approach to the spatial effects of television that is as elastic as the medium's relationship to its environment proves itself to be.[7]

I place some emphasis on this issue because, although it might be easy to accept that television's presence in the *home* is a complex form, with many uses that do not conform to a dominant orientation, the utopian ideals attached to public space in criticism and theory can make it difficult to attribute an equivalent complexity to television, and the uses of television, in such arenas. Specifically, idealistic notions of public space as a polis under siege cannot help but erect flattened caricatures of the mobile modern subjects who move, recreate, and work in the ephemeral and transitory spaces that television occupies outside the home. A priori assumptions about the "degraded" character of televisual spaces like shopping malls or theme restaurants translate too easily into contemptuous ideas about the populations whose needs and desires such places serve.

An article in the *Times* of London will serve as an emblematic instance here. A smarmy review of the Planet Hollywood restaurant in London, it describes the space as a chaotic postmodern jumble, its TVs showing "montage with no regard for narrative, meaning or even cinematographic style. They are pointless pictures, evidently silent; they are wallpaper, moving posters. But they are watched." The viewers, however, are apparently the most revolting thing about the place to the reviewer. They watch, he writes, "with open mouthed attention so that you can watch their masticatory kit. They watch because this is what they do at home."[8] The article bestows a metonymic nickname on Planet Hollywood's viewer-diners, one drenched in class hatred, calling them simply "tracksuit bottoms" (sweatpants, to an American). It is hard to read this image as anything other than a condensed representation of two major targets of upper class British cultural contempt: America and the working classes. Planet Hollywood's televisual festival is the epitome of this fear, and it shows in the accompanying illustration, a depiction of the proverbial "snotty-nosed kid" posed in a "hyperreal" atmosphere filled with movie props, while his dead-eyed parents consume both food and, if their offscreen gazes are any indication, videos. It might be easy to distance ourselves from such class-enveloped descriptions of televisual spaces like the theme restaurant as, simply, the place where "those awful people" go. But when we approach such televisual spaces from the start as the decline of public space or as, in one critic's words, "the theming of America," without asking more detailed questions about them as well—what realities they occupy, what roles they play in work-leisure relationships, in urban development, in the political economy of cross-promotional branding—we risk reinstating such attitudes.

Of course, as vernacular locales of modern life, these places are certainly standardized by institutional aesthetics, part of a recognizable category of everyday places. The doctor's waiting room, the car-rental office, the store, and the tavern are all places more unremarkable than spectacular, defined less by dwelling than by mobility. We do not own these places, nor do we want necessarily to remain in them for a longer period than our missions therein dictate. They are places in which we make contact with strangers and friends, places where we work, sit, eat, play, and pass the time. And certainly, the television screens in these places obey conventions in the forms of their installation as well. Examples would be the frequent placement of the screen overhead, the placement of signs on the front of the console instructing us not to touch, the surveillance monitor placed at the entrance to a store as a visual deterrent against shoplifting. Our use of the screen in public places, as at home, is similarly conventional—we frequently find ourselves waiting, eating, or shopping in TV's presence—although in both places we may not even notice the screen as we carry out these activities. However, although public TV places are generic and conventional, defined by the authoritative mandates of, variously, such institutional spheres as aviation or retailing or managed care, we miss an opportunity to understand more closely how the rhythms of particular places shape what media are and what they do when we call the airport, the mall, or the hospital waiting room a "non-place." [9] Nor should we assume that the relationships we form with these places are generic, standardized, disengaged. The Bonaventure Hotel may be disorienting to the conferencegoer, but this is not the case for the people who work there, people who are all too familiar with the tarnished gleam of its wacky postmodern architecture. Similarly, Baltimore's Harborplace urban entertainment destination may exemplify a particular ideal of postmodern leisure architecture, but it doesn't feel like a "stage set" or an "architecture of spectacle" when you work there, as I did one summer.[10]

The class and gender politics embedded in the judgment of placelessness become particularly apparent when we consider how it applies to that most reviled site of "placelessness" in American culture—the mall. For whom, after all, is the mall a "nonplace," a "simulation," exactly? As Meaghan Morris argues, the aesthetics of the mall, for women who spend household work time there, are "a set of managerial props for the performance of inventive scenarios in a drama that circulates endlessly between home and the pub and the carpark and Green Hills [the mall] and back again to home."[11] Genericness thus does not necessarily entail emptiness; indeed, attempts to characterize a place as generic say much more about the speaker than about the place itself. An influential essay by Alice Kaplan and Kristin Ross on the legacy of situationism sums up the politics of genericness concisely: "the political . . . is hidden in the everyday, exactly where it is most obvious: in the contradictions of lived experience, in the most banal and repetitive gestures—the commute, the errand, the appointment."[12] If this is the case, then the routine implantation of screens in transit stations, banks, and waiting rooms—the precise arenas in which these "banal and repetitive gestures" take place—would seem to be a crucial phenomenon for assessing the nature and direction of a politics of public space and the everyday.

Although there are many overlaps between the politics of the domestic screen and the screens we encounter in these other places, some major differences shape the meanings and occasions of television outside the home. If we consider the home and public space as parallel categories for a moment (recognizing, however, that their asymmetry prevents us from sustaining this parallel very long), we find that the public screen is generally assigned more overtly *authoritative* tasks within its environment. Institutional, directive deployments of the TV screen are legion in public space. This is the case not only in obvious ways (for example, closed-circuit surveillance systems, information monitors in transit areas) but also in such pervasive televisual forms as "point-of-purchase" TV designed to direct traffic through the store, and, one could even say, TV in the space of the bar, where conviviality and its social pressures set limits on how and what we watch therein. Of course, some structures of authority similarly constrain domestic viewing, enmeshed as it can often be in the power dynamics of the enduring institution of the family. Still, because the vernacular category "public space" encompasses such a broad range of sites, examining the screen's roles outside the home does reveal a similarly broad array of institutional mandates routinely issued to television and its spectator.

Ambient Television's focus on the institutional and the routine means that its account of the cultural politics of television outside the home places more emphasis on the banal than the spectacular dimensions of screen culture. In this respect it deviates from standard, journalistic accounts of T V in public. It is a set piece of news reporting to visit T V viewing sites (most often bars) in order to gather evidence of public opinion on media events, from wars, to scandals, to sports matches, to elections. The most frequent form of this convention is sports journalism, in which reporters often visit sports bars to interview fans. More politically charged examples of media events in which bars became informal polling stations include the famous "coming out" episode of the sitcom *Ellen,* when journalists descended on gay bars to gauge the reactions of gay and lesbian fans to the event.[13] On some occasions the physical space of the bar provides journalists with even more specific indexes of opinion in particular cultural constituencies — when the crossdressing flamboyance of Chicago Bulls basketball star Dennis Rodman was a hot news item in 1996, a *San Francisco Chronicle* reporter discovered a gay sports bar and polled basketball fans about whether Rodman was a "positive" or "negative" role model.[14] In such conventional moments of cultural reporting in American journalism, particular places become metonyms for entire identity communities — reinforcing the belief that people who share an identity affiliation must necessarily share opinions. In other cases, though, the screen's presence in a public space becomes a way of gauging not the reactions of one singular "community" but rather the tensions between communities. This phenomenon was particularly noticeable in the televised coverage of the O.J. Simpson murder trial in 1995. In article after article reporters recounted fierce interactions and eruptions of debate around the trial and its verdict.[15]

Although such moments of collectivity and shared engagement will certainly figure in the stories this book tells about televisual places, especially bars and other communal leisure sites, these spectacular formations of spectatorship are merely the more visible and mediatized ways public screen practices materialize political forces of everyday life. Such collective, dramatic moments of public viewing are relatively rare compared to the myriad, far less sensational, relationships among screen, subject, and space that are formed, and deformed, outside the home. My interest in the nonspectacular aspects of the physical space and material object of the screen is unorthodox in its movement away from an analysis of the excessive visuality of the TV image, but it seems a less distracting way to concentrate on how media become material culture, on the spatial features of television that can get eclipsed when we define the medium as, wholly, an electronic stare at the remote other, a portal that places eyeballs directly on battlefields, a spectacular and promiscuous way of looking at the world. Without denying the prevalence of such hyperbolic aesthetics in television, I want to explore other aesthetics of television and space than its seductive visuality. The notion of spectacular visuality is virtually the only thread through which critics connect the small scale of television (conventionally metonymized as the living room) to political "theaters" constituted on larger scales. Media events are important sites of political drama, constituting the "imagined community" of the national audience, but they are not the sum total of television's manipulation of space and time, its ability to link the site of reception to other ideological and geographical places.

In short, then, this book is interested in continuing a certain strain of cultural studies' historical intervention in the mission of the humanities by focusing on the more *unremarkable* and *everyday* forms of the apparatus, everything, almost, *but* the image.[16] Yet it is equally concerned with broader and more abstract processes, in that it continually asks how local dimensions of the TV set and its relation to space — where it sits, who it addresses, for example — also implicate sites and subjects of reception within wider networks of power and contestation. The adaptability of TV as an environmental medium means that there is as much rich material for analysis in the technological and positional forms TV assumes in a space as there is in the images it displays. Building on this basic assumption, I suggest that on occasion the material elements of the "television setting" play as important a role as the image in the positioning of subjects both in the site of viewing and within wider geographies of power and knowledge.

This returns us to the site-specific qualities of television and to its "facticity" as a medium. In the next section I outline the spatial theory that underlies my approach to the relationship between screen and site. As has often been noted, television technologies are complicated spatial forms, at once "global" in their scope and infinitesimally "local" at the point of reception. If TV is on the one hand a site-specific apparatus of spectatorship and on the other hand a figure for the modern collapse of space, then how exactly these spatial operations fit together in any given place is a concern that deserves some explanation. The screen's ability to span geographic scales and degrees of materiality figures crucially into the analyses of screen places that constitute the chapters that follow, and I want to outline now the key geographical terms that figure into my subsequent assessment of the cultural politics of screen and space.

Theorizing Site-Specific TV: Scale and Place

Instead of looking for signs of the privatization of public space, the approach to television's relationship to public space I adopt pays closer attention to the *variability* of television's relationship to all spaces in which it appears. To take such a stance is to become immersed in the complicated epistemological networks of geography as an academic discipline, and in particular one distinctly difficult and flexible category of geographical knowledge: *scale.* As Neil Smith defines it, scale is the "language of spatial difference."[17] The term addresses differences that range from global to local, but these terms in themselves have no set meaning—they are fundamentally relative, constituting each other only through their differences. Scale is thus an inherently political concept in cultural studies. Like determinations of privacy, determinations of what counts as "local" are imbued with power: "geographical scale . . . defines the boundaries and bonds the identities around which control is exerted and contested."[18] For Smith the politics of scale are easily illustrated by the social experience of homelessness in the American city: the state of homelessness limits the individual's activity to the local scale of the street and disempowers collectivities formed on that scale because it prevents them from linking up with the workings of justice and power on the larger, institutional level. It closes off participation in the civic sphere, given that entry into the latter is rooted in a more significantly scaled space: the home, site of proprietorship, money, employment, consumption.[19]

The concept of scale is central to the study of television and not merely because it lies at the heart of certain methodological debates, as in political economists' critiques of cultural studies (the latter charged with "celebrating" the local and the specific, although it often seems that merely acknowledging the indeterminacies of the local is enough to draw this damning charge).[20] Rather, scale is central to the study of television because it generates much of the complexity of the medium itself, a complexity signaled in the tensions between the placeless generality of the image and the specificity of its terminal forms as they appear on screens of all sizes and in all sorts of spaces. As John Hartley notes of TV in domestic space, "Each TV programme may be the same for all the millions of its viewers, but what's 'on TV' — literally on it — is never the same; it's always personal, private and significant."[21] At base, then, to ask what the television screen is doing in the immediate space around it — the "microlevel" of reception — is to ask how these two scales are connected, to explore how the standardized "elsewhere" of the image takes material form in a particular place. It involves an awareness of the fact that TV's role in an environment takes shape on multiple levels, in the case of this study, from the quantum social forces that give certain types of places their particularity — even "nonspaces" like airports — to the top-down institutional systems that attempt to impose models of spectatorship on them.

The complex politics of scale shapes my exploration of TV as a site-specific cultural form in several distinct ways. First of all, it should be noted that a sense of discrepancy between the general and the specific is always bound up in the analysis of the everyday. Tensions between modes of subjective experience and objectifying knowledge, between the anonymity of mass culture and the ineffable specificity of its myriad appropriations by individuals and cultures, are not just analytical problems to be solved but rather distinctive features of the social production of space on the microlevel. As Luce Giard notes, the analysis of everyday life "is doomed to an incessant coming and going from the theoretical to the concrete and then from the particular and circumstantial to the general."[22] Television is caught in this movement, not easily mapped onto an opposition between the individual and the institutional, the local vs. the mass, "place" vs. "space." Rather, time and again environmental discourses and practices of the public screen show these apparent opposites crossing one another and indeed serving as vehicles for each environment's grammar of social space. A site-specific approach must therefore be finely attuned to the scale on which actions, gestures, and speech acts are formed through television's presence within particular environments, examining both what de Certeau might call the *strategies* of the TV set — its use in standardizing, institutionalizing practices of space — and *tactics* of television — in which the screen might serve as a resource to be exploited in the momentary and discontinuous operations of users as they pass through a space on individual itineraries.[23]

Although they are overly binarized, as critics have pointed out, de Certeau's twinned categories offer a useful framework for thinking about the relationships that situate the TV screen in public space.[24] Because they focus our attention on the processes through which institutions, and challenges to institutions, take *material form* on the microlevel, they provide a vocabulary for thinking about the texture, and visibility, of power in places where media dwell. In airports, for example, television screens construct networks of strategy that plot the spatiotemporal coordinates of the spectator as a traveler, serving as a kind of institutional voice. Announcing arrivals and departures, easily updated via computers, the monitor coordinates traffic and supplants human information-givers with a standardized table of destinations. As Patricia Mellencamp notes, these screens support "the mission and desire of being 'on time' while feeling timeless, contextless, unmoored, noplace, in an anonymity of suspended time."[25] Commercial practices within such sites similarly work to impose a grid of meanings on the site, via branding strategies. In the case of the CNN Airport Network, car-rental commercials, sponsored weather reports, and references to destination cities are program forms that — in the political economy of audiences — commodify the spectator's position in space for sale to advertisers.

Yet such highly policed, commercial network strategies are also available as instruments of user tactics. On a very simple level they provide a way of resituating oneself away from the immediate place of interaction in which one sits. When I visited the food court of a shopping mall to watch another CNN venture in action — Café USA, the Food Court Entertainment Network — I found that parents with children were constantly looking at the screen while their children ignored it in their squabbles and play. The screen, clearly, was a tactical resource that parents used to escape the world of the family for a few moments.[26]

In more extreme cases the TV set can help expand the scale of oppositional or tactical maneuvers within a space. Consider, for example, a recent news report on an incident involving the TV screens at Bangkok's Don Muang airport. In this situation, detailed in the *Bangkok Post*, an apparently disgruntled employee of the airport's internal television system interrupted viewing of the championship soccer match between Thailand and Vietnam with a twenty-second clip from a hard-core pornographic film. Following the incident, the *Post* reported, the firm announced that it would "air an apology on the airport's video screens every hour for seven consecutive days." Moreover, the article noted, Charnchai Issarasenarak, assistant secretary to the transport minister, said that the ministry "had the right to sue Media Networks [the closed-circuit company] for allegedly tarnishing the country's reputation."[27] In this instance the strategic institutional blanketing of a space with television is momentarily disrupted by an unruly, tactical action, and the consequences of this action, moreover, resonate over a long temporal duration and along networks wider than the immediate space of the screen. Indeed, the hourly apologies, directed at spectators in transit who are unlikely to have seen, or even heard of, the initial affront, only amplify its effects in social space. A twenty-second clip thus became, in the sensitive and patrolled environment of the international airport, a rupture in the position of the nation in wider international relations.[28] This small-scale example of airport TV is only one of many cases in which television helps shift the scale of tactical, anti-institutional operations within a site, giving rise to both contingent and permanent forms of social contest and control in the spaces it enters.[29]

Television's implication in both strategies and tactics in the microlevel is not the only way the politics of specificity and scale shape this book's analysis of the relationship between screen and environment. Another one, no less important, might at first seem merely a conceptual or terminological or methodological problem. It is the fact that when we search for TV in public places, we find a dense, ambient clutter of public audiovisual apparatuses that fall, strictly speaking, only within the penumbral definition of television: video walls and touch screens, coin-operated consoles and projection screens, tape players, cable systems, network images, and laser-disc players, to name but a few. How can we probe TV's role in everyday terrains of power, routine, and pleasure when it seems so difficult to define the medium in straightforward technological terms? Indeed, it may seem at this juncture that I am using somewhat slippery terminology in defining my object of study; *television,* after all, is a rather too general term for the very heterogeneous forms of video and broadcast imagery one encounters outside the home. What does the Diamondvision screen in New York's Times Square have in common with the small black-and-white console perched on a homemade shelf in the corner of my local laundromat? The scale of their address, revealing the indeterminate scale of all television, seems to suggest that they belong to different "species" entirely.

Ultimately, I think, we must understand this slipperiness as part of the specificity of television as a medium, a characteristic of its peculiar adaptability as a media object in social space. It might be tempting to see the vague generality of the word *television* as a reason for making a preliminary methodological choice between one technological form or another when we embark on an analysis of the TV set. Or alternately, it might seem like an occasion to explore the expansive terminology of television as a theoretical problem that, once solved, yields a more precise and "correct" definition of the medium. But a less pedantic option, one that might preserve the dialectical qualities of TV as an object in space and as a relationship between spaces, is to recognize that this technological diversity is a reflection of TV's site-specificity, its *flexibility* as an environmental media apparatus. Unlike film, TV does not require great physical and technical alterations within a site; it operates without supervision and without much alteration in ambient light; its programming sources are easily accessed; and its screen size and volume are variable. Television blends with other electronic devices, other media forms, and other commercial displays from site to site. It can be encased in a kiosk and hooked up to a minimal digital information retrieval system, accessible through interactive features like the touch screen in the subway station, or it can be embedded in a floor, playing silently underfoot, at the NikeTown store. This ability to dissolve into a place's structures, to mesh the authoritative and persuasive discourses of institutions and commercial interests with the inscrutable practices of space on the level of reception, is a fact of TV technology.

The complexity of scale and its value as a concept for the analysis of television's site-specific operations in particular places is most apparent, however, when one considers the relation of the site of the screen to the spatial operations that are generally attributed to TV as a medium. As many theorists of television as a technological apparatus have noted, television is a preeminent expression of the spatial processes of (post)modernity. As a source of images from elsewhere, a technology that interacts with the ethereal, unlocatable physics of the electromagnetic spectrum, TV does not exist solely on the immediate social scale of the place where it is viewed. The very simple fact that it is a medium of transmission, of communication across distance, means that televisual representation—often charged with an aura of temporal immediacy—is seen as linking disparate places. This is what literary philosopher Samuel Weber calls "space-binding"—the ideological impression that electronic media are able to shrink space. The metaphysics of transmission link the terminal point of the network, the screen, to other places — the studio, the disaster area, the remote news location — and this linkage somehow collapses the distance between these spaces and the space where the screen is located. Whether called "liveness," "space-binding," or, to coin a phrase, "scale-shifting," these properties of spatial manipulation, and the myths of temporal simultaneity they sustain, make the TV screen a peculiar kind of *thing* indeed.[30]

But the "thingness" of television signals another register of its spatiality, one that exists alongside the ideology of spatiotemporal compression. As Spigel has noted, television is characterized both as a "window onto another world" and as a piece of household furniture.[31] The cultural fantasies and anxieties she traces in television's postwar arrival in the home centered not only on TV's perforation of domestic space but also on the interior rearrangements of the gendered social space of the home that the screen seemed to initiate. Television is a thing that exists, in Weber's words, "in at least three places at once."[32] If TV devours space and time, leading critics to point out that it colonizes regions and localities and standardizes spectators as "the masses" or "the nation," it is equally true, as the vast literature on domestic viewing practices illustrates, that TV is a medium we integrate into the quantum routines of our daily spaces, to serve local needs quite distinct from the macrolevel forces of space-binding.[33] As Bruno Latour puts it, "even a longer network remains local at all its points."[34] The fact that we can approach television as a spatial instrument that is at once a physical object in social space and a source of enunciations originating in, and displaying, other places, suggests that the screen not only exists in more than one place but also on more than one scale; it is the physical space where local processes meet the "global" determinations of the image.[35]

Furthermore, as a spatiotemporal force that establishes social relationships within and between places and between scales, television is clearly a social apparatus with highly *dialectical* qualities. In materializing the unlocalized space of the image within particular spaces, in site-specific ways, it seems to exemplify David Harvey's succinct definition of dialectical reasoning: instead of focusing our attention on "the self-evident world of things" television's spatial complexity embodies "a much more confusing world of relations and flows that are manifest as things."[36] From this perspective the two scales of analysis — the macrolevel of the political economist and the microlevel of the cultural researcher — are not really incompatible after all. Rather, they are both absolutely essential for our understanding of the cultural politics of TV sets and TV settings. Indeed, the local flexibility of television technology that I have outlined here is analogous to wider economic and social notions of flexibility. As Aihwa Ong notes, "while there appear to be different sources and domains for the rise of flexible concepts and practices in modernity, they all point directly and indirectly to the workings of global capitalism."[37] Her persuasive analysis of how karaoke systems introduce "slices of Singapore, Hong Kong, and Taipei" into the everyday spaces of mainland China demonstrates the TV set's crucial role in localizing different modes of transnationalism, a role toward which this book, with its largely American and institutional focus, can only gesture.[38]

Thus, although this book is concerned with the local specificity of the physical place of the TV screen, it is equally concerned with understanding how larger ideological processes of the medium take material form within this site. For if, as I have been suggesting, TV's cultural politics on the microlevel of screen and setting look very different from place to place, then perhaps the overarching ideologies closely associated with TV—its space-binding, its obscene visibility—can also be, paradoxically, highly *localized* in their meanings and operations. When we attempt to define television's operations across time and space, it helps to stop and consider that media ideologies might acquire quite variable and contextual meanings when they are made concrete by the screen in particular places.[39] As I will argue, we can perceive many new aspects of TV as a cultural form, and spectatorship as a part of the built public environment, if we avoid a premature resolution of this discrepant relationship between TV's effects on different scales. If we accept, in other words, that TV encompasses *both* space-binding and what I have been calling site-specificity, then we may gain a far clearer sense of the political geography of everyday media practices and the mechanisms that connect small-scale screen practices to the global networks of power that define media corporations. For example, frequently in this book I examine various ways that TV installations in different sites represent the televisual ideology Jane Feuer calls liveness: a charged sense of immediacy, presence, and direct representation that emerges from TV's technological capacity to transmit and receive signals simultaneously, regardless of whether the broadcast in question is "literally" live or not.[40] In evoking this ideology of spatial connectivity and collapse I seek to demonstrate how it is grounded in particular contexts, acquiring different meanings within each one. There are a great many differences between the "liveness" of a collectively viewed sports broadcast in a bar and the "liveness" of an image of oneself glimpsed unexpectedly on a monitor attached to a display model camcorder in an electronics store. When we pay attention to the distinctive mix of standardizing and individualizing forces that cohere in the screen's relationship to its environment from site to site, from the physical conventions of screen placement to the construction of the spectator in managerial discourses about what TV can do, we can better understand the internal contradictions that characterize the institutions that govern these sites. And we discover, most important of all, that cultural agency in relation to the TV screen is formed not on one or the other scale — the micro or the macro — but in the particular ways that the relationship *between* scales takes shape in any given setting.[41]

This explains this book's comparative approach, its focus on multiple settings and institutions. I have found it necessary to limit the scope of my analysis, leaving out, for example, certain key sites of nondomestic TV, the two most obvious ones being closed-circuit video surveillance systems and the high school–based network Channel 1, on which pupil-oriented news and commercials play. Still, I have tried to visit a variety of sites, from the mall to the train station to the snack bar, to emphasize that the screen's complex relation to geographical scale is best communicated when we explore its operations in more than one place. The comparison, moreover, must extend beyond an appraisal of the differences between domestic TV and what *Advertising Age* calls "out of home TV" — a term that foregrounds the fact that television outside the home is often defined in terms of domestic space. Such comparisons are unavoidable in certain cases, especially as they are so frequent in popular and professional discussions of nondomestic TV. However although this book also compares spaces in this fashion, I have tried to focus as much on differences *among* out-of-home TV settings as on differences between the domestic and nondomestic screen. This provides a less binary sense of the site-specific forms of TV and of the way different televisual ideologies acquire specific form and meaning from one place to another.

This leads to a final geographical issue that I must define in relation to TV in public space: the idea of "place." Currently, "place" is a concept applied primarily in media studies to particular regions of a country or federation of nations, and it is most often invoked in discussions of the region's relation to national broadcasting systems.[42] The concept of place on which I draw is the one advanced in recent geographical theory, namely, that ideas about place are also ideas about how the relationship between scales, and between perceptions of specificity and generality, are produced in various localities through particular arrays of discourse and practice. Place is, I want to suggest now, a central concept for understanding the relationship between local, site-specific forces of TV and the apparatus's globalizing ideologies of space-binding and "scale-shifting."[43]

What kind of geographical object does this word *place* designate, exactly? Place is a true "keyword" in that, as Raymond Williams put it, "the problems of its meanings [are] inextricably bound up with the problems it [is] being used to discuss." As a concept, it poses particular methodological challenges for geographers and philosophers of space. This is because, on a linguistic level, the word *place* serves as both a commonsense category of spatial differentiation, one that we use every day in various contexts, and a theoretically complex unit of geography's scientific representation. This tension between experiential and objective designations is what J. Nicholas Entriken calls the "betweenness" of place—the fact that its meaning lies somewhere between vernacular and empirical spatial lexicons, at the point where memory and subjectivity brush up against cartographic and quantitative sciences.[44] For Marxist geographers such as Doreen Massey and Harvey these tensions between specificity and generality are political as well as epistemological. Each argues, in a different way, for a dialectical understanding of place: place, they assert, is not insular and timeless but rather "a particular moment in larger networks of social relations" (Massey).[45] A site acquires its distinctive character, they suggest, not through inherent, fixed properties of culture and community (often conceived as timeless, although imperiled by forces of modernity) but rather "through the working out in that place of interventions and influences from outside" (Harvey).[46]

When we approach places from these more dialectical perspectives, namely as "relations and flows that are manifest as things,"[47] it is easy to see how television and video in public places are less agents of destruction, perforating a bounded and coherent unity, than they are agents of a place's *con*struction. For if, in Massey's words, place is "the focus of a distinct *mixture* of wider and more local social relations" in which "juxtapositions of these relations may produce effects that would not have happened otherwise,"[48] then surely television plays a crucial role in this process of mixing and juxtaposing the local and the global in one physical site. The geographical approach to place, and to television's role as a passage between scales and spatial relations, thus matches the observable ideological flexibility and material adaptability of the TV screen in its everyday environments, allowing for a less deterministic account of TV's role in spatial change and transformation than the one offered in rather more predictable narratives of television as "no sense of place."[49]

Most scholarly accounts of television's relationship to particular environments must approach the television set through what Entriken calls the *generic* idea of place. Generic place is not a unique location on the earth (what he calls "chorographic place," after chorography, the study of regions) but rather the categorization of place based on contiguities such as comparable scale, social similarities, institutional relationships. We signal a generic understanding of place by using the definite article — *the* home, *the* bar — when we talk about these environments.[50] But place also can mean a unique location on the earth — from the ambiguous category of "the region" to the more specific category of a particular village, down to an individual dwelling, an actual home. The spatial stories I tell in the following chapters encompass both "generic" places and particular, "chorographic" ones.[51] I focus generally on the screen's role in supporting particular generic qualities in places — spaces designated as sites of transport, of leisure, of consumption, of bureaucratic administration. But I also propose that we cannot understand what TV is doing in the generic space of the working-class bar, or the middle-class home, or the discount mall shoe retailer without knowing something about the wider historical processes — movements of industry, investments in urban development, population relocation — that shape such places within the life of the urban neighborhood, or the suburb, or the growing landscape of retailing. And such an understanding requires a chorographic sense of place as well as a generic one. For these processes are regionally specific, governed by localized processes of uneven development — urban renewal policies and factory closings, for example, are different from city to city. Thus, on occasion I supplement my readings of the rhetorics and practices that surround TV in certain generic sites with analysis of the chorographic processes of actual regions.

A second way in which the following spatial stories of television encompass both generic and chorographic notions of place is marked in the division of this book into two parts. The first half focuses primarily on institutional discourses on TV's relationship to particular places — stores, waiting areas, bars. Somewhat historical, these stories trace how institutional agents have, at selected points in TV's histories, thought about the implications of spectatorship as a site-specific relationship among subjects, spaces, and images. The stories of the second half trace the material practices of the TV screen in unique sites—actual stores, bars, restaurants, malls, and waiting rooms I visited and observed over the course of writing this book. This focus on specific screens in actual locations is thus chorographic, and it uses photographs or artist's renderings based on photographs to grasp the very concrete and tangible forms that institutions and cultures of the public screen take in social space. Yet in both parts I am interested in crossing over between the generic sense of place—the bar, for example—and particular senses of place—an actual bar, its actual TV set. The result, a somewhat Latourian mixture of sources, data, and impressions, seems to me to be the most appropriate way to really grasp how television itself serves as an agent of forces of generality and specificity within a site.

Methods and Maps

If TV is site-specific, materializing wider institutional ideas about the subject and tracking the subject's individual itineraries within diverse, microlevel sociological terrains of everyday life, then the best way to approach it is through a critical practice oriented toward what Lawrence Grossberg terms "the peculiar logic of cultural studies: it begins with a context that has already posed a question; yet the question itself defines the context."[52] This means that when we ask how the screen's flickering display, its italicizing musical bursts, its position in a room mediate the relations between organizations and clients, strangers and acquaintances, coworkers and companions, policy makers and publics, we must expect that the way we pose and answer this question will differ from place to place. And when we ask how localized TV practices help designate forms of spatial belonging, of community even, we must understand how constructions of community emerge from particular situations. In practice this means that a diverse array of textual and visual materials bears witness to TV's public life, and I have had to synthesize quite different methodologies, and draw on a number of very different archives, in order to carry out this study. Some of these sources are more reliable than others, but all are symptomatic in some sense of the kinds of meanings—gendered, racialized, class-inflected—that attach to public TV screens.

Over the course of researching and writing the following chapters I have immersed myself in diverse professional literatures, some of which are at once alien and curiously similar to the well-aligned worlds of film, television, and cultural studies in which I was trained. In particular I found that the discipline of retail merchandising is a key arena in which to discern the networks of practice and institutional power that position television outside the home. This immersion process was in some ways an uncanny experience. Like film and television studies, retailing is a discipline that produces both academic analysts and practitioners, and each of these constituencies participates in ongoing debates over the longings of the subject: as a body and an agent in social space, as a knowing participant in the exchange networks of capitalism, as an irrational creature with drives and emotions accessed, and constructed, by visual culture. Tracing the history and geography of television outside the home, one must adopt a somewhat more aerial perspective on television than these institutional viewpoints. For one inevitably must compare and tabulate theories of spectatorship offered in highly distinct professional spheres, ones that have nothing in common other than their fantasies about what to do with TV in particular places. The disparity is signaled in some incongruous juxtapositions in my source material—*Department Store Economist* and *Medical Economics, Progressive Architect* and *Progressive Grocer.*

This book's archive also includes the public culture of TV companies, preserved in the industry trade press and in manuscript collections. Both contain a rich selection of texts to interpret, including details of the design principles of screens for public viewing, photo documentation of particular screen sites, and written proposals for programming strategies for specific places. Where relevant, the book also addresses discussions of public viewing in popular magazines and newspapers, discussions that often seek public opinion in the scenes of spectatorship that surround media events, whether they be broadcasts of sports, scandal, or foreign wars. And my materials also extend to encompass anthropological literature and site-specific studies of particular locations. What I have tried to do with images in this book is not visual anthropology, exactly; given that I tried to respect and preserve the alterity of TV viewers in public places with the camera, these images are better described as documentations of television's material culture. Yet I have learned a great deal about how to read social space, and televisual space, from anthropological sources, and I hope that the discourses and practices of public TV screens described in this book will be of some value to researchers in that area.

A final, and crucial, archive on which this book draws was assembled using photography. As a prop that appears in the scenography of everyday institutional places like shopping malls, what is interesting about the television set is the way it blends in so closely with everyday space—so closely, in fact, that we tend to ignore or forget about it. In order to halt the screen's disappearing acts, and to help me focus very materially on the role of the screen in its public environments, I began to carry a camera and to photograph public TV screens over the course of this study.[53] I have used the resulting images of everyday life to chronicle the conventions of placement and usage that embed TV images (and the screen on which they appear) within everyday environments. A small number of them appear in the second part of this book, either as photographs or as artists' renditions of scenes I photographed that were, for one reason or another, impossible to reproduce in black and white. These images facilitate "thick description" of the ways in which the simple placement of a TV set in public can have profound effects on the relations of space and time, of public and private realms, of personal practices and institutional norms, therein. They have also allowed me to discern continuities in the patterns of TV's placement in places otherwise quite distinct from each other. A passenger jet and an Internet café may have little in common, but their TV screens perform quite similar functions, conforming to a larger system of protocols for usage and placement even as they interact with the more localized environmental features that give each place its particular identity.

As I have already noted, this book is divided into two parts. The first explores the institutional ideas of site-specific spectatorship that emerge in and around three key locations of out-of-home TV. The first two are physical locations — the bar and the store — and the third is a more general arena of institutional discourse on site-specificity: the "out-of-home network." Rather than offering an exhaustive historical survey of TV's role in these respective locales from 1945 to the present day, I trace in rather narrow historical case studies how certain ideas about viewing arise at particular, and instructive, moments in American TV history, what institutional logics give rise to them, and what local social processes the screen is perceived to enter and alter. The conceptual thread that runs through these case studies is the development of an enduring institutional formula for thinking about spectator identity, and TV's effects. This is the notion that the viewing subject's identity, needs, and desires are related to, even produced by the screen's location. The second part of the book is a guided, illustrated tour of the everyday practices of screen placement through which institutions and individuals bring TV to public places. Whereas part 1 looks at the rhetorics of site-specific TV formed within institutional spheres, part 2's "eye-level" account of TV in public space connects such rhetorics to the embodied spatial practices of particular everyday spaces: the waiting room, the megastore, the pizza parlor, the station, and so forth. Although the sites examined vary greatly, each illustrates TV's peculiar ability to render visible the social forces, and contradictions, that shape particular places as arenas of institutional, or quasi-institutional, power.

Close analysis—of discourses, images, and places—is the guiding method of both parts of this book. Much of part 1 is taken up with an explanation of the public landscape of TV in the very early years of its introduction. This narrow historiographic focus may be explained by the fact that the period represents a level of interest in nondomestic television unparalleled until the 1980s and the growth of the "place-based media industry." In these years TV's widespread introduction in numerous places outside the home seemed a definite reality. Some of these were "one-off" installations in diverse sites—prisons, hospitals, buses, airports, cars, trains, planes—that would not become taken for granted as televisual sites for many years. Others, most notably the bar and the store, would endure to the present day.[54] Discussions of TV in public places gradually faded away as network TV broadcasting and domestic receiver sales took off in the 1950s. By that time the geography of television outside the home seemed fairly stable: "theater television" was an accepted method of transmission for special sports events; tavern television was a routine and unremarkable form of entertainment; and department store TV had, for the moment, proven too costly for regular adoption. It is in the imaginative speculation and experimentation with nondomestic TV systems that took place in the years surrounding the war, therefore, that we find perhaps the most extensive cultural and institutional expressions of the geographical and site-specific features of TV spectatorship outside the home. This narrower focus thus provides us with a more in-depth picture of how TV's relation to its environment takes shape within particular discursive horizons than a comprehensive survey can convey.

In chapter 1 I examine the debates over community and spectatorship that emerged when TV first entered the tavern. With the arrival of TV the tavern became a site of masculine domesticity; tavern keepers were encouraged by the hospitality trade press to minister to the needs of their sports-viewing clients and to increase the flow of liquor during televisual games. Yet the screen also brought with it very many social fantasies and anxieties about the degradation and corruption of working-class leisure, leading to a host of reformist strategies designed to supervise and discipline the tavern audience, particularly the child spectators who might try to sneak a glimpse of TV in the bar. By looking at the history of TV's arrival in the tavern, we can discern how rhetorics of TV spectatorship, particularly its collective versions, express particular site- and class-specific forms of knowledge and power.

In chapter 2 we move to a very different site of consumption and leisure: the department store, the first retail institution to test point-of-purchase video advertising, now a pervasive part of retail visual culture. In detailing institutional debates on TV's effect on middle-class female shoppers within the retail environment, I argue that although TV's presence therein was strictly temporary and experimental, it was nonetheless symptomatic of wider discourses on femininity and the consumer gaze in the 1940s and laid the groundwork for the contemporary use of video in retail spaces as a fantasy technology for controlling and automating the unpredictable behaviors of shoppers. As in the tavern, TV in the department store provides us with an opportunity to examine how managerial and popular conceptions of a link between class/gender identity and viewing environment produced particular spectator relations. When we look closely at the terms in which these relations were envisioned, we can see how ideas about spectatorship are constructed from a "spatial dominant" that is constantly being asserted and reproduced within the discourse networks of social and economic organizations.

Chapter 3 takes up this point within a more expansive focus, exploring the political economy of this equation of spectatorship, identity, and location in a more contemporary context. It details the emergence of "place-based media" corporations like Turner's Airport Network in the 1990s and shows how these networks defined their spectator's bodily and demographic characteristics in topographic terms. This emergent industry systematized the inchoate equations of place and identity detailed in the previous case studies, producing a marketing theory that would allow firms to sell particular populations, for example air travelers, to advertisers by asserting that they constitute particular demographics (in this case, business persons). This discursive process, I suggest, produces the out-of-home TV audience as a mobile and elastic commodity, in contrast to an increasingly devaluing home audience, thus striving to alleviate the crises over audience measurement that plagued the advertising industry in the 1980s. However, as we shall see, in extracting value from hypotheses about the contextual relationship between the highly idiosyncratic itineraries of anonymous, everyday subjects and the institutional spaces in which they move, place-based media corporations also demonstrate the limits to, and contradictions within, site-specific theories of television's effects.

Chapter 4 examines the common physical positions the TV console occupies as an object in space, focusing on how these positions shape concepts of public and private in different ways across a spectrum of commercial spaces. It lays the groundwork for a practice of "reading" the television setting in detail by analyzing how seemingly unremarkable conventions of the public screen — its placement overhead, the use of multiple monitors, the construction of individual and more public viewing situations — are statements about the position of the spectator and the place of viewing within the wider geographies of public and private, work and leisure, consumption and distraction that define contemporary public space.

Chapter 5 examines the sculptural conventions of the point-of-purchase TV set — the extensive use of video as a sales device and form of retail display in stores and businesses of all categories. It focuses on a few examples of the vast array of audiovisual details that link TV images to merchandise, and to other images and objects, within the retail environment, focusing on the contradictory notions of space, spectatorship, and "televisuality" they embody. The redundant presence of TV advertising at the point of sale, I suggest, reflects the corporate anxieties about brand visibility that define the contemporary retail environment. The video screen synthesizes the different visions of consumer behavior that shape the design of retail space, linking demographic identity to brand identity in marketing's ever expanding "science" of consumer motivation.

Chapter 6 focuses on a temporal convention of the public screen: the use of TV as a way of measuring, or warping, time for site-specific purposes. It examines the discourses and practices of TV programming in waiting rooms and other zones of transition and access in which we commonly "mark time" and suggests that TV's long-standing mobilization of tensions between habit and crisis acquire a charged, site-specific meaning within the institutional networks of access and delay, boredom and anxiety that define the experience of waiting in modern public settings. By looking so closely at these conventions of "television settings," I hope to expand our understanding of the site-specific politics of space and time that television initiates in the cluttered visual landscape of everyday life.

The distinction between institutional rhetorics and material practices is a continuum as much as a switch. Although it is a distinction that divides the two halves of this book, it is a line that almost every chapter crosses constantly. However, it is not until the conclusion that I examine the implications of these crossings in full. Here, by way of two different artists' video practices designed to "intervene" in public space, I explore ways in which what de Certeau conceives as institutional strategies and user tactics can blend together in TV's public environments on the micro-level, and I speculate on how public practices of the TV screen, whether or not they call themselves art, might exploit this confusion to activate the dialectical forces that the TV screen embodies in a site, in the service of progressive cultural politics.

PART I

HISTORIES AND INSTITUTIONS:
RHETORICS OF TV SPECTATORSHIP
OUTSIDE THE HOME

CHAPTER I

TV, CLASS, AND SOCIAL CONTROL
IN THE 1940s NEIGHBORHOOD TAVERN

Press shots of TV viewers in bars are among the earliest representations of TV spectatorship in postwar American culture. Like the scenes of deeply packed crowds outside appliance store windows and in high school auditoria photographed in the same period, such images depict TV viewing in public as a potent sense of collectivity. Although its specialized, Lacanian connotations make it a less than ideal term, *gazing* is the only word that really pinpoints what the people in these photographs are doing. Photo after photo captures TV viewing as a single structure of looking that binds persons in the space, a scene surprisingly close to the figures of collective *domestic* spectatorship captured in the image of TV's "family circle" that was so prevalent in this same period.[1] The image of TV viewing in both sites is a tableau of faciality. Picture after picture shows us a scene of total absorption, of wide-eyed, open-mouthed people whose vision is directed toward a central point. But whereas the familial hearth pictures generally seem to adhere to rigid principles of sex balance in their representations of collective viewing, the TV audiences captured for posterity in the tavern tend to be almost all male.[2] Often wearing hats and ties, this square-shouldered spectatorial fraternity gapes transfixed, cigarettes and drinks forgotten, in a pose often parodied in newspaper cartoons and mimed (hilariously) at the time by comedian Ed Wynn in his 1949 TV variety show.[3]

However, despite the perception of the tavern as a masculine preserve, these images of the barstool audience sometimes reveal a woman sitting somewhere in the crowd. In figure 1 she is unusually conspicuous, sitting at the bar, wearing a boldly striped blouse, and biting her lip as she stares at the screen. This female spectator reminds us that although the prevalent image of early TV spectatorship in the tavern may be the kind of homoge-

FIG. I
An unknown photographer captured the male collectivity of tavern spectatorship for *Time* magazine in 1947. Note the lone and conspicuous female viewer.

neous masculine collectivity described above, it should be taken as a normative belief, not an empirical document, of what the tavern viewing experience must have been like. Indeed, her pronounced visual incongruity within this sea of men in hats is an allegory for the pervasiveness of perceptions of tavern spectatorship as a masculine phenomenon in American culture of the postwar period.[4] Press reports invariably depicted the bar as the province of male viewers and the home the space of female ones. "The bar and grill set prefers sporting and news events," an article in *Business Week* reported, "and there aren't enough . . . to fill television's broadcasting hours." Noting that "the studio programs designed for home listening do not appeal to the watchers in saloons," the article concluded that the audience manifested a "split personality."[5] *Newsweek* reached a similar conclusion: "Other television shows feature fashion shows and special events, but bar owners find sports telecasts more popular."[6] *Business Week* further surmised that the two audiences occupied different class positions. Working-class people watched in bars, whereas those with "more comfortable incomes" watched at home. Such reports also treated this large bar-viewing constituency and home viewers as very distinct audiences. Some surveys, conducted by the alcoholic beverage industry and by TV stations, estimated that most TV viewers watched from the neighborhood tavern; this led the advertising industry magazine *Sponsor* to conclude in 1948 that "the product using TV most successfully to date is beer" — a perception no doubt reinforced in the explicit references sports announcers on television made at the time to viewers in taverns and bars.[7]

These discussions of television viewing in its earliest years are striking in their emphasis on *location* as the basis for knowledge about the audience. In the 1940s, given the novelty value of television, it seems likely that the audience watching in public drinking establishments was highly diverse, comprising gawkers and other unconventional spectators for whom the TV set, rather than the sports events often displayed on it, was the main attraction.[8] But journalistic coverage of TV in bars nevertheless described such sites in very particular terms, as masculine arenas of white, working-class, urban culture. This is not in itself surprising. Not only was the thick-accented tavern drunk something of a cultural stereotype, parodied on radio by vaudeville performers like Wynn, but the white working-class tavern was popularly depicted as the site of community values in urban public culture — a mythic site revered and celebrated by writers like Damon Runyon, as well as newspaper nightlife columnists like New York's

Earl Wilson.⁹ But the press's narrow focus on a particular version of the tavern audience does highlight the rhetorical value in associating TV viewing places with particular social groups and with particular configurations of collectivity and sociality as well.

Although they are unlikely to be true, such speculative links between the audience's location and its identity illustrate a wider ideology that continues to define much commercial discourse about television outside the home, namely, that there is a direct correspondence between social space and social subjectivity. Today's industry rhetorics of site and spectatorship are, to be sure, far more precise in their representation of this correspondence—the short-lived "Trucker TV" network, for example, targeted truck drivers at highway rest stops—but the construction of the tavern audience as a masculine, sports-viewing collectivity in the postwar years is exemplary as an early institutional fiction that used the habitual character of public spaces as a way of "knowing" the TV audience located out there on the other side of the screen. But the public discourse on tavern spectatorship in this period is also an opportunity to explore the field of cultural politics that comes into being through such spatial constructions of spectatorship. As I will detail presently, the debate and conjecture sparked by the arrival of the bar as a new venue for sports spectatorship gave expression to wider concerns about, and actions against, working-class leisure and entertainment in the postwar period.

In this respect the words and images through which we can trace television's arrival in the bar also reveal how uncertainties about the TV set's effects took on the accent of the social conflicts that defined the bar as a cultural space. As in the home, TV in the tavern occasioned questions about the medium's exact nature as an object in social space and as a window to other places—as a piece of talking, gaze-channeling furniture that needed to be integrated into the routines of everyday life within its location. But in popular and professional press coverage of tavern viewing, one can quickly discern how these questions about television's role in bars were at once comparable to those expressed around home viewing yet quite distinct in the meanings they assigned to particular televisual phenomena. Television's ability to collapse distinctions between public and private space in each location, for example, was judged to have very different effects, depending on the environment in question. Broadly speaking, one could say that whereas at home TV threatened to bring the anonymous and unpredictable realm of the outside world into domestic familial space, in the tavern TV provoked concerns about the "privatization" of the bar by undermining its traditional, masculinist ideals of free entry and conversational democracy—a concern that remains active, in different ways, around TV's presence outside the home to this day. By noting the points where the postwar construction of television spectatorship in these two arenas overlap and diverge, we can start to distinguish the broader mechanisms of site-specificity that suture television as an object and a spectacle into the human processes of its immediate environment.

This chapter pursues this opportunity, focusing on how a range of American cultural texts, from a beverage industry trade journal to the newsletters of social reformers, represented the screen's power to configure, and reconfigure, social relations in the bar. Television's emergence in the neighborhood tavern, as in the home, embodied contradictory cultural sensibilities and forms of social power. The tavern was a cultural arena in which liberatory ideals of democratic socializing met the privatizing forces of commerce and insular expressions of community. It was a space where the disciplinary desires of social reform constantly bumped up against the sediment of local practices, of explicit and implicit norms of behavior and socializing. It was a masculinist utopia in many ways, and yet its parodic representation in the press and popular culture of the postwar years reveals how often perceptions of this masculinity hinged on class contempt. The following account of television's arrival traces how TV gave expression to these and other contradictions that defined the tavern as a cultural space. It is a history in which class-based forces of social regulation feature prominently; the social questions TV raised for both the denizens of the tavern and its critics were intimately linked to the longer history of the bar as a working-class social space. Specifically, the prevailing discourses on TV's ability to alter space and to structure leisure time in the bar were inseparable from the institution's historical evolution as a space of working-class leisure and its position in the moral geographies of reform movements. When, at the end of this chapter, we visit a tavern that has managed to weather changes in neighborhood culture far more damaging than the arrival of TV, the extent to which anxieties about television's arrival prefigured larger structural changes in urban working-class lives will be apparent.

As I will argue, the history of tavern spectatorship in the 1940s is also a history of how very localized rhetorics of screen and place come to embody more diffuse processes of power and regulation. The debates over the tavern screen anticipated concerns about the impact of collective sports viewing on the economics of leisure that arose with the postsatellite rise of the commercial sports bar. In each case the thrill of the crowd was seen as the key to the bar as a reception context, and it introduced an intangible and even threatening element to the way other institutions of visual entertainment and recreation—baseball and movies in the case of the 1940s tavern, commercial sports broadcasting in the case of the sports bar—interpreted the TV viewing experience as a form of competition. Anticipating more contemporary concerns about TV's intrusion in various public places, the postwar tavern screen is thus a valuable lesson in how to think about the social impact of the TV screen in public places today.

Commerce, Culture, and the Tavern Public Sphere

The rise of satellite networks designed for drinking establishments in recent decades was not the first occasion for the commercial exploitation of a barstool TV audience. In the postwar years TV manufacturers quickly realized that the characteristic spatial arrangement of the bar gave rise to very particular viewing conditions. A number of companies developed large-screen receivers (both projection and "direct view") to accommodate the bar's collective viewing situation.[10] Whereas larger companies such as DuMont, RCA, Philco, and GE added these models to their existing lines of home sets, at least one company, the United States Television Manufacturing Corporation, specialized in receivers for public places. One model, the "Tavern Telesymphonic," had a nineteen-by-twenty-five-inch screen and retailed for two thousand dollars.[11] The tavern TV market also encouraged the early participation of alcoholic beverage companies in TV advertising. Even before the days of network broadcasting, *Beverage Media,* the trade journal for New York tavern owners, was filled with advertisements from local breweries announcing the sports events they were sponsoring on TV. Such advertisements addressed the tavern keeper as the proprietor of a convivial space for sports spectatorship, promulgating the image of tavern viewers as a masculine collectivity.

Such conceptions of the neighborhood tavern as a masculinist space reflected some of its enduring characteristics as an institution. Internal, informal systems for vetting entry and participation in tavern culture on the basis of gender as well as age were common in this period. The potential for hostility toward women in the tavern is vividly conveyed by the content of the following "humorous" signs found posted above the bar and collected in a 1947 survey of taverns in Manhattan and the Boroughs of New York:

Danger! Women Drinking
Notice! No Back Room Here for Ladies
Good Ale, Raw Onions, and No Ladies
No Unescorted Ladies Permitted at Bar[12]

Although no legal interdiction barred women from the tavern, signs like these would severely limit their participation in the social life of taverns in working-class neighborhoods. Still, this does not mean that women were entirely absent from tavern culture. One sociological study in this period found that "women were more likely to affirm the importance of the tavern in providing a meeting place and satisfying unmet social needs." One woman even stated, "If my daughters are eventually going to drink I would rather they go to the tavern than to go to private places."[13] Her implication, presumably, was that the visibility of the tavern as a space allowed the watchful eye of the community to monitor the activities of women and men therein.

This sense of the tavern as a community hub marks the tavern's historical role as a neighborhood public sphere. Working-class neighborhood bars, before and after prohibition, were a hub of male (and sometimes female) recreation and social interaction.[14] The author of the above-cited study of bar signs in New York characterized the tavern as a place "frequented by men and women who call each other by first names, who know what their drinking companions work at, the number of children each has, whether so-and-so is getting married, and who, in short, feel comfortable, natural, and at ease in each other's company."[15] Regular customers thought of their local taverns as informal social clubs rather than as places to get drunk: "Many who wish to drink may do so at home or in other private ways," one patron noted. "Often [the tavern] is the only place a man can go unless he belongs to such clubs as Madison, Club, Elks club, et al., and including country clubs."[16] This was echoed by a number of patrons, who felt that "everyone is equal in a tavern — whereas schools and churches all have their caste systems."[17] The tavern was thus understood as a social institution distinctly more democratic than others, practiced by its patrons as a nonhierarchical social space.

This ideology of the tavern as a barrierless space for exchange and communication bears some resemblance to the "classical" bourgeois public sphere excavated as a historical form and promoted as a normative political ideal by Jürgen Habermas, although its class contours and physical arrangements differ sharply from those of the eighteenth-century London coffeehouses Habermas examined. Indeed, Habermas would no doubt dispute such connections, given that he blamed the lack of a critical public in the twentieth century on mass cultural patterns of amusement and leisure.[18] But by most accounts, prior to the arrival of television tavern and saloon life *combined* conversation, community participation, and recreational activities; one could say working-class drinking spots consolidated their community roles as public places by offering both amusement *and* discourse.[19] People came to the bar not to escape but to do a number of things: "talk, exchange ideas, discuss their important problem, and have fun playing cards and shuffleboard and listening to the juke box."[20] In addition to the jukebox many other visual and auditory amusements were available in the tavern: movies were often screened in neighborhood taverns, and all had mirrors, and sometimes murals, to spice up the visual spectacle of the interior.[21] This sense of the tavern's visual culture as a key element of its public life is corroborated in Roy Rosenzweig's study of turn-of-the-century labor movements. Rosenzweig depicts the history of leisure and recreation in the United States as not simply a progressive decay of agency through a commodified desire for passive amusement but rather a reflection of class conflict over working conditions. The saloon was a particularly contested topic in workingmen's demand for leisure time, a demand voiced in quantifying terms—"eight hours for what we will." This was because the right to congregate (and consume) publicly within saloons intensified middle-class reformers' and institutions' efforts to design more appropriate forms of recreation for the working classes.[22] Thus, rather than simply depoliticizing the space, saloon amusements were recreational forms that laid the groundwork for television's presence in the bar, and they were the material result of a long-standing political struggle over leisure.

When television spectatorship arrived in the tavern, it was understood, similarly, as a social and recreational practice that marked the temporal relations of the workday, although discussions of this function also revealed how much the cultural politics of leisure that formerly framed urban drinking had faded from view. An article in *Beverage Media*, although it situated television within a longer history of barroom amusement traditions, hinted that tavern life was hardly an alternative to the ossified structuring of time at work. Rather, the article suggested that the tavern might itself be a habitual space of deadened, wasted leisure time: "There's really nothing new about the tavern owner being in 'show business.' If you own or rent a juke box, you're a showman. If you have a shuffleboard game, you're a showman. You have already discovered that in supplying some form of entertainment to your customers you can attract more people, and you can keep them longer by breaking up the monotony which a normal routine without such features would induce."[23]

The tavern, this suggests, could be a space both for the experience of the tired routine of the daily grind and a space where normal time could be suspended and changed by visual spectacle. The television screen's relation to this environment was potentially transformative, akin to what Walter Benjamin saw as the cinema's transformation of "our taverns and our metropolitan streets, our offices and furnished rooms, our railroad stations and our factories" by the "dynamite of a tenth of a second."[24] But it also harbored the possibility of a further inured and deadened populace of working people for whom even the process of relaxation was becoming mechanized.

This latter possibility certainly occurred to many observers of TV's postwar arrival in the tavern. Television's widespread takeover of the bar in the late 1940s, prior to the rise of household viewing, was an early occasion for a lament that has become commonplace with the arrival of television screens in all areas of public life: the worrisome fear that the screen is an intruder in the environment it inhabits and, moreover, one that might bring other intruders in its wake.[25] Numerous postwar writers speculated about what the new medium would do to the local tavern as a particular kind of social space. Their questions, detailed in the following sections, included the following: would TV eradicate conversation from a neighborhood public institution, turning the convivial "working man's club" into a theater? Would the appeal of watching a baseball game with the tavern crowd lead fans to desert the stadium? Would televised sports also attract children to this adult male space, and should municipal authorities attempt to divert them with alternative TV viewing clubs? Such questions echoed the nascent concerns about the invasion of the domestic, familial sphere that were emerging around television's installation in the home. In each case concerns about the effect of TV's installation on social space revolved around the medium's ability to warp time and space and to change the environment it entered. However, the terms in which these invasion anxieties were figured in the tavern, as in the home, were profoundly site-specific. Although TV in both places drew concerns about the corruption of children, the tavern screen did so not because it brought inappropriate images into the space of the family but because it brought children to an inappropriate, nonfamilial environment. And although TV in each space posed a perceived threat to stadium sports attendance, home viewing was believed to do so because it offered a way of *bypassing* crowds; in contrast, bar viewing was seen as a way of bringing the crowd experience home to the neighborhood.

Television's entrance into the gendered space of the working-class tavern thus inflected discourses of spectatorship with site-specific cultural politics — it entered into the particular relations of public and private, of class, gender, and age, that defined the tavern as a space. Rather than repressing or eradicating these local social relations, TV extended their range, linking them to new institutional arenas: the business of live sports promotion and the moral geography of social reform, in particular. When we trace the terms of this postwar discourse on tavern spectatorship in greater detail now, it will become clear that the television screen's appearance in public space was from the first a social mechanism that gave material form to wider conflicts over the cultural meaning of leisure, conflicts that had historically structured the perception of the tavern as a working-class environment.

The Social Space of the Tavern Screen

Let us turn first to the question of the physical changes that the arrival of television wrought within the space, moving subsequently to the wider social controversies that TV precipitated as it became intertwined with the rhythms and routines of working-class leisure outside the home. As is evident in the illustrations accompanying this chapter, the conventional overhead placement of the barroom TV dates back to this period. This foregrounds how, from the very beginning, television's popularity, particularly its sports broadcasts, meant that tavern owners needed to position the screen very carefully for maximum sight lines. Although actual data on audiences are rare, press accounts from this period stress the magnitude of the crowds TV brought to the bar. On one fight night, for example, one reporter at a small New York bar counted 37 customers at 9:15, 162 when the bout ended.[26] Although several expensive large-screen models were marketed specifically for taverns, many screens were no larger than nine inches across. This called for inventive measures; *Colliers* explained that "taproom tycoons use mirrors to enlarge the screen's pictures and multiply the visible surfaces," and other bar managers placed magnifying lenses in front of the screen to make the picture larger.[27] Many of these smaller receivers were initially placed directly on the bar, but later it was more common to find them on shelves near the ceiling, a placement that made them easier to see and discouraged customers from fiddling with the knobs.[28]

Given the need to accommodate large crowds and to provide everyone with visual access to the screen, it is not surprising that a series of viewing protocols emerged around the contingencies of space, especially when big events were broadcast. In crowded bars, patrons were asked to remove their hats and stay seated during important programs. A sign on one tavern's set read, "You're not transparent. People back of you can't see the screen. Please don't stand there."[29] Tavern owners found ways to arrange crowds efficiently. According to the *New Yorker,* the owner of one bar seated the audience that gathered for the 1946 Louis-Conn bout in a predetermined pattern: "seventy in straight backed chairs on the floor, fifty more in booths along the wall, a couple of hundred standing at the bar, and several dozen outside peering through the window."[30] *Colliers* reported that one restaurant owner in the Bronx converted his back room into a television theater and claimed that a New Jersey tavern proprietor had constructed wooden bleachers around the walls of the bar.[31] A good example of a theater-like presentation style is shown in figure 2 — a photograph of a tavern TV screen taken from a very early collection of photographs commissioned in the early 1940s by the Jersey City, N.J., furniture store that installed TV in numerous local establishments. (These images now reside in the Smithsonian among the papers of Allen B. Du Mont, New Jersey television pioneer, set manufacturer, and network owner.)

From 1947 to 1949 the trade journal *Beverage Media* often addressed its tavern-keeper reader as a subject in need of education on the social conventions of the screen, recounting many such innovative examples of techniques for dealing with television's arrival in the space of the bar. Lecturing the tavern owner on how to serve a distracted audience and "make them feel at home," the journal's advisory style strongly paralleled the "lessons in managing the resident's gaze at the screen" that Spigel traces in women's magazines of the same period.[32] A special issue on television in 1947 presented a comprehensive survey of tavern owners with TV sets, outlining their experience of the medium's value, and its potential drawbacks, for the business of beer and liquor sales. Article after article in this issue offered detailed advice on diverse topics ranging from the logistics of seating large crowds, how to answer inquiries from customers about the way television actually works, and the importance of tending to customers' drinks while they watched TV. Like the womens' magazines of the

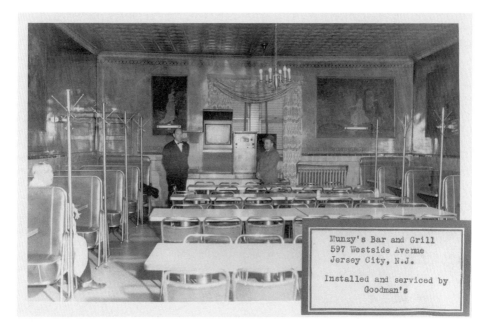

Munzy's Bar and Grill
597 Westside Avenue
Jersey City, N.J.

Installed and serviced by
Goodman's

FIG. 2
Munzy's' television set ended up in the back room, near elaborate
saloon-style wall murals depicting courtiers in eighteenth-century dress.
(DuMont Collection, Archives Center, National Museum of American
History, Smithsonian Institution)

period, *Beverage Media* depicted TV proprietorship as a responsibility that combined labor and nurture. As one article lectured,

> One thing is certain, any tavern owner who ventures into television will have to be definitely "on the job" when the television is working for him. He must keep his employees on their toes, not watching the television screen but watching the customers and taking care of them. He must circulate among the customers and make them feel at home in his bar. By seeing that glasses are picked up as soon as they are emptied, he will thus suggest another drink. Tactfully suggesting another drink to the customer obviously nursing his drink might also help.[33]

This advice parallels the readerly address of popular magazine articles on domestic TV in the way it encourages attentiveness and polite supervision of the needs of others. Indeed, one can discern a quasi-maternal sense of domestic pride in such passages, as well as in the commercial material promoting tavern television in *Beverage Media*. As a DuMont TV set advertisement's address to the tavern keeper in this same issue proposed: "Your patrons have come to expect the finest of everything from you. The confidence and goodwill you have worked so hard to build deserves the finest in television."[34]

Perhaps because the screen drew attention to, and brought about changes in, the bar's interior decorations, these trade discussions of television tended to foreground the tavern's cultural status as a space of male-oriented comfort, a status referenced in patrons' descriptions of the space as a lodge, a club, or a "home away from home."[35] Such characterizations of the televisual bar fostered an ideology of "masculine domesticity" that paralleled, in some respects, the address to male TV owners that Spigel traces in the culture of the home screen.[36] Do-it-yourself, one of the signal features of masculine domesticity, was a skill bar owners honed when they bought TV sets;[37] when McGary's Tavern in the Bronx borough of New York remodeled and became McGarry's (*sic*) Broadway Cafe, the owner built a precarious structure to house the bar's large (and presumably heavy) TV set: a "wheeled stand about seven feet high."[38] The positioning of the screen on specially constructed stands can also be seen in figure 3, another Goodman's photo from the Du Mont Collection and one of several that show affable, white-coated bartenders beaming at the camera as they stand beside their brand new TV receivers. In this one the bar-

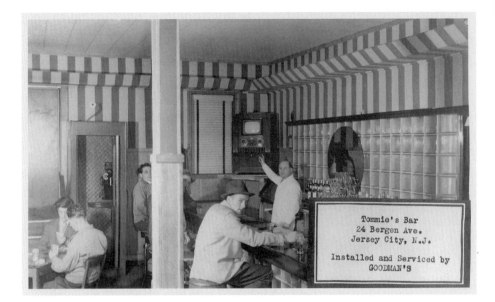

Tommie's Bar
24 Bergen Ave.
Jersey City, N.J.

Installed and Serviced by
GOODMAN'S

FIG. 3
Specially constructed stand elevated the TV set to pride of place in the
overhead space of the room, changing the visual architecture of the
tavern in the process. (DuMont Collection, Archives Center, National
Museum of American History, Smithsonian Institution)

tender gestures proudly to the expensive and ornate console that sits on a platform in the corner of the bar.

Pride was at stake in the domestic men's culture of the tavern in another way, too. One of *Beverage Media*'s advice articles recognized the proprietary role of the bartender within the social environment of the tavern, giving bar owners a "crib-sheet" for explaining how TV works. Knowledge of the principles of television broadcasting was important, the article noted, because "when Mike the bartender and Henri the waiter begin to discuss *Iconoscopes* and *Kinescopes* you'll know they've been initiated. They belong to the lodge. The boss has bought a television receiver and the boys have been learning the language. They've found out how it works."[39] Emphasizing technological mastery and social status and depicting bartenders as initiates in a televisual "lodge," this statement links the male domesticity of the tavern to stereotypically masculine anxieties about authority and technology.

In other cases, indeed, television's presence within working-class masculine leisure space was figured as a potential invasion of the tavern's hermetic, homosocial community. In 1948 *Variety* reported that television had brought an unwelcome transformation in some bars, citing a report from the New Jersey Alcoholic Beverage Commission officers that stated, "Bar owners are jerking [TV sets] out as bad investments." Their reasons, the article claimed, were that people came to the bar to watch TV and not for the social drinking experience, that patrons drank too slowly, and that they tended to leave as soon as the show was over. "The novelty of TV has worn off and . . . non-paying barflies keep customers from the bar. . . . Patrons fail to agree on which programs they want to look at, with noisy debate resulting from such disagreement," the article noted.[40] Another complaint about television in the tavern that aired in the popular press was that it killed conversation. Several journalists bemoaned the loss of talk and conviviality in the local tavern: "It used to be practically a barroom must to engage in badinage and raillery with a hapless, elbow bending neighbor. Television has invoked the silence of the tomb on the bar," one writer claimed. This silence was broken only by "the grunts, groans and roars emanating from a ten inch screen perched precariously over the far end of the bar."[41] Contrary to Leo Bogart's assertion that TV in bars "provided a common denominator of experience which may . . . have stimulated some conversation among people with little in common to talk about,"[42] these commentators asserted that conversations in tav-

erns had become "furtive, sandwiched in between strikeouts, odes to cigarettes, and hysterical hymns to men of muscle."[43] One *New York Times*
editorial, entitled a "barroom lament," explained:

> The saloon . . . has been the favorite forum of the man with something
> on his mind. In it he could air his preferences, his prejudices, and his
> heresies; fulminate against his employers, his relatives, and the status
> quo, voice his grievances against mankind, calypso singers, and park-
> ing regulations. . . . The saloon now harbors a horde of mutes. Thanks
> to the intrusion of a garrulous pictorial contraption called television,
> the thirsty talker has had his forum shot out from under him. . . . As a
> business bait, television may offer momentary rewards; as a curb on
> freedom and continuity of speech it can only breed resentment.[44]

The tavern patron in this depiction was a sodden rambler to whom calypso
singers and the status quo were equally irksome; he talked regardlessly,
with or without listeners. Despite the affirmation of talk and conviviality
as public functions of the barroom, this was the general tone of many
articles on tavern TV. It betrays a disdain for the tavern and its patrons and
a derisive dismissal of the possibility that it might serve a public function
in urban communities. As the above quote demonstrates, such articles
tended to affect the rhetorical style of a hiccuping, W. C. Fieldsesque barstool philosopher. Another editorial, entitled "Video Kayoes the Barroom
Bore," welcomed television's intrusion as a way of silencing such incessant
talkers. It heralded the defeat of the drunk whose "bleary face, unrelent-
ing elbow, and incoherent phrases disturb his suffering neighbor on the
bar stool."[45]

   This image of the working-class tavern-going public in dominant journalistic accounts of television's impact on the bar offers little insight into
the day-to-day role TV played in the lives of tavern patrons, revealing instead how much tavern spectatorship embodied middle-class ideas about
working-class identity. Contrary to these press accounts, I would suggest
instead that television spectatorship in the tavern, as in other places, no
doubt quickly became part of the rhythms and patterns of neighborhood
life. This possibility is suggested in the techniques tavern owners used to
publicize their TV screens; *Beverage Media* announced that, in addition to
attracting viewers with cardboard or neon signs, interior displays, displays
provided by the manufacturers, handbills distributed around the neighborhood, and postcards mailed weekly, tavern owners used the neighborhood's oral networks to pass along television-related news: "Your bar-

tender is in a particularly advantageous position to tell his customers about 'the big fight on the television show on Friday night.' " [46] These forms of publicity locate the tavern and its screen within a local print and oral culture, suggesting that the screen's presence could reinforce community ties, albeit for commercial gain, as much as fray them.

However, it is clear that TV did commodify certain aspects of barroom social relations, most notably in its transformation of the bar patrons into an identifiable collective of predictable and regulatable audience members. Although it was illegal to charge admission to taverns, tavern owners found other ways to pass along the cost of television to the customers. Some raised prices, imposed drink minimums, and suspended draft beer sales in favor of bottles during important sports games.[47] A bar in Brooklyn was reported to seat viewers during important games according to their drinks: "The front row is reserved for scotch drinkers, the second row for the bourbon, rye, and blend trade, third row for devotees of the grape, the last row and standing room for the ordinary and beer drinking fare." [48] Whether true or not, such statements reference the extent to which television may have introduced new terms for social hierarchy within the tavern. One complaint among tavern owners was that the customers TV attracted were worthless because they didn't buy drinks. Jukebox manufacturers and operators sought to capitalize on this complaint by marketing coin-operated devices capable of supplying six minutes of television, radio, or phonograph music for a nickel. Promotional copy for one such machine, called the Solotone, emphasized its profit potential for tavern owners: "The mechanism . . . [keeps] people seated and therefore not so preoccupied that they forget eating and drinking. It also is said to eliminate 'floaters.' " [49] Another device of this type promised to help bar owners avoid "the non-profitable 'free show' customer." [50]

These ways of thinking about barstool spectators suggest a perceived transformation of the tavern into a kind of theater. Television's spatial effect on the bar, they indicate, included the reconstruction of conversational space as a standardized, visually based arena of spectacle. Like the home-theater metaphor circulating in other areas of TV discourse at the time, this idea arose from a longer lineage of class-coded ideas about spectatorship.[51] But whereas the home-theater metaphor embodied an escape from the world of public amusement, the theater metaphor brought the tavern closer to other spaces of commercial visual entertainment, like the movie theater and the stadium. Its perceived similarity to both raised important questions of legality, policy, profit, and even ethics for various state, corporate, and civic bodies. The screen's transformative potential within its immediate environment thus had consequences that extended beyond the four walls of the tavern, as it also shaped the latter's relationship to a wider geography of gazes, bodies, and commercialized amusement in the postwar American city.

For motion picture exhibitors TV turned the tavern into a theatrical space for viewing images, one that was not subject to the same heavy licensing laws and fees as movie theaters. In 1948 a group of New Jersey theater owners called a meeting with legislators to discuss the "alarming threat" television posed for the film business. A survey in the area had disclosed that, in *Variety*'s jargon, "most theaters are now surrounded by a belt of bistros which offer tele entertainment as a cuffo chaser to the drinks."[52] (Translation: a number of lounges and restaurants with television were located near theaters.) To stave off the possibility that people might prefer a night of TV and drinks to a movie, exhibitors suggested that bars be required to purchase licenses as places of amusement. The effort was probably futile, as the Internal Revenue Service had ruled the year before that taverns with TV were not eligible for federal amusement taxes when the set was "not coupled with other amusements."[53] In all likelihood these theater owners were motivated by the 1947 precedent set in nearby Philadelphia, where the liquor board ignored the IRS ruling and instituted a $120 amusement tax on taverns with TV.[54] When tavern owners protested, the Pennsylvania Supreme Court held that "video was in effect motion pictures" and authorized the tax in a move that undoubtedly pleased both sports promoters and theater owners.[55] Such judicial rulings placed television within the legislative arena of public amusements, where municipal and commercial interests could jointly patrol the borders of the tavern as a commercial space.

For sports promoters tavern TV was part of general debates over the commercial impact of televised sports in the late forties. This debate centered on whether the medium would create new fans or decrease stadium attendance.[56] In 1948 *Variety* ran an article that characterized the tavern sports audience as a potentially greater threat to gate receipts than were home viewers. The article reported that baseball league executives had "expressed [the] conviction that tele, if confined to its rightful place in the home, could help them by converting some of the public into new fans. They voiced considerable misgivings, however, about the number of bars that advertise in bold window cards 'see the baseball games here.'"[57] To stave off "the competition tossed in their faces by tavern and bar sets," baseball owners announced that they would ask set manufacturers and distributors to warn bars against advertising games in their windows. If tavern owners did not cooperate, owners of sports teams warned that "they might prohibit baseball telecasting in the future. And that . . . would cut a deep swath into the pull of taverns." [58] The popular press lent support to this fear; in 1947 *Time* quoted a Chicago tavern owner's perspective on television's ability to aid business (*Time* also attempted to represent his accent in print): " 'Bout coupla months ago we was losin' money but fast. . . . I figure maybe dese guys is goin to hockey games or fights, an I say, why not bring hockey or fights here, so guys can see sports and drink atta same time." [59]

The idea that barstool TV viewing was an experience just as "live" as stadium spectatorship, and one that featured the added attraction of alcohol, lay beneath the humorous situation illustrated in figure 4, a cartoon clipped by Allen B. Du Mont in 1946. In this tavern scene, a bemused bartender and patron watch an inebriated press photographer aim his camera at the TV screen, on which the baseball game he is supposed to be covering appears. This image allows us to discern some of the broader cultural continuities that underscored sports magnates' concern with the tavern as a space of spectatorship. Though it plays off the midcentury stereotype of journalism as a hard-drinking profession, it also recycles a joke scenario as old as the 1902 Edison film *Uncle Josh at the Moving Picture Show*. In each case, a stock character's encounter with a new technology of vision raises the possibility of confusing the two-dimensional space of the image with the reality it depicts. But whereas in "Uncle Josh" the joke lies in seeing the bumbling bumpkin try to enter the world onscreen, in this cartoon it lies in the fact that the medium's perceptual collapse of spaces, of appearing to be in two places at once, may be cunningly exploited to confuse others and get away with something.

Postwar concerns with the economic impact of the bar as a location for sports spectatorship hinged upon similar perceptions of the tavern-goer as a viewer who was getting away with something. This perception reveals the site-specific dimensions of early conceptions of television's effects on its spectator. In the debate over the lure of tavern sports, television was seen as an apparatus capable of shaping microlevel social processes and viewer desires in different ways depending on its environment. For commentators who feared TV's effects on stadium sports in particular, the *context* of the screen greatly determined the effects of the images it displayed. The specific source of sports promoters' displeasure with tavern TV was

FIG. 4

This 1946 cartoon satirizes major league baseball's concern that the bar was a more appealing place to view—or cover—a game than the stadium. (DuMont Collection, Archives Center, National Museum of American History, Smithsonian Institution)

the fact that fans were drawn to the tavern as a viewing environment more local and comfortable than the stadium but just as "live" and participatory.[60] Home TV, on the other hand, fostered an interest in the real thing. Writing in *Variety*, ABC executive Paul Whiteman explained, "Bellowing opinions is part of the fun of attending a ball game or a fight and I think that television will create fans who buy tickets."[61] One ad executive stated, "I've already gone to more games than I did last year. Television increased my interest in getting out to the park."[62] Television technology's space-binding ideology was thus rendered in nonidentical, site-specific terms from home to bar, encouraging different modes of "liveness" in each one. The home was understood as a site that produced a distinct yearning for the live event in the fan, whereas the tavern was a place where the televised event and the ringside experience seemed to blend together.

The difference in TV's perceived effects from site to site reflects the very different status of tavern and home as cultural spaces. One is fully commercial, the other considered outside the province of commerce. One was, in the 1940s, a space of homosocial, collective recreation, the other a space defined by familial gender relations in dominant discourse. The next section details another dimension of the cultural status of the tavern: the fact that it was a highly policed space. Much of the postwar concern with the television set's immediate social effects in the tavern lay in the potential scandal of underage viewers. Reformist concerns in this vein reflected a longer lineage of debates over the corrupting effects of the saloon on poor communities in urban America. As we shall see, the solutions that reformers proposed for the problem of child tavern spectatorship were designed to combat the harmful potential of the screen's embedded relationship to its social milieu, through the physical relocation of viewers.

Challenges to Tavern Viewing

Some aspects of reformist concerns with tavern TV can be traced back to the Progressive Era, when both the saloon and the movie theater were sites of commercial leisure considered unsanitary, unfit places for mothers and children. Both were crucial battlegrounds in the moral geography of reform movements.[63] If the theater was a place infested with gangs of "juvenile delinquents," the saloon was the place where these delinquent subjects were formed, in the young crowds who congregated at the swinging door of the saloon to gawk at the spectacle of drunkenness inside.[64] Reformers used spatial strategies to combat these unsavory spaces of working-class sociality. Many groups attempted to block the corrupting influence of both saloon and theater on youth by establishing separate clubhouses that used structured play activities to instill a sense of responsibility and moral rectitude in young people. One play reformer noted that "the immediate necessity is to get hold of the child, and in early years create such interests and ideals that the future man and woman cannot be drawn into the lower life of which the saloon is the exponent."[65] For adults temperance groups established social clubs that replicated the social function of the saloon, minus the alcohol, in spaces equipped with billiards, newspapers, and tables and chairs for conversation.[66] Progressive Era reformers thus mapped leisure in working-class communities along an axis that traversed inappropriate spaces, such as saloons, dubious ones, such as movie theaters, and appropriate ones, such as social clubs and playgrounds.

A similar set of reformist spatial strategies emerged in the controversies surrounding children's inevitable presence at the doors and windows of taverns with TV sets. To combat children's attraction to the tavern, benevolent groups established their own TV sites as alternatives.[67] These "television clubs" sponsored by churches, park districts, civic groups, and private individuals were considered ideal venues for keeping children occupied. One minister commented that "child welfare leaders have recognized that television has given them a 'natural' for attracting children to the church and to supervised clubs."[68] As this suggests, youth viewing sites also allowed adults to monitor children's activities. A successful Presbyterian TV club in Greenwich Village led a writer in the *Christian Century* to observe that although the site's "primary purpose was to get young people out of the taverns . . . the only places where most of them had a chance to see telecasts," it also allowed the church to "keep a watchful eye on the audience."[69] Several other reports noted television's disciplinary effect; as one organizer exclaimed, "one has only to witness a group of vigorous, hard to handle boys sitting meekly before a televised professional or college football game to realize the interest value of this new form of entertainment."[70]

Removing children from the unpredictable social arena of the tavern, where they might be exposed to the sight of drunken adults, TV clubs assembled youth within one space and directed their energy and attention toward a single point. The goal was, clearly, to organize and standardize youth social activities, creating watchers who were themselves more easily watched.[71] In spatializing TV spectatorship by age these TV clubs were an

early and forceful example of an administrative use of TV to control behavior and standardize audience identity in public space. Indeed, they are
surpassed only by retail TV installations at the point of sale in their treatment of the screen as a device that can "micromanage" the behavior of
subjects in social space.

However, as with all attempts at micromanagement, it should be immediately noted that whether these disciplinary uses of TV in juvenile
recreation were *effective* is another question entirely. In one instance several factors combined to thwart a juvenile viewing site's good intentions
quite spectacularly. The site in question was the Louisville, Ky., public
library, which employed college students as "television sitters" to "keep
the sets adjusted and protected, and to supervise the crowd." [72] The library
experienced problems with this youth TV scheme almost as soon as it
was established. A local newspaper article reported that "some of the kids
are throwing things at the operators, the machines, and the windows."
In addition, parents were using the library TV as a babysitter while they
"went merrily to parties," not returning until late in the evening to collect
their children. The article also claimed that adult drunks were crashing the
show—a situation that surely ran counter to one of the general purposes of
juvenile viewing sites: preventing children from witnessing the spectacle
of adult drunkenness. [73] Furthermore, library board members complained
that the programs children were watching were highly unsuitable. Father
Felix Pitt, secretary of the city's Catholic School Board, expressed hor-
ror that the young viewers had been allowed to watch a broadcast of the
movie *The Private Life of Henry VIII.* Rather than discontinue the project,
the library handed responsibility over to the city's recreation department,
replacing the college student "sitters" with personnel trained in juvenile
management. [74]

Another controversy over young viewers is perhaps more revealing,
however, because it exemplifies in very concrete ways how much administrative rhetorics of TV viewing judged the medium in site-specific terms.
For it was a controversy based on the assumption that the screen's physical
environment has more effect on the spectator than the image it displays.
It happened in 1948, when Patrick "Parkey" Radigan, a Hoboken, N.J.,
tavern owner, decided to close his tavern to adults for an hour in the afternoon and invite neighborhood children in to watch *Howdy Doody* and
Small Fry Club. Radigan's motives were philanthropic and reformist; as he
told the *New York Times,* "most of [the kids] come from poor families and
can't afford to see a big ball game, or, for that matter, too much of any kind

of entertainment. And besides, it seemed like a good way to keep them off the streets."[75] But the state Alcoholic Beverage Commissioners quickly put a stop to the "children's hour." With or without patrons, they argued, the physical space of the tavern was a corrupting influence. As one official put it, "A barroom hardly constitutes the proper setting for a 'Children's Hour.' . . . Longfellow would turn in his grave."[76] An area veterans group stepped in to carry on the custom, adding a TV club room to its lodge.[77]

This relocation communicates how inflexibly site-specific conceptions of the tavern as a space of adult spectatorship could be. At the heart of this "Saga of Parkey Radigan" was an unauthorized coupling of space and spectator, one considered incompatible with the wider forms of social regulation that defined the tavern as a space. Inviting children in to watch TV was a gesture of masculine domesticity that confused the rigid segregation of adult and child recreation that the tavern historically represented. Community versions of family "togetherness" could not, apparently, be formed safely within the seemingly autonomous sphere of adult leisure. In contrast, viewing sites established by church and civic groups upheld the segregation of adult and juvenile spectatorship.

Reformers were not alone in their efforts to achieve particular goals through the relocation of children from the tavern to other, more child-oriented spaces. Official juvenile viewing clubs, exposing large numbers of children to television, were also a great commercial opportunity for broadcasters. They fostered a potential home market for both set manufacturers and retailers, and TV corporations cultivated them by donating receivers or by establishing generous installment plans for charitable group viewing sites.[78] Such philanthropic gestures, creating goodwill for manufacturers, might eventually catalyze the parental decision to purchase a set for the household.[79] This was the explicit goal of the National Association of Broadcasters when it recommended that new television stations encourage viewership by establishing public youth viewing sites in theaters: "In effect, the theater would . . . [operate] as a public relations magnet to attract people to buy sets and to develop a station's audience."[80]

The tavern television screen's influence was thus quite extensive. It helped to segregate two TV viewing formations spatially: the barstool viewing collective and the juvenile viewing collective that loitered at the door. Although neither audience was targeted by a particular commercial address *on* the screen (with the possible exception of brewery-sponsored sports telecasts aimed at tavern viewers), their presence within these particular television locations made them fertile commercial markets, for set manufacturers and for the bar owners who saw television as a way to improve business.

The rise of the home audience in the late 1940s and early 1950s meant that the tavern screen was not a distinct force of spectatorship for long. Indeed, home viewing seemed, to some in the tavern trade, eventually to pose a threat to the social space of the bar. Like theater managers and sports promoters, tavern keepers apparently perceived a loss of business from the rise of household TV ownership. As early as 1950 *Beverage Media* found it necessary to ask, "Is there an answer to television for the tavern and restaurant trade? Television has hurt, without question. Top flight programs are keeping prospective customers at home."[81] As a solution *Beverage Media* suggested a spatial reorganization of the tavern environment: "Television cannot be fought by ignoring it. On an increasing scale, operators are providing television screens that give patrons at the bar *and* tables maximum visibility to enjoy TV programs as they do at home *with* the inducement of the bar's conviviality."[82] It is quite possible that this reference to "patrons at . . . tables" is also a reference to women, as tables were often seen as the designated place in the bar social environment for women. Several tavern owners I interviewed in the course of writing this book noted that their remodeling in the postwar period involved adding "tables for the ladies."[83] Television, this suggests, ultimately helped to bring women into the tavern—a possibility that returns us to the image of the female tavern spectator in figure 1, a patron whose acceptance within the space of the bar may have been made easier by the screen's presence there too.

This 1950 complaint against television in the tavern can also be read in a wider historical context, though, as a portent of the large-scale transformation of working-class urban culture that would take place in the decades to come. The postwar years brought increased geographical and social mobility to urban residents, many of whom left the city for suburban areas in this period. The result was a downward turn in the fortunes of urban neighborhoods, which saw dramatic changes between the 1950s and the 1970s: the progressive erosion of an urban manufacturing base, the construction of a highway system that would cut through neighborhoods and the spatial ties of interconnection that helped forge them, and the processes of urban renewal, or "negro removal," as James Baldwin called it, that would balkanize city neighborhoods along racial lines.[84] If the neighborhood bar declined as a social space in the postwar years, this decline surely had more to do with these wider material processes than with the television set, whether at home or perched atop the bar. The impact of a thirteen-inch screen on the social space of a particular tavern does not compare to the impact of a factory closing right next door to it or a two-level four-lane highway passing by its front door. The next and final section of this chapter pursues these historical implications in the present day, focusing both on social-spatial circumstances, like postwar urban decline, and forms of technological change, like satellite broadcasting, to trace the contours of barstool spectatorship as a continuing part of everyday public leisure.

From Starr's Tavern to the All-Star Cafe

Although it was a shift in methodological gears, I made a pilgrimage when I was near the completion of this chapter's historiographic narrative. I wanted to understand the effects of the postwar years' place-altering spatial processes on the tavern, both as a social space and as a public environment for the TV screen, in material terms—as sensory facts, in other words, if only partial and "unrigorously" collected ones. I therefore sought out the five Jersey City bars—among them Tommie's bar and Munzy's Tavern shown in figures 2 and 3—that someone from Goodman's Furniture Store photographed in the mid-1940s. In many ways Jersey City was a perfect place to seek answers to the question of the afterlife of the tavern in the changing urban world of the postwar decades. Located between New York City and Newark, Jersey City is a place where national networks of transportation and communications converge as they enter New York from the west. Criss-crossed and shadowed by train trestles and highway interchanges, it is a town that is constantly being rebuilt. Indeed, it was Jersey City's aura of being permanently transitional that prompted urbanist Kevin Lynch to choose it as a case study in spatial confusion in his classic 1960 text on the urban experience, *The Image of the City*.[85] I suspected that these tavern photographs, taken during the 1940s, represented what might be called the city's boom years. In this period Jersey City was both a major manufacturing center and the site of some extensive New Deal building projects, including a huge public hospital and a baseball stadium.[86] I wondered if this prosperity might explain why these neighborhood tavern owners had chosen to spend money on television sets, even before regular broadcasting had been established. But I also knew that Jersey City's prosperity had not lasted. The decline of manufacturing, a ruinously corrupt local government, and a series of drastic urban renewal projects combined to change the social and commercial climate of Jersey City dramatically over the years since these images were taken.[87]

Given these changes, I doubted when I set out to look for these bars that they would still exist. Still, I wanted to know what had become of them and the working-class, manufacturing-oriented districts of the city in which they were located. Sure enough, in the years since these photographs were taken, one of the four neighborhoods represented in this collection of images had been entirely razed. Two other bars preserved in these photos, including Tommie's bar (fig. 3), had been knocked down to make way for other buildings. But perhaps surprisingly, the two remaining bars are still open today. One (formerly Munzy's tavern, fig. 2) is now a private club for the Knights of Columbus, but the other, Starr's tavern, is still open to the public. And, as I discovered when I visited on a warm summer afternoon, many of its features seem to recall the 1940s, when the photograph in figure 5 was taken.

But rather than become starry-eyed about the timeless durability of urban working-class culture, I found that Starr's tavern as a present-tense institution reflects the changes that have occurred in urban neighborhood life over the years. As figure 6 indicates, the layout of the space is now quite different. The worn, twenty-foot bar had been moved to the other side of the room in the 1950s to accommodate the expanded short-order kitchen and to make way for more tables. Business was good in this period, and the bar was transported manually, with the lifting power of a large group of customers. The story of this event seemed central to the history of Starr's; over the course of my visit two customers, as well as the bartender, told it to me, I think to convey a sense of bygone networks of sociality. The decline of these networks is indicated in the fact that the long bar shelves stocked with row after row of liquor bottles have disappeared, and the large area in the back has been given over to storage. And nowadays the doors close at 5 P.M. on weekends, sometimes before the baseball game ends.

The story of what happened to this tavern and its neighborhood since the 1940s is a familiar one. When the owner, Frank Starr, purchased his two TV sets in the 1940s, the bar was packed every day with workers from the nearby American Can Company plant. The company remained in the neighborhood until the 1970s, when it moved to nearby Edison, N.J. After that patronage dropped off dramatically. Apparel mills and print and machine shops eventually moved into the empty factory building, now renamed the American Corporate Center. The retention of the initials is sig-

Starr's Tavern
854 Newark Avenue
Jersey City, N.J.

Installed and serviced b
Goodman's

FIG. 5

Starr's Tavern, c. 1944. The bar is on the left, and the screen sits high in the corner above it. (DuMont Collection, Archives Center, National Museum of American History, Smithsonian Institution)

FIG. 6

Starr's Tavern today. When the long bar was moved to the other side of
the room in the early 1950s, the TV set moved with it. Still a small-screen
model, it now sits on the left, next to the Heineken sign.

nificant, perhaps, suggesting the original owner has remained identified with the building in local usage long after it changed hands. Yet despite the major changes Starr's has undergone, many features from the 1940s remain. The cash register is the same, as are the tin ceiling, the glass door (now alarmed), and the wood paneling. The TV set is still a small one, and it still perches high above the bar, next to an old menu board on which updated prices written on scraps of paper have been taped. The bar still serves its culinary specialty, perfected by the owner's brother in the 1930s: a crisp, deep-fried foot-long hot dog.[88] And it is still a stop on the itineraries of the (now primarily Latino) labor force employed in the light industry of the ACC building and other nearby plants. Several workers stopped by at the end of the day to cash their paychecks during my visit, although they did not stay to drink or eat.[89]

What does the local narrative of Starr's history tell us about the social space of spectatorship that materialized around the barroom TV? In some ways it puts this space into a radical kind of perspective. Although I do not explore this point until later in this book, my encounter with Starr's history called attention to the concrete, material processes that shape the screen's environment, forcefully conveying the inadequacy of theoretical characterizations of television's spatial effects as, simply, the eradication of a place's specificity. In a Heideggerian turn, Weber describes TV spectatorship as a process in which the screen "takes place" by undermining "the unequivocal determination of place and bodily situation" and by fracturing "the space defined by the television set."[90] But what I witnessed in Starr's was a very different relationship between screen and space than what Weber understands as the fundamental "undecidability" endemic to the medium's physical form. What transformed Starr's tavern from a central hub of neighborhood work-leisure relations into a residual cultural site was not TV; its impact on the bar's social environment was nothing compared to other local forces. The patterns of work, community, and leisure that gave television viewing in the tavern its gender and class identity in the first place threatened the livelihood of the tavern when they themselves changed. Television's intrusion could not compare to the far more powerful intruder narratives that were being produced in white urban culture at the time, "racial-spatial" narratives of the reorganization of social relations in the city.

But perceptions of television as an agent of destruction for neighborhood taverns are very persistent. Starr's is precisely the kind of local, beer-drinking institution that commentators mourned when the televisual institution of the sports bars arrived on the scene in the late 1970s and early 1980s.[91] It might be tempting, indeed, to adopt Lawrence Wenner's schema and view ageless neighborhood taverns like Starr's as "authentic" spaces of social interaction and sports spectatorship, wholly opposed to the escapist, theme-park fantasy of the "postmodern" sports bar that "is designed as an 'experience' as opposed to a real place." [92]

Insisting too strenuously on this distinction between the "real tavern" and the "inauthentic sports bar" not only leads us toward reductive binaries, but it also obscures some of the deeper historical currents that bind the two spaces together. As I want to detail now, by way of conclusion, the rise of the sports bar bears several similarities to TV's introduction in the tavern. Like the latter it is a social, commercial institution that grew with a new communications technology and industry sector, in this case commercial satellite broadcasting. Indeed, if we compare the site-specific discourses on spectatorship produced around the sports bar as a historical and economic institution with the ones that accompanied TV's entry into taverns like Starr's, a similar process rises to the surface. In each case the screen's relationship to its environment is shaped by the latter's location within wider contexts of commerce and social power.

Like the postwar tavern's TV set, the sports bar screen opened up a new site of audienceship in the sports and entertainment market. And similarly, its spectatorial environment raised issues of regulation and policy in the commercial sphere of audience markets. The substantial number of viewers in sports bars who were watching the satellite feeds that networks transmitted to their local affiliates led sports magnates to ask whether sports bars were, in a sense, siphoning off a portion of the regular broadcast audience. To be sure, there are important differences between the regulatory challenges brought against the postwar tavern and the sports bar. In the former the exhibition of live sports images was defined as unfair competition for ballparks; in the latter it became equivalent to theft. But this difference only indicates the "progress" of industrial strategies for commodifying both broadcast transmissions and localized audiences in the years between the two moments. It should not obscure the fact that objections to the sports bar audience bear a remarkable similarity to those that baseball owners and film exhibitors brought to bear on the tavern.

Sports bars were first accused of "stealing" network audiences and signals in 1989. The NFL successfully sued several sports-bar owners for receiving broadcasts of sports events directly from network feeds, via satellite, rather than tuning in to the local network affiliate's retransmission of this signal. The practice was illegal, NFL officials argued, because it effectively "shortchanged" local and regional advertisers, preventing them from reaching a sector of the markets they had paid for.[93] The following year, a month before the September opening of the football season, the organization announced plans to scramble its telecasts so that only local affiliates would be able to receive the signals, something it had threatened to do for many years.[94] But after sponsoring breweries sided with the bar owners, the NFL relented and agreed to license games to subscribing sports bars in packages that would be prorated to accommodate different-sized audience commodities (the most well-known is the Sunday Ticket plan, started in 1994).[95] Local teams ostensibly agreed to take responsibility for prosecuting bars that pirated the NFL signal, although this system was apparently less than effective.[96]

As this regulatory narrative indicates, both the tavern and the sports bar gave rise to institutional anxieties about audience activity and its economic impact, rooted in TV's ability to alter, if only symbolically, the *scale* on which a place and its population figure in wider markets of spectacle and amusement. The sports bar may produce a more refined and advanced audience commodity than the tavern did in the postwar years, and it may be a more mediatized space with its multiple video screens and other sports-related amusements; but, at least in policy terms, it is an extension, rather than a violation, of the tavern's collective relations of spectatorship.

Another continuity between the taverns of early TV and sports bars is the way both offer environmentally enhanced "live" sports experiences, although in the latter case the architectural and technological forms that construct spectatorial spaces in the bar are far more differentiated. Sports bars are filled with innumerable technologies of sports vision: satellite screens, on-site broadcasts, boxing rings, skeeball, foosball, shuffleball, indoor golf courses, batting cages, basketball baskets, videotex score updates, computerized "rotisserie" leagues, tailgate parties, and video games like Sport Active Football, in which players "coach teams of real athletes and watch them compete on TV before a stadium of cheering spectators."[97] These technologies deliver many different ways to participate in the spectator sports experience. When the two-floor Original Sports Bar in Baltimore opened in 1989, for example, it promised its patrons a variety of televisual scenographies in which to combine live sports and drinking: in addition to the bar and cocktail tables, it featured separate lounges with a "press box area" and offset booths equipped with private TV sets. Like the TV screens in sporting goods and apparel stores today, this proliferation of delivery options offers multiple embodiments of a "live" sports experience — coach, athlete, reporter, viewer, crowd participant.[98] Although some critics might assert that this spectacular space is different than the old-world charm of the 1940s bar, it seems to me that the postwar TV tavern offered similar promises — recall the ersatz bleakers and prosceniumlike presentation described in press reports. And then as now, TV sports at the bar served as the cultural emblem of a particular kind of masculinist, collectivity, a place where sports journalists go to gauge fans' reactions to the home team's failures and successes.

Perhaps the most instructive aspect of the comparison between the sports bar and the tavern, however, is the fact that, although the dollar value of the barstool audience may be far greater now, tavern viewing was one of the first occasions for linking TV audience identities, and their values in the political economy of broadcasting, to the screen's presence in a particular place. Whereas in the home *time* was, and is, one of the central means of distinguishing viewer identities (for example, the assumed female viewer of daytime TV), the gendered geography of everyday life outside the home made it possible to classify viewer identities in *spatial* terms as well. This location-based idea of the spectator would later come to define the political economy of TV audiences for "out-of-home" networks, a process described in chapter 3 of this book. However, as the following chapter suggests, the tavern was not the only place in which equations of space and identity formed the basis of commercial TV practices outside the home. The fact that the department store was conventionally considered a middle-class female space meant that the installation of the TV set within it was a discursive process that took correspondingly gendered forms. The prototypically male, working-class sports fan constructed in press reports of the TV tavern had little in common with the ideal female shopper-viewer that department store executives imagined in their point-of-purchase TV experiments in the same years. But each of these site-specific discourses of the spectator illustrates how TV's presence in particular spaces occasions new forms of strategic social "knowledge" about the people who inhabit them.

To understand how such location-based ideas about the TV viewer emerged, and the cultural politics they gave expression to in the process, we must grasp the distinctive features attributed to each of these TV sites in the postwar period. The extent of the distance between the department store and the bar as TV institutions can be gauged in a 1947 TV industry survey of department stores and their various television projects. According to this survey, one reason that some department stores were hesitating to embark on TV sponsorship was "the bar and grill trade." The article explained that store managers believed "that the greatest number of sets are concentrated among this group—with store feeling being that the best time to influence customers and sell merchandise is *not* when they're sipping a drink." [99] What remained unspoken here was the idea that the tavern audience, perceived as male and working class, was not a target market for the department store's commercial appeals. Collating space and identity to match a certain vision of what TV was and what it could do, the rhetorics of spectatorship associated with both places thus reflected particular (gendered) institutional histories. The postwar history of television as a point-of-purchase display technology in department stores, a history recounted in the next chapter, is therefore instructive as much for its *differences* from tavern TV as for its similarities.

CHAPTER 2

GENDERED FANTASIES OF TV SHOPPING
IN THE POSTWAR DEPARTMENT STORE

Contemporary visitors to the department store may be jaded enough now to ignore the commercial appeals that continually blare from unattended video screens on the sales floor. But in the years surrounding World War II, shoppers lined up in droves to see the television receivers that were starting to appear in department stores across the country. Most often these receivers were presented to the public as a new form of merchandise—a new commodity. But sometimes, especially in the days before widespread network broadcasting, the goals behind TV's exhibition in the store were more elaborate. Many large retailers heralded the medium's arrival by staging free exhibitions of television technology for the education and edification of the general public. These exhibitions were in line with other kinds of gala events held in department stores at the time, events that mirrored museum displays in the didactic views of art and industry they offered store visitors. Held in large auditoria or even on the sales floor, these festivals of progress placed an inordinate emphasis on the consumer applications of the modern technologies and artifacts they displayed. For example, noting in 1938 that "lectures and lessons . . . are two of the most popular department store services," a *Reader's Digest* article listed examples of numerous store exhibitions and educational shows, each of which clearly had an underlying commercial appeal, including "enlarged models of moths . . . shown at their horrid tasks [with] improved scientific methods for dealing with the insect."[1] Such exhibitions in addition marked the department store's high cultural position, its claim to a community status that went beyond that of a commercial establishment. They were aspirational displays, designed to elevate the store by aligning it with other marketing spectacles of the modern state like world's fairs and expositions.[2]

The department store's affinity with the space of the world's fair made it a useful, if not crucial, space for receiver manufacturers and broadcasters like RCA in their efforts to publicize commercial television. Mixing commerce with pedagogy, stores could teach the public about the new medium in three ways at once: as a modern technological marvel, as a novel new form of entertainment, and as an object available for purchase. Store managers in turn welcomed a connection with TV because it allowed them to discharge their duties as modernity's vanguard in consumer culture and affirmed the department store's historical role as a site for what venerated turn-of-the-century retailer John Wanamaker called the "education of desire." Indeed, after RCA presented the new medium to the public at the 1939 World's Fair, eighty-eight department stores, from Portland, Oregon, to Manchester, New Hampshire, sponsored a nationwide tour of the exhibit, showcasing "live" TV images to an estimated three million people.[3] As at the world's fair, this traveling exhibition presented visitors with a "Television Test Certificate" showing that the bearer had appeared on television. However, this tour surpassed the fair's presentation in that it emphasized television's value as a medium of commerce, as well as a technological wonder. Its viewers, like many of the urban publics who would see the new medium in the department store after the war, were treated not only to a glimpse of TV but also to a series of prototypical television advertisements featuring store merchandise.[4]

After the war several TV exhibits adopted the model of the television tour of 1939 and presented television advertising as a merchandising device designed to stimulate sales in the store by directing the shopper toward products in featured departments. These presentations, experimental in nature, were the first occasion of what is now one of the most widespread uses of video outside the home—as a sales tool at the point of purchase.[5] The idea of using TV in the store this way was an abiding retail dream. As early as 1930, modernist architect Frederick Kiesler predicted that television broadcasts of "fashion news would be a regular feature of window display" and speculated that they might help to train shoppers in their purchasing decisions.[6] Kiesler's passing reference to fashion indicates that the target audience of in-store TV advertising was from the very beginning imagined as female; indeed, a decade or so later, when department store managers and broadcast professionals first speculated about what in-store TV advertisements could do for sales, they often invoked a gendered equation of space, identity, and consumer desire. As numerous historians and critics have noted, the social architecture of department stores gave material form to institutional fantasies of the female gaze throughout the twentieth century. Professional ideas about how women look and move formed the basis of detailed techniques for the display of commodities and for moving shoppers into and through the store: striking window treatments, curved counters, escalators, mannequins, and more.[7] In Anne Friedberg's words, the store's visual spectacle of material things was "a sheltered refuge for itinerant lookers" designed to incite in the bourgeois female spectator of everyday life—the *flaneuse*—"the indirect desire to possess and incorporate through the eye."[8] It seemed only logical that TV could enhance this gendered visual culture of consumption with its powers of detailed display and demonstration of products on the sales floor.

But although TV and the store seemed like an ideal pairing, gala experiments with advertising on the sales floor were surely thinly veiled publicity stunts. They provided free exposure for TV stations, introduced the new medium to its potential owner-viewers, and trained them as an audience all at once. This is evident enough in the fact that by 1949 retail experiments with in-store TV advertising systems ceased, dismissed by most observers as costly and ineffective. Still, their ephemeral nature does not mean that these store TV systems are historically insignificant. Although they were short-lived, they have an important place in the history of TV outside the home. They prompted a wealth of discussions in the pages of journals like *Department Store Economist* and *Display World* about how advertising in the store might appeal to a female shopper-viewer and what they might do for sales. These ideas about television's spatial effects, circulating among retail professionals, can teach us about how institutional theories of television spectatorship emerge from site-specific discourses of space, in this case the motivational, persuasive architecture of the store, which had historically embodied cultural ideals of consumer spectatorship and desire. And, as the contemporary proliferation of in-store media networks indicates, postwar visions of TV shopping were also prescient forecasts of a future trend. Indeed, the manner in which these retailers explained the desires of the consumer shopper in architectural terms anticipates the manner in which on-site networks today hypothesize a link between their audience's identities, their receptivity, and their location—a logic detailed extensively in a later chapter.

This chapter traces how TV became integrated into retail space and charts its role in the visual and spatial ideologies of consumption associated with department store display and architecture. Television's early

arrival on the sales floor of department stores materialized postwar retail ideas about female consumer vision, occasioning an enduring institutional discourse on the TV screen as a technology for micromanaging
both the literal and figurative mobility of subjects in consumer culture.
Examining these early retail attempts to "televisualize" the sales floor, we
can glimpse how particular televisual forms — advertising forms like the
product demonstration, in particular — get taken up in architectural theories of longing and motivation. These theories extended to encompass
professional assessments of the differences *between* spaces of TV viewing.
Department store discourses on TV's relation to its environment in this
period had a strongly comparative flavor; many conceptions of commercial TV on the sales floor sought to differentiate the imagined female shopper's visual desire in the store from her consumer attitudes in the home.
For example, retail expert E. B. Weiss, an early proponent of mass-market
methods in department store retailing, suggested in 1948 that *in-store*
TV could never "overdo" advertising messages, as TV in the *home* might:
"Broadcast television will tend to overemphasize merchandise. That's because broadcast television goes into the home, where the atmosphere is
quite different. But in a store, and particularly in a department store with
its vast variety and assortment of fashion merchandise, the appeal of [tele-
vised] merchandise to the woman shopper is *supreme.*"[9] The accuracy of
this confident pronouncement is suspect, to say the least. However, what
makes it striking is the site-specific perception of television's effects it
presents. Weiss's tellingly "local" understanding of the spectator not only
places a strong emphasis on the role of the environment in determining
the image's effects, assigning the commercial screen different roles within
different spaces of women's work and recreation, but it also situates the
TV image on a continuum with the sales floor's distinctive aesthetic and
its layout.

Like the networks that install TV commercials in the food courts of
shopping malls today, hoping to place some items on the viewer's post-
prandial shopping itinerary, Weiss — and other retail commentators on TV
in this period, as we shall see — understood the screen as a speaking object
that could reorganize relations of commerce within a place. In this respect
his remarks demonstrate the longevity of what is now a pervasive institutional theory of television's effects outside the home, namely, that it is
capable of altering the experience of space and time within its locale for
immediate commercial gain. But the fervency with which retail professionals like Weiss embraced the idea of in-store TV and imagined its effect

on women shoppers suggests something more, too. As I will later detail, retailers approached the new medium as a kind of solution to some of the problems and uncertainties they faced in their professional attempts to control female consumer vision within the store, especially given some anticipated transformations in retailing that would take place in the postwar decades.

Department store TV also teaches us something about the way local, pre-network TV sponsors approached advertising in the home, using broadcasting to situate domestic space within a regional geography of commerce and consumption. To write the early history of TV in the department store is also, necessarily, to write the history of the department store's appearance *on* early TV. In addition to tracing the use of TV *in* the store, this chapter looks at the commercial programming conventions stores used when they advertised on local broadcast television. Department stores were among the first sponsors for the few stations that were on the air right after the war, when the fact that only a small number of TV households existed meant that sponsorship was as much a way of garnering prestige as it was a technique for increasing sales.[10] Store and screen were frequently paralleled in broadcasting rhetoric, which often represented TV to sponsors as a form of show window in the home. This metaphorical collapse of store and home became a slogan for at least two TV corporations; a DuMont brochure from 1944 hailed TV as "the best show window in the world," and the following year RCA called TV sponsorship "a new show window in the home."[11] The programs I examine, which bore an uncanny resemblance to today's home-shopping programs and infomercials, sought to demonstrate store merchandise to the viewer at home. But like early point-of-purchase TV experiments, they were inherently *regional* phenomena, embedded in the retail economies of a particular metropolitan area. Examining how the space of the store and the space of the home were figured as televisual sites of consumption is therefore also an important case study in how institutional discourses of the television screen as an environmental technology, capable of interweaving with and shaping behaviors in space, extend beyond the space of the sales floor and into wider regional networks of consumer mobility.

Retail display, the institutional context in which department store professionals envisioned television as a site-specific apparatus for micromanaging consumer's movements, was the historical precursor to the brand-driven in-store sales tool known today as "point-of-purchase advertising." This category of commercial speech needs some explaining; it is distinct from other advertising categories in that it specifically targets a consumer who is, as the folksy vernacular of retail writing puts it, "aisles, not miles" away from the product and from the cash register. Point-of-purchase advertising includes window display, mechanical and live demonstrations, manufacturer promotions, and even package design. As a category it grew steadily in the 1930s, along with other changes in the spatial form of retailing. Most notable among these was the rise of self-service sales floors, a form inaugurated with the introduction of chain stores and supermarkets and that spread rapidly across a host of retail categories in the postwar years. As a design concept self-service changed the way retailers and manufacturers envisioned the consumer's relation to the commodity. At base, self-service required that the product "speak" directly to the buyer in a way it never had before. Advertising on the sales floor consequently also gained a greater prominence in managerial conceptions of the shopping process as self-service systems continued to spread throughout the retail industry. In the absence of salesclerks, point-of-purchase advertising strengthened the product's "voice" in the marketplace; it helped to direct shoppers through the commercial space of the self-service sales floor, beckoning to them and pointing their bodies and vision in particular directions (ending up, of course, at the cash register).

Because self service retailing assigns point-of-purchase advertising the double task of initiating both a desire and a sequence of actions based on this desire, it is to this day highly dependent on marketing theories of consumer behavior.[12] In the postwar years, as today, these theories were often explicit in their categorization of behaviors by gender and other identity information. As detailed later, the first professional advocates of point-of-purchase television advertising advanced their arguments on the basis of empirical market research. Although their retail visions of spectatorship are probably best viewed not as empirical truth but rather as a new chapter in the wishful patriarchal narrative of quantifying female consumer desire, we should not underestimate their power. For to this day they are a means by which commercial institutions construct women's activities in public realms as practices that can be channeled, predicted, and made more profitable by spatial and technological means.[13]

Television's adoption as a form of advertising on the self-service sales floor was no doubt aided by the fact that commercialized moving images had been a staple fixture of the store environment since the beginning of the century. Window displays were not static tableaux; often they were animated spectacles. Mechanical devices such as spinning pedestals or animatronic mannequins were popular attention-getting devices, and some window displays even featured live models. The store was also enmeshed in wider networks of downtown metropolitan recreation and consumer amusements. In particular, throughout the first half of the century department stores' dense visual spectacles were closely linked to the cinema institutionally, architecturally, and spatially, a link that stimulated sales with a regular cycle of Hollywood merchandising tie-ins.[14]

But film preceded TV as a point-of-purchase merchandising apparatus more directly, too: department stores regularly placed small, portable rear-projection film systems to demonstrate products on the sales floor.[15] The kind of spectatorship these filmic images encouraged was not of the same order as narrative film's sutured absorption; it was, rather, closely bound up with the particular characteristics of the store as a commercial environment. Institutional perceptions of what shoppers wanted meant that particular genres and topics predominated: how-to demonstrations, manufacturer films about the production process, and institutional messages of consumer goodwill. Trade press discussions of these commercial films in the store provide some clues to the overall commercial role that screen spectatorship was assigned within the retail environment around the time of television's introduction. In 1944, for example, a producer of commercial films for in-store exhibition explained in the *Journal of Marketing* that such visual aids were an ideal application of "machine methods" to retailing. Just as the "machine principles" of automation had increased production, so, he argued, could they increase consumption as well, by "standardizing the sales pitch" and ensuring "uniformity in . . . quality and character."[16]

This rather extremist theory of retail spectatorship, Taylorizing consumption with images, reflected a particular vision of the store that emerged in this period—the idea of the store as machine. Richard Longstreth, a historian of commercial architecture, notes that this metaphor gained rapid popularity among retail professionals in the years surrounding World War II. The rising influence of architects like Morris Lapidus and Victor Gruen led to the emergence of a set of design and display principles in the department store that could, Gruen declared, turn department stores into "machines for selling."[17] One model of the store as both a space of spectatorship and kind of commercial machine is evident in the illustration shown in figure 7, an advertising image made by the DuPont chemical corporation at the end of the war. Produced as one of a series of institutional ads demonstrating the company's commitment to

Sitdown Shopping?

COULD BE! The department store of the future would shock all of us—if it suddenly appeared today, fullfledged with innovations in selling methods.

Instead of weary shoppers trudging past the merchandise, perhaps the merchandise will move past the shoppers. Certainly, bright ideas will develop self-service and impulse buying far beyond what we know today.

Brilliant displays of merchandise will make today's shops look strangely old-fashioned. Packages will be more efficient, more appealing, more self-selling. Prevention of spoilage and soilage will also be a "must" for every package.

In the post-war world to come, keener competition and improvements in merchandising and distribution methods will demand the maximum in scientific packaging skill.

FIG. 7
A midcentury vision of futuristic shopping in a factory-like department store. (DuPont Collection, Hagley Museum and Library)

the bright future of technological change, this image of the "store of the future" shows a fantasy of the impending transformation of everyday activities, such as shopping, that the end of the war would bring. Female shoppers sit in front of a conveyer belt on which an endless variety of consumer goods flows, and telephone lines link the shoppers to a group of store operators who take their orders in a nearby room. As the copy for the advertisement explains, "Instead of weary shoppers trudging past the merchandise, perhaps the merchandise will move past the shoppers." No doubt a product of its historical moment, namely, the wartime production economy in which conveyor belts staffed by women played a crucial role, this image exemplifies the machine ethos of the midcentury store. Like the commercial film producer cited above, it projected the modernist fantasies of efficiency and mechanization, materialized specifically here in the conveyer belt, onto practices of *consumption*.[18] Immobilizing the shopper and animating the commodity instead, it suggests a utopian ideology of retail desire and mobility, imagining a visit to the store in which all noncommodity-oriented distractions and physical movements are eliminated in order to concentrate the shopper's gaze on one thing only: the merchandise.

Although this image is not a representation of television spectatorship, it is strikingly parallel to its theoretical depiction in several ways. The conveyer belt loaded with commodities recalls Raymond Williams's famous description of television programming as a segmented flow—a flow that, as Patricia Mellencamp has noted, places TV spectatorship within a modernist economy of production based on the assembly line.[19] Moreover, its use of the telephone, a technology of domestic consumption often combined with radio to promote shopping in the home in the years before TV, might be taken as a reference to the period's idea of "interactive media." Such parallels between fantasies of the store of the future and the visual relations of television viewing are not surprising, however, given the strong ties between broadcasting and the store at the time (see note 12). In the period when this image was produced, articles on the selling power of television, which often proposed that TV could mechanize the shopping trip in similar ways, appeared thick and fast in the three major retail trade journals, especially *Display World,* for window and sales floor decorators.[20] Some observers even predicted that interactive closed-circuit television would replace the traditional system of written communication via pneumatic tubes in department stores.[21]

Before tracing how these ideas about TV as an instrument that could mechanize shopping emerged, it is worth pointing out that other, more pragmatic factors shaped retailers' initial interest in in-store TV as well. Much of TV's value lay in its ability simply to attract people to the store. Its mere presence gave the impression that stores were modernizing their merchandising techniques in preparation for postwar abundance. In 1945 the president of Gimbel's in Philadelphia explained that "with the centrifugal pull of chain, neighborhood, and drive-in stores, a center city department store needs to be more and more an interesting, as well as convenient place in which to shop. The use of television can be an important factor in accomplishing this."[22] Such hopes for television reflected the changing retail landscape of the city at midcentury; shifts in the geography of consumption that were beginning to occur in cities like Los Angeles before the war returned unabated in the postwar years.[23] Increased automobile traffic and congestion in downtown areas led to concerns among retailers that people preferred to shop outside the city center. More stores began to construct suburban branches with parking lots, and companies such as Macy's and Saks began the expansion that would transform them into nationwide chains. Competition from chain stores such as Sears, J. C. Penney, and Woolworth's intensified, especially as such stores had already captured the burgeoning suburban market. The department store was rapidly appearing old fashioned in relation to this growing chain and variety store trade; store executives' interest in television, and more generally, in mass marketing, surely reflected these changing circumstances.

As Lynn Spigel has detailed, futuristic ideologies of TV as a technology of space-binding and remote vision were common in this period.[24] These tropes of spatial collapse were easily integrated in the techniques department stores adopted to compete with chain stores and other newer types of retail establishments—self-service, open floor plans, more stock on the floor.[25] This is evident in the publicity surrounding the first postwar test of point-of-purchase television, held at the Gimbel's store in Philadelphia shortly after the end of the war. This "experiment" was designed to find out whether screening in-store TV advertising might help direct traffic to far-flung areas of the store and stimulate impulse buys, in addition to generally attracting more shoppers. It should be noted that Gimbel's use of television to achieve these effects on the sales floor differed from contemporary point-of-purchase television in some respects. Whereas the TV image generally appears today on a free-standing console or wall-mounted screen placed close to merchandise on the open sales floor, Gimbel's isolated its TV viewers spatially, in small rooms equipped with rows of chairs. This setup recalls the visual relations of cinema spectatorship, although it must also have produced a cozy, domestic atmosphere for the fantasy of "sit-down shopping" it offered. Later analyzing the event, the store president presciently predicted that future installations of TV imagery in the department store would be placed on the open sales floor to attract traffic from afar. However, he noted, the enclosed screen was the only practical way of dealing with the large crowds expected to gather in front of the screen. His predictions were accurate; over a three-week period 250,000 people visited Gimbel's to view ten minutes of live advertising shot in the store's auditorium and transmitted to small TV receivers located in the twenty-two "telesites" dotted about the store.[26]

Television's value as a prestige-building sales technology of the future is also apparent in the way Gimbel's advertised its vision of television in the store to the Philadelphia public. The general tone of the store's description of the TV shopping trip was celebratory, promoting an experience both entertaining and efficient. Full-page advertisements in the *Philadelphia Inquirer* invited store visitors to participate in "an experiment that may change the shopping habits of a nation!" In an effusive tone it posed — and answered — the following question to its readers:

> Wouldn't it be wonderful if hours of weary shopping could be reduced to one wonderful, walloping piece of entertainment? Because we feel nothing in this modern age is impossible — not even being in three places at the same time — we're going to try and make these things come true. It all started with one idea — an idea that through the electronic wonder of our time, the almost magic, mysterious, scientific miracle — TELEVISION — you could relax in any one spot in our store, see a whole parade of products, and decide on anything from playpens to permanent waves without wasting a step.[27]

The shopper-spectator implied here is unquestionably female; in addition to playpens and permanent waves, other store products and services featured on the screen were "Millinery, scarfs, furs, nursery furniture, toys, curtains, interior decorating, and hair styling."[28] But what is perhaps more striking about this invitation is the way it highlights television's space-binding powers ("being in three places at the same time") and its ability to alter the experience of time within a place. Conceived as a spectacular form of live-action display case, Gimbel's TV thus offered store visitors the ocular power Friedberg calls "virtual mobility": the promise of a viewing experience in which the gaze substitutes for the physical exploration of space.[29]

It should be noted, however, that the experience of shopping that Gimbel's constructed via TV differs from the peripatetic pleasures of looking and wandering that Friedberg describes. In keeping with contemporaneous machine ideologies of modern retailing, Gimbel's version of television shopping aimed at making shopping's constant process of imagining and desiring more "productive" (of sales). In classic marketing style its ad copy presented this manipulation as a desire on the shopper's part—as if shoppers had somehow petitioned the management and requested that the tiresome problem of having to walk through the store be replaced by a better, more "efficient" way of shopping.

These ideas about TV viewing as efficient mobility emerged from existing ways of thinking about the store as a space in retailing, existing paradigms for linking commercial images, store architecture, and the temporal structure of the shopping trip to consumer behavior. The prewar idea of the store as a "machine for selling" led architects to refashion the postwar store as an ever more concentrated, systematic structure of physical and visual persuasion. The resulting idea of commercial architecture as a sales *system* echoed a concurrent shift in advertising's attempts to understand and predict the consumer. This was the shift business historian Merle Curti identifies as a turn toward highly behaviorist, "scientific" methods of market research.[30] In retailing this meant a new institutional discourse of merchandising that reconfigured the customer as a behavioral assemblage of eyes, legs, and pocketbook moving through a giant visual assembly. The broad ideological promises of television, its oft-touted "space-binding" powers in particular, meshed easily with professional fantasies of a mobile, visually motivated, feminine viewer-shopper.

The first of these "scientific" principles to enter retail design in this period involved a new approach to the bodily motions of shoppers as a mass. Mobility, as Margaret Morse has pointed out, was a central trope in postwar spatial reconstructions of the ideal subject of the American city and its environs, a subject privately transported to other visual worlds via television, retail space, and the freeway system.[31] Mobility was certainly of paramount importance for advocates of the machine-store model, who placed a high-premium on efficient traffic flow. In the 1920s, Longstreth notes, the fantasy image of the store of tomorrow had been a skyscraper surrounded by multistory highways, airplanes, and other transportation networks. But in the postwar period, he adds, this "earlier vision of . . . emporia towering thirty or forty stories, would have seemed as foolish to . . . merchants as the multilayered speedways through these towers seemed to traffic engineers." In these years the reigning paradigm in store construction was a "continuous selling space" with fewer stories and departments that flowed into each other.[32]

This new design principle, known as "free-flow planning" or "the fluid planning system," was an attempt to organize the movements of shoppers more precisely, transforming them into a ductile mass. The base of this architectural model was the idea that the ideal shopping trip was a form of "flow."[33] Descriptions of blueprints for sales floors based on this system imagined shoppers guided unconsciously toward merchandise by a "streamlined process in which traffic is automatically directed through desired channels, where all obstacles or resistance are removed."[34] Through a centrifugal action, customers entering a sales floor constructed by fluid planning would be "whirled away to the outermost selling reaches by a compulsion that can almost be felt in study of the [floor] plan."[35] In these calculated attempts to govern consumer mobility, postwar retailers transformed the perennial concern with traffic flow in store design into a rational science for wholly managing the movement of the shopper.

When broadcasters "pitched" point-of-purchase television to retailers, they often invoked it as a solution to traffic concerns and as an indispensable component of "fluid-planning." In 1945, for example, a DuMont representative told a meeting of department store executives that TV would create precise itineraries for shoppers: "by use of television specials you can direct traffic to upper floors and basement, and you can train customers to come in the early morning and mid-afternoon hours. By the use of strategically placed receivers, you can raise the volume of impulse buying [and] do a super job of suggestion selling for add-on sales."[36] Testing this possibility was the announced intention of Gimbel's' point-of-purchase TV experiment, which located its TV screens "with a view to guiding traffic through the store to certain departments."[37] A few years later journalist Grace Neville, writing "on behalf of the woman shopper," disputed the retail wisdom of using TV to direct traffic to undervisited departments: "There's a plan that could succeed so well that Milady—who traipsed all the way downtown with a fur jacket in mind—never *does* run the obstacle course to the fur department but goes home with an underprivileged egg-beater or bathmat—but think of the pangs of conscience that could set in later!"[38] For Neville TV images might impel customers *too* easily; in issuing a corrective to what she joked were clearly male views of the female shopper, she only reinforced the idea of the latter as fanciful and suggestible, impelled into motion, and purchasing action, by the television image of commodities.

A second set of scientific principles to color retail rhetoric at this time originated in the department store's postwar acknowledgment of the "mass selling" methods chain stores were using with great success. The trend toward open sales floors with more stock on display, intended to increase traffic flow and facilitate self-service, signaled the fact that department stores had begun to adopt mass-marketing methods in the postwar period. Along with this shift came a new understanding of the function of display within the store. The jargon term *visual merchandising* was introduced in this period as a more dynamic alternative to the rather old-fashioned and static connotations of the word *display* (eventually, the trade journal *Display World* would rename itself *Visual Merchandising*). As the phrase implies, visual merchandising endeavored to increase the *sales* impact of display techniques, influencing the decision to make a purchase by controlling the visual field of the customer.

Visual merchandising's proponents claimed to be compiling a repertoire of detailed, heavily researched display techniques guaranteed to make sales. The Visual Merchandising Council, formed in this period, conducted empirical studies of the eye movements and traffic vectors of the shopper, yielding such "facts" as the suggestive declaration that "eighty-five percent of all buying is through the eye"[39] and motivational adages such as the axiomatic pronouncement that "what's to be sold must first be seen."[40] The movement's rhetoric was also heavily weighted with pseudoscientific terms; visual principles were often presented as infallible edicts ("Goods should be exposed in a plane as close as possible to a right angle of moving sight") and mysterious formulae ("conceal all duplicates of the items shown, as close as possible to the point of sale").[41] Commonsense ideas were often reworked in the rhetoric of visual merchandising as quantifiable variables. Describing the shopper's visual habits, for example, retail professor Howard Cowee explained that "traffic has direction, speed, position, vision, and pronounced preferences with respect to the location and execution of displays."[42] Whether these ideas about the display's viewer as a maneuverable body were successful in increasing sales is another matter. But as an *ideology* of display, visual merchandising certainly presented itself as effective, claiming that the correct placement of display cases, counters, and signs could revolutionize store sales by training eye and body to shop more efficiently, or simply to shop *more*.

For all its scientific weight, certain elements of the discourse of visual merchandising suggest that at base the increased value of in-store display to the postwar store's sales campaign resulted from the pragmatic, cost-cutting methods department stores had also adopted from their chain store rivals. When display experts like Cowee called for a new emphasis on informative visual selling and on shoppers "automatically" guided by visual displays, it was because they knew that fewer and fewer salespersons were available to perform that task in person.[43] The department store's move toward a self-service sales floor, relying on packaging and manufacturer displays to address consumers and answer their questions about the product was accompanied by a steady reduction in staff in the postwar years. E. B. Weiss suggested that the move toward staffless selling in postwar department stores reflected the increasing "low level" of department store sales personnel training. Poor quality salesclerks, he argued, mandated an increased use of machinery as a tool for presentation. Weiss proposed that point-of-purchase TV was itself a form of mechanical demonstrator that could essentially automate the sales pitch, removing the need for "flesh-and-blood sales people."[44] In a similar vein a GE representative asserted that intrastore TV would eliminate other disadvantages of personal contact with salespeople in the store as well: "everyone is fascinated by a [live] demonstration, but many people are embarrassed to go near . . . because of the high pressure look-you-in-the-eye salesmanship usually involved. With television, you know no-one is breathing down your neck or holding out his palm, so you feel you're making up your own mind."[45]

Television's mechanized commercial appeal, such testimonies suggest, was a way of removing all the "noise" that interpersonal contact was perceived to bring to commercial interactions in the store. Its visual attraction was strong enough, one 1945 article anticipated, to integrate fully into the way women organize their time in the store: "As the regular customer becomes conditioned to your telecasting time schedule he or she (more likely) will be on hand to watch the special items advertised for the day such as the latest thing in millinery, which may have just come out of the marking room."[46] This idea of television imagery as a mechanized demonstration, Pavlovian in its effect on shoppers and seductive as both entertainment and information, helped justify the anticipated downsizing of department store sales forces later in the postwar period.[47]

However, over and above its pragmatic, labor-saving value, the televised in-store demonstration was attractive to retailers for more speculative reasons, deriving from long-standing concerns about the precise pathways of motivation of women shoppers. The fascinations of the product demonstration were perceived time and again as answers to the visual desires of women. At Gimbel's, for example, the point-of-purchase commercial presentations that aired for the Philadelphia public "every hour, on the half hour" presented stereotypically feminine merchandise in a series of continual direct addresses to the camera by an employee or spokesperson. Themes included "Hair Restyling, where an operator transformed coiffures, and . . . Scarf Magic [which] demonstrated how smart new uses of scarfs could change the same old dress." [48] Although the extensive surveys of viewers in the store did not prove that either format elevated sales of the items advertised on the screen, they did support the idea that viewers preferred these demonstrations over acted commercial scenes. [49] This "fact" immediately yielded interpretations saturated with gendered assumptions. E. B. Weiss pronounced Gimbel's TV advertising successful because "there is no greater *entertainment* for women when they are in a department store than *merchandise!* . . . Show merchandise—describe merchandise—demonstrate merchandise—talk merchandise." [50] Weiss's reference to "women" is especially significant given that photographs published in trade journals show many men, including servicemen, visiting Gimbel's to see the new medium. Weiss saw the fascinated spectator as female even though TV's novelty at the time meant that as many men as women could have been interested in seeing it, something which makes his interpretation notable primarily as a marker of the way retail professionals gendered the fascinations of the product demonstration.

Weiss's description of female consumer desire as an affect triggered automatically, simply through images of merchandise, provides some clues to the mental anatomy of the spectator figure that Gimbel's TV experiment constructed from wider retail ideas about women's visual preferences. Note that although its context is the utopian possibility that TV might mechanize the shopping process, Weiss's perception of fascinated female vision is not particularly Fordist. Rather, it reflects a parallel sense of women's relationships to commodities in consumer culture at the time, relationships considered highly irrational and unpredictable. As Mary Beth Haralovich has shown, this was a period in which the consumer products industry's empirical studies of women homemakers intensified dramatically, along with the rapid growth of market research as a profession. These studies of female consumer desire often produced an institutional image of female shoppers as spectators enthralled by the sight of consumer goods. These images were sometimes laughably extreme; one empirical study, conducted by Ernst Dichter, the (in)famous pioneer of Freudian-based motivation research in advertising, found that "women reacted with favorable emotions to the fresh, creamy surface of a newly opened shortening can."[51]

In the 1940s department store the emergence of visual merchandising was inflected with tensions between a rationalist architecture and an irrational shopper. This contradiction was tenuously reconciled in the new institutional paradigm of scientifically measurable relationships among vision and emotional and behavioral effects. Calls for a more scientific approach for store management reiterated women's inscrutable qualities as consumers. In 1944, in one of the first uses of the phrase "visual merchandising" in the retail press, display consultant Albert Bliss declared "before considering how we can sell through visual merchandising we must think about the person we expect to sell to — the customer. I doubt whether we have a clear picture of her."[52] What little picture retailers had of the shopper at this time was certainly a fractured one, based on a dualistic notion of department store shoppers' motives and desires. On the one hand, she was seen as highly suggestible, easily swayed by the visual image of merchandise, as Weiss suggested. But other professional studies described the store patron, especially in the new era of self-service, as a consumer who valued information in retail display. Driven by "an interest in . . . efficiency," this shopper was believed to prefer displays that told her "the price and [let her] appraise the value by herself, in the shortest possible time" over "dramatic, traffic-stopping showmanship."[53]

This strange view of female desire as both goal-oriented and easily distracted was by no means new in retail discourse.[54] What was new, however, was the idea that television's affective and technological manipulation of the space and time of shopping might somehow help resolve the contradiction at the heart of such views. W. L. Stensgaard, the display artist who designed Gimbel's' TV exhibitions, wrote that point-of-purchase TV was a form of showmanship, but one that could also "demonstrate and educate." It was a device "to illustrate and prove technical advantages such as many times are not visible."[55] Although they might disagree on whether women desired information or entertainment from advertising, retailers generally seemed to concur that women consumers could always, at base, be manipulated by displays that exploited visual details. In another article Stensgaard told his (presumably male) retail professional readership that because of television, "Retail stores will come to be more specific with selling facts such as cut-away models of products and technical tests and demonstrations. . . . Yes, you will even sit and enjoy a vacuum sweeper demonstration."[56] These assessments of the demonstration's particular appeal, focusing on its combination of small-scale visual fascination and theatricality, are an early instance of the gendered logic of the detail that Mimi White discerns in home-shopping programs today, a logic in which idealism and realism, ornament and everydayness, combine to form a televisual discourse of feminine consumption.[57] The aesthetic of home shopping, and indeed of infomercials and product shows in general, rewards viewers and producers who narrate the details of the commodity and animate it as a singular, ownable thing.

The intricate aesthetic of the product demonstration led many retailers to see television's postwar introduction as an opportunity to rethink retail visuality entirely, using the space-collapsing, visual promiscuity of television to extend the sensory space of the sales floor and its merchandise into the home. For the author of a 1949 treatise on visual merchandising entitled "Seeing Means Selling," television was a metaphor for the power of display; he claimed that the visual attraction of merchandise for women was a law that governed commercial displays on both sales floor and screen: "the picture presented on the home screen is only an extension, however important, of a principle that operates all the way from showing the customer a towel in the linens department to turning a switch at her own fireside. That principle is that she SEES the merchandise."[58] Similarly, when E. B. Weiss insisted that home-viewed TV programs should minimize direct commercial appeals, he exempted local store-sponsored shopping shows from this rule because, in his words, "Women will look at and listen to these store video programs because department stores know how to make merchandise of absorbing interest to them."[59] In such characterizations the department store shopper and the TV viewer at home were identical subject positions founded on the visual fascination of the retail demonstration.

It is worth noting here that such assertions of a single visual principle underlying women's TV both in the store and in the home point to the *limits* of television's site-specific rhetorics of spectatorship. For they suggest that some televisual ideologies are constant, regardless of place. It seems that, no matter where they happen to be located, female viewers are always represented as a group highly receptive to a consumerist televisual lesson. This continuity between retailers' depictions of the female consumer in both the store and the home no doubt stemmed from the fact that both were sites of women's domestic labor. It must have been easy for retailers to imagine their housewife spectator as a "pupil" of television's consumer education. Bloomingdales' vice president in charge of the store's television activities proposed in 1944 that "after the war, new electronic cooking equipment will make the pressure cooker look as primitive as a fireplace with a kettle on the hob. Complete re-education in cooking and other household tasks will be required to utilize new equipment, and television will be the medium through which it will be done most effectively." [60]

The remainder of this chapter traces the application of this idealist vision of televised product demonstrations as forms of consumer pedagogy in the local "shopping shows" sponsored by department stores on early television. Such programs were often envisioned as a means of bringing the sales floor closer to the home; in designing these programs display professionals sought to translate their ideas about the movements and desires of the shopper on the sales floor into techniques for reaching consumers in their living rooms. In their careful consideration of television's particular relationship to the lived, social environments of home and store respectively, the retail sponsors of these shows demonstrated an acute awareness of the local spatial operations of the television screen. These programs, airing on local stations in a particular metropolitan area, sought to redesign the home as a point of purchase — a commercial space made adjacent to, or annexed by, the store through the visual, space-binding powers of TV. This idea of television as a material object that can symbolically connect sites of consumption within the itineraries of everyday life is one of the more enduring ideologies of the site-specific screen, as we shall see in the following chapter. My purpose in concluding the present one with a consideration of retail television advertising outside the sales floor, and within the visual culture of postwar local commerce, is to illustrate the kinds of representational problems that institutions face as they formulate strategies for altering space, and people's spatial pathways, with TV. Although sites and circumstances change, the kinds of solutions to problems of remote influence I detail here continue to shape site-specific modes of commercial address in television to this day.

As a TV genre, the shopping shows of the postwar years were no doubt based on the shopping programs that were a staple on local radio. However, they were endowed with more powerful consumer qualities by virtue of their visuality.[61] At the end of the war, when broadcasters "courted" department stores and devised various publicity meetings to showcase television's advertising powers, they particularly encouraged stores to sign on as early sponsors of such programs and to try out intrastore TV. They pitched TV as a means for retailers to have more control over the consumer's processes of product selection and purchase decisions, proposing that the new medium was a way of maintaining a watchful presence in the spaces where consumers live and visit in the routines of daily life. The copy of a DuMont television catalog printed in 1944, for example, mapped home and store as different sites in a geography of feminine consumption. It depicted the former as the place "where women talk and the urge-to-buy is born!" and the store, contrastingly, as the domain of "shoppers who are on the spot and ready to buy." [62] In 1945 Paul Carlson, a DuMont executive, described a hypothetical store-based program to a group of home-furnishing manufacturers and retailers as a way of controlling the consumer at home, as well as in the store: "Between the visual and the aural impressions given the audience via television, it will be an easy matter to implant in the minds of the audience the trade name of the store, the address . . . and any other messages." [63]

Although none of these shopping programs survives for contemporary viewing, their titles—*Shopping at Home, Let's Go Teleshopping,* or *Shopper's Guide*—leave no doubt that they were hybrid progeny of existing forms of commercial exchange in the domestic sphere, not only radio shopping programs but also store magazines, mail-order catalogs, and phone ordering.[64] But television also updated these older consumer forms in the home. Specifically, it reflected the emergent domestic ideal of the postwar period, in which, as Spigel details, the home was depicted as "a well-run machine" and the homemaker as "a lab assistant and efficiency expert who knew how to handle modern technology." [65] These mechanized metaphors surfaced in network ideas about how daytime programming for women could aid women's work, although, as Spigel notes, they likely misjudged the level of the female viewer's desire for domestic education.[66] Judy Dupuy, a staff member at WRGB, offered a more realistic view of women's attitudes to the commercial pedagogy of televised product demonstrations when she suggested in her 1945 manual of television production that such presentations would need to be extremely seductive to succeed: "It will take little coaxing to give the man who is interested in sports a television lesson in flycasting or pocket billiards right in the comfort of his living room." However, women, she claimed, must be "*intrigued* into watching a studio cook whip up cake batter or turn ice-box leftovers into a tempting dish, or *intrigued* into watching a washing machine demonstration." [67] Although Dupuy reiterates the professional image of women as visually

fascinated and motivated beings, her call for more "intrigue" in advertising recognizes the rather unappealing connection between commercial
viewing and domestic labor, a connection that might only be broken by
an extremely fascinating visual display.[68]

For retailers, however, the drawbacks of home shopping seemed to lie
in the medium, not in the potential resistance of the viewer they targeted.
Some rejected the idea that television was simply a seamless continuation
of the sales floor's methods of display and demonstration. With a skepticism born from years of experience in the world of product display, a few
stores declined to advertise on television because its picture quality made
it unable to convey "the quality of line or texture of higher-priced fashions
or household commodities."[69] Others were highly sensitive to the spatial
and temporal contingencies of retail sales, and they questioned TV's power
to influence purchasing decisions remotely. The fact that the space of the
store contained both the merchandise and the means of owning it was a
crucial factor in stimulating sales. As the editor of *Display World* wrote:
"Televised display will have the disadvantage now possessed by newspaper
and magazine advertising; that is, the prospective customer is at a distance
from the store where the merchandise can be bought. To a displayman,
accustomed to the obvious advantages of bringing the merchandise to the
attention of the shopper when she is at the point-of-sale, this is no small
drawback."[70] The importance of time in this mental and behavioral map
of shopping is striking. It depicts women's decisions to buy as the result
not of a sustained longing but rather a flash of inspiration triggered by
the sight of merchandise. The layout of the sales floor, comprising product, display, and cash register, lent itself to this temporal situation, as it
compressed the temporality of desire and action into one relatively small
space. As the "aisles, not miles" catchphrase of point-of-purchase advertising insists, the effectiveness of store display hinges on the fact that the
shopper is a short walk from the sales counter. Intrastore TV conformed to
this spatial logic of shopper mentality, but broadcast TV, with its inherent
separation of consumer and product, was quite a different matter.

This retail skepticism goes some way toward explaining why the broadcasters with whom store sponsors worked in early TV placed so much
emphasis on the idea that television could collapse the distance between
home and store. An industry writer reporting on RCA's intrastore TV experiment at Gimbel's speculated that TV might supplant the sales floor
in the housewife's itineraries of consumption: "with the trend toward de-
centralization of our big cities slated for steady growth . . . special daily

shopping features, during which a few selected items are shown, the selling points explained, and a brief demonstration given, together with full information on prices, sizes, delivering and ordering instructions, is [*sic*] predicted as a television natural."[71] In their more utopian moments retailers agreed with such visions of home shopping: one article in *Department Store Economist* presciently forecasted today's on-line shopping when it suggested that in the future television retailing would be so streamlined that landmark downtown stores would disappear altogether, replaced by "the customer at a home screen telephoning a store for pictured merchandise carried prepackaged, ready for the delivery label, in a remote warehouse."[72] But although such apparently fanciful predictions may have spurred some stores to advertise on TV, in practice early retail TV sponsorship seemed to operate according to a rather more *local* sense of the screen's influence, one that drew on what retail professionals already knew about the regional patterns of commerce in urban areas. Trade accounts of store-based shows invariably included a description of how the sponsors viewed the relationship between the store and the home, a detail that suggests that sales managers did not see TV as a substitute for the store. Rather, they seemed preoccupied with figuring out its role in in-store sales as a new visual technology of home consumption.

Thus, for example, some shopping shows endeavored to represent the sales floor as a space one might want to leave home for and visit physically, attempting to attract customers with the promise of participating in a television show, as well as promoting the store to people watching at home. Such shows targeted viewers in both places. In 1949, when Gimbel's sponsored a "Television Breakfast Carnival" on WPTZ, the producers took great care to train the vision of the *in-store* audience on the merchandise being displayed. As the store's sales promotion manager explained, "Our commercial demonstrations would have a greater possibility of influencing and stimulating the studio audience to buy *if it was seated right next to the actual selling display*—with a trained sales force ready to follow up."[73] Although it presented itself as a form of home shopping, this show placed a higher premium on TV's immediate effects in the space and time of the shop, as if its persuasiveness might diminish as its images traveled in space and time.

Such evident concerns with the precise spatial coordinates of the targeted viewer, and with the effects of her distance from the cash register, provide us with an interesting example of how ideologies specifically associated with television's conquest of space and time—ideologies of liveness, of space-binding, of telepresence—acquire local properties as they "touch down" in particular spaces and institutions.[74] In the above example Gimbel's used the promise of seeing TV in production to attract home shoppers to the store; shoppers were then handed over to in-store display for the final "pitch." Together with in-store display, the store broadcast *mapped*—as much as conquered—the distance between the space of the home and the space of the store. It was the physical movement of the shopper from one to the other, and not just the fact of the TV signal linking them, that made the two spaces contiguous zones of commerce for Gimbel's.

Accounts of other store-based shopping shows suggest different beliefs about how to stimulate sales remotely. Some envisioned the home viewer as a remote but telepresent pair of eyes in the store's system of movements and transactions, a subject equally as impelled to purchase by the sight of merchandise as the store shopper. Shows of this type emphasized customer orders over the phone much as home-shopping shows do today. When the Fair Store sponsored *Let's Go Teleshopping* over WBKB (Chicago) in 1946, *Television* magazine reported that "no mention is made of department locations, since they [The Fair] feel that most teleshopping will be done over the telephone."[75] This suppression of the sales space of the *actual* store in order to encourage phone sales, unlike the Gimbel's program described above, treated home and store as competing, rather than complementary, points of purchase.[76]

However, although it used phone ordering to replace physical mobility and counter queues, *Let's Go Teleshopping* still retained the space of the store as a template for its temporal structure. Its format was not, like today's home shopping, a non-narrative sales pitch addressed directly to the viewer. Rather, it staged its serial product demonstrations as a surrogate trip through retail space, conducted for the benefit of shoppers at home. The show followed a fictional male shopper with a long gift list through a studio mock-up of the store, tracking his humorous encounters with sales staff and focusing on the ways they displayed and demonstrated merchandise. One can imagine that these commercial moments were somewhat crudely integrated into the "noncommercial" narrative address of the program, as in many early commercial television programs. Still, at the time, it was covered in the trade press as an innovative show; as *Television* magazine noted, the studio set of *Let's Go Teleshopping* was designed to facilitate easy camera switching among displays, eliminating the distance between them and cutting down on time spent moving from one to another.[77] More crucially, though, this layout was the ideal sales floor in visual merchandising terms because it effectively condensed the shopping trip into a flow of contiguous sales addresses and completely guided the vision of the home "shopper." A "virtual" shopping trip, the show replaced the movement of the customer with the movement of the camera. Although it used narratives and played for laughs, it nevertheless articulated a retail dream of television as a way of managing and automating the visual experience of shopping, replacing the "labor" of shopping with the pleasure of looking.[78]

It is striking that *Let's Go Teleshopping,* like other shopping shows, played for laughs with its emphasis on the plight of a helpless male consumer lost in the "ladies paradise" of the store. This narrative structure positioned the female viewer in an attitude of superiority, reinforcing the idea that shopping was a skilled form of household work. The show interpellated the female viewer by suggesting that, unlike the bumbling man on the screen, she was an expert shopper and a seasoned navigator of the space of the department store. It pitched its appeal, in other words, to a viewer knowledgeable in matters of consumption, constructing a reflexive image of the spectator as a no-nonsense, informed appraiser of commodities. This respect for the viewer's consumer abilities links *Let's Go Teleshopping* to a more pared down version of the shopping show, a telephone-based program entitled *Shopping at Home* (KTLA, Los Angeles, 1944–1948). The show did away with the narrative of the tour of the store and the mise-en-scene of the sales floor, offering only product demonstrations, one after another. Describing the show, *Television* noted that "no attempt is made at dramatization or story"—as if these would be annoying—"but care is taken in selecting telegenic merchandise . . . always shown in use wherever possible."[79] Incidentally, the phone ordering system made it possible to track the effect of these demonstrations on consumer behavior; *Sponsor* noted that the show's telephone log functioned as an index for measuring purchases in relation to display that in turn generated valuable sales data for attracting new sponsors.[80]

If DuPont's Store of Tomorrow represented the ultimate fantasy of feminine consumption as an immobilized, technologically connected, constantly changing visual relation, then local shopping shows like these might be seen as domestic versions of the same dream. Like the DuPont fantasy, their department store sponsors used images of modern technology to locate the consumer in a particular space of consumption and to envision her as a being poised to buy at the sight of goods. And like the DuPont fantasy they represented shopping as an experience in which commodities simply flow past an eager, attentive, "comfortably seated" viewer. The obvious parallels between the postwar retail ideology of efficiently displayed and serialized commodities and the contemporary organization of commercial televisual flow seem to confirm Margaret Morse's observation that both shopping mall architecture and TV broadcasting reflect an everyday aesthetics of mobile privatization that would come to dominance in the postwar years.[81] But although both the mall and the TV image can be described as "derealized," virtual spaces, this should not eclipse the fact that they are cultural forms produced in actual sites, within institutional and experiential networks of problem solving and debate. As the shopping show's complex and comparative mapping of home and store spectatorship suggests, quite particular spatial rhetorics of the screen distinguished the "meanings" of TV and TV images from site to site, and these *differentiating* logics of space were as important to TV's historical relationship to commercial architecture as were the parallels between broadcast and retail theories of spectatorship. It helps at this point to recall TV's simultaneous appearance in the masculinist space of the tavern, an institution that like the department store would change dramatically as an urban institution in the postwar years. Television was less an agent of these changes, as metaphors like "derealization" suggest, than it was a "rhetorical figure" for concurrent anxieties about the reorganization of particular social spaces in postwar life.[82] And the solutions that TV seemed both to provoke and to provide were different from place to place, comparable only in the fact that they consistently appropriated and transformed the spatial effects of television as an image source and an object on the local level. Thus the comparative visions of spectatorship articulated at the moment of TV's arrival in store, home, and bar illuminate the deeply site-specific nature of television rhetorics and, consequently, of its institutional uses as a form of communication and a material object even when it might appear phenomenologically to create a sense of "non-space."

I have suggested here that TV's arrival in the store, as in the tavern, was bound up in the challenges retailing faced as an institution in the postwar years. The emergence of the visual merchandising movement of which it formed a part indicated a larger set of changes that included the relocation of downtown stores to the suburbs, the introduction of self-service, the deskilling of the labor force, and the consolidation of national department store chains.[83] As a later chapter will detail, the continuing uncertainty of supply and demand that defines retailing has led eventually to a video display practice on the sales floor that *materializes* in ever more literal ways institutional concerns about consumer motivation and identity. If you know what you are looking for, it is easy to discern a panicked "hail" in the interpellative excess of the point-of-purchase installations one routinely encounters not only in department stores but also in the modern retail superstores known today as "category killers" and other contemporary retail sites.

In the postwar years, site- and gender-specific constructions of retail TV spectatorship were a means for department store executives to think through the changes that were taking place in the social space of retailing and urban life in the postwar years. Their attention to television as a revolutionary apparatus of consumer vision, at a moment when broadcasting and receiving stations were thin on the ground indeed, underscores how much the medium is a powerful touchstone in capitalism's fantasies of effortless systems of distribution and consumption. Still, it does not provide much sense of what the reality of shopping by television was like. Retailers' visions of the female viewer, both at home and in the store, embodied the utopian and wishful dimensions of advertising discourse, invested as they were in an idealist understanding of the relationship between seeing and buying merchandise. Utopias are historical fictions, changing as the social conditions to which they stand as oppositional alternatives change themselves. The utopian image of TV as an efficient, streamlined consumption tool reappears at other moments of spatial and media transition in retailing—it is certainly part of the emergent field of e-commerce today. But as chapter 5's tour of contemporary commercial establishments suggests, TV's role in contemporary sales floor promotion is a response to a different set of problems, ones associated with the rise of brand-based marketing that has changed the visual culture of retail substantially in recent years. And as a problem-solving practice point-of-purchase video continues to express contradictory institutional ideas about consumer desire in the spaces of everyday life. But before we can turn to the concrete scenes of spectatorship that are staged on today's sales floor, the task of the next chapter is to introduce the more recent institutional and economic history that explains exactly why commercial TV monitors are a staple component of other areas of public visual culture today, in the shopping malls, airport gates, and other places that we move through as we go about our lives outside the home.

CHAPTER 3

OUT-OF-HOME NETWORKS IN THE 1990s

In 1988 a short-lived in-store advertising venture made its debut in American supermarkets. Called VideOcart, it was a satellite TV network beamed to grocery stores and transmitted as a low-power signal to flat electronic screens installed on special hi-tech shopping carts. VideOcart was designed for viewing during the act of shopping, and its silent transmissions mixed national advertisements with "information on local prices and store configuration . . . games, and weather."[1] The system also used digital technology to match its programming to certain products in the store. As the shopper approached hidden sensors in each aisle, VideOcart triggered advertisements promoting one of the brands on display. According to a report in *Advertising Age,* these commercials, "containing graphics and animation similar to those on computer displays (but without sound), could be changed at a moment's notice with new commercials or animation sequences programmed from advertisers' or ad agencies' personal computers" (6).

An animated, interactive visual companion to the shopper as she or he chooses from the multitude of brands crowding the sales floor, VideOcart was a retail fantasy of consumption in which the shopping process is controlled down to the last minute by customized, reprogrammable techniques of manipulation. As we saw in the previous chapter, this techno-fantasy of training consumer desire and behavior remotely, via television, dates back to the postwar years, when retailers and manufacturers first experimented with TV as a way to control the bodily movements and physical pathways of shoppers in department stores. VideOcart demonstrates the enduring nature of this belief, although it takes its promise of a close, customized relationship between consumer, screen, and space much further than postwar retailers dreamed in their speculations about "the store of the future." Still, it is difficult to imagine a closer realization of early point-of-purchase TV advertising's ideal of a totally managed shopping trip than this odd image, both science-fictional and curiously homely, of the televisualized shopping cart.

As this historical continuity suggests, we can think of VideOcart as the product of an ongoing corporate imaging process. It is part of a continuous cycle of innovation and imagination in retail display, giving rise to ever new techniques for promoting brand awareness, like the automatic coupon dispenser in the soup aisle or the "got milk?" sticker on the banana. But like early visions of TV in the department store, in which the experience of space would be transformed by fashion broadcasts on every floor, VideOcart is also very specifically a fantasy about *television* as a consumer apparatus capable of altering behavior in its immediate environment, with up-to-the-minute, "live" eruptions of commercial speech. And like the store TV systems of the postwar era, it visualizes and materializes institutional ideas about TV's particular qualities and their value for retailing—honing in, in this case, not only on TV's promise of immediacy via customized, triggered ads but also on the medium's capacity for embedding itself in the mundane architectural props of its locale. Advocating for brand-name products on the microlevel of daily life, VideOcart's tightly focused strategy of influencing, and monitoring, decision-making processes at the point of purchase has a surveillant edge that earlier store TV systems lacked. Tracking the shopper and responding immediately to his or her movements, VideOcart brought the digital economy's postfordist paradigms of "flexible specialization" to the plebeian realm of in-store advertising.[2]

But this added sense of responsiveness and watchfulness in point-of-purchase media should not be interpreted merely as a by-product of technical advance nor for that matter as a product of trends in macroeconomics. For it very directly reflects institutional shifts in the economic relations of retailing between the present moment and the 1940s. Not only does VideOcart's mobility and its targeted brand exposure index how much, in the intervening years since "intrastore TV" at Gimbel's, market research techniques for measuring consumer behavior have intensified; it also reflects new corporate perceptions of the local level of the store and the national firms whose name-brand products it distributes.[3] Because market research now suggests that the store is where most consumers make purchasing decisions, manufacturers of brand-name products perceive the sales floor as the place where battles for brand equity (the intangible "value" attached to the recognizable and trademarked image of the corporation) are won and lost.[4] In the words of anthropologist turned retail consultant Paco Underhill, "Products live or die by what happens on the selling floor."[5] As this martial metaphor might suggest, marketing trade journals depict point-of-purchase advertising as a kind of arms race, constantly reporting that manufacturer expenditures on point-of-purchase advertising are on the increase and carefully tracking new and innovative techniques for hailing the consumer while he or she is shopping.[6] The emergence of a retail display technology as novel and improbable as VideOcart is an effort to exploit manufacturer struggles for brand equity, capitalizing on corporate anxieties about the visibility of brands in the marketplace by pushing the envelope of in-store display ever further.

However, despite the hype surrounding the introduction of devices like VideOcart, it would be unwise, at the very least, to attribute fantastic powers of manipulation and control to such devices. Even the point-of-purchase advertising industry concedes that of all in-store display advertising, including product labels and window posters, "in-store television monitors, electronic signs with moving words, and in-store radio rank lowest in attracting shoppers' attention."[7] Advertising on television screens in public places, one might imagine, would seem particularly unattractive to sponsors because such audiovisual display forms are doubly problematic; on the one hand they can "blend in" too easily with the environment, yet on the other they risk angering the people who are forced into spectatorship by their presence. But no doubt because of stronger market forces, such disadvantages have failed to prevent both large, diversified media corporations like Turner and Whittle and small start-up companies like VideOcart's IRI from exploring the possibilities of selling out-of-home television advertising for brand-name products on the sales floor and in the spaces adjacent to it, in the waiting areas and ante-rooms where the itineraries and errands of everyday life take place.

The focus of this chapter is the dramatic rise in the 1990s of such networks for public and semipublic spaces, among them the Airport Network,[8] the Food Court Entertainment Network, and the Commuter Channel. As full-blown *networks* these TV systems are worlds apart from the localized coaxial cable systems that transmitted product demonstrations to "telesites" in the postwar department store. Their prevalence and wider scope provide us with a far more sustained opportunity to explore the political economy from which institutional, commercial discourses on the spatial properties of TV sets and images emerge. Addressing very direct debates over how to tailor programming to fit the everyday locations in which people wait, eat, work, and pursue leisure, and how to target these people as demographic collectives, the institutional speech of networks for public places offers us detailed accounts of how the quantum world of the screen is negotiated and "managed" as a potentially valuable economic resource among advertising professionals. The sensory, bodily relation between the built environment and the users who move through it is an obsession of the executives who promote TV networks for such environments, and out-of-home TV networks are best thought of as case studies in a corporate media discourse of the local. Later chapters on particular screen installations detail how some of these negotiations of scale take visual and material form in the screen's immediate environment, from the eye-level perspective of the user. Here, however, I trace the ways the screen's spatial powers are figured as institutional "facts" and how knowledge systems based on these facts rewrite the audience environment as a raw material from which information commodities may be fashioned—the commodity, in this case, being the audience profiles produced by advertising's measurement systems.

Although it should come as no surprise that TV networks for particular places are highly concerned with the social processes of locality, exploring the terms in which this concern is expressed also provides some useful perspective on the spatial logics of media networks, as corporate and cultural systems, in general. Out-of-home network rhetorics of space are a routine, banal repertoire of marketing theories and consumer-spectator concepts, but as a media geography they allow us to glimpse how corporations negotiate the complexity of place, endeavoring to assimilate small-scale sites with specific characteristics into a standardized, networked framework of spatial knowledge. This corporate rhetoric on space and place creates a deeper context for the kinds of "readings" that we perform in social space—readings that identify wider social transformations in the mundane, and spectacular, forms of everyday space and that include the analyses of TV's role in the built environments that make up the second half of this book. For if the cultural and economic logics of postmodernity (Jameson and Harvey) or "the space of flows" (Castells) are indeed visible and materialized in physical social space, then it is crucial that we ask how this process is conceived institutionally and what spatial politics inform it, and that is what this chapter sets out to do. Television's presence networks places like the waiting room or the store, aligning them with other more abstract human processes that are happening elsewhere.

A "spatial reading" of these operations is particularly illuminating when it addresses how the commonsense epistemologies and practical operations of commercial institutions make abstract geopolitical or economic hierarchies palpable in the micropolitical terrain of social space and everyday architecture.

As this chapter explains, although the corporate discourse on out-of-home commercial TV may absorb the topoi of everyday life into a series of networked places, the process of connecting places and shifting scales through TV is nevertheless fraught with contradictions and tensions. Various conceptual and pragmatic difficulties hinder institutional attempts to "map the great global multinational and decentered communicational networks in which we find ourselves caught as individual subjects"[9] into media architectures, and they rise to the surface when we start to look closely at corporate understandings of everyday systems of flux, transit, mobility, and information exchange. By tracing these tensions we can unpick the "Ariadne's thread" of practice and discourse that links different scales, relations considered "global" and ones considered "local," in the conceptual maps of media institutions.[10]

Returning again and again to issues of how to "localize" the "global" or how to manage and control the ways that TV materializes consumer market categories in the built environment, these networks endlessly play out in miniature broader corporate ideologies of expansion and distribution. They apply arguments akin to the multinational corporate ideology of the free flow of culture across national and regional boundaries, for instance, when they rationalize TV's crossing of the less territorialized, unpoliced borders of the waiting room, the train station, or the mall as the dissemination of information and news as a public service to waiting, shopping, traveling populations. As corporate entities forever puzzling the problem of interweaving television invisibly with the habits and protocols of particular places, these forms of "local network television" thus offer an in-depth opportunity to explore the ways that site-specificity becomes the basis of profit-making structures for out-of-home media companies. Corporate subsidiaries like Turner Private Networks—a cluster of lifestyle news channels freed from the journalistic standards that freight the parent corporation's news ventures—exist solely to extract revenue from particular locations, in the form of site-specific knowledge about human behavior. As I will explain, the print materials produced by and around these networks might be viewed as a handbook for the commodification of spaces and their audiences via television. They are, essentially, a set of directives for translating large-scale, "globalizing" institutional strategies that annihilate space with airtime into microlevel protocols of spatial management.

It is worth noting at the outset that these strategies do not always succeed; at the end of this chapter I sketch the micropolitics of space that emerge around such networks when their presence in public arenas is contested. These moments of minor resistance to TV's presence parallel an earlier moment in the history of television outside the home, namely, its midcentury arrival in the bar—a debut that, as we saw in chapter 1, caused some public alarm. Television's presence occasions moral outrage among journalists and consumer advocates confronted by the squawking display of audiovisual billboards, although it is seldom prolonged. In 1991, for example, irate gym members boycotted sponsors of Health Club TV, a network of news, fashion, and entertainment programming for gyms; but nowadays health club television networks are a commonplace, unremarkable part of exercise culture. Still, regardless of their duration, such complaints focus attention on the limits of TV's abilities to adapt to an environment and generate revenue in the process. Because of their parallels to "local" responses to "global" media imperialism in the geopolitical arena, these instances of antimedia activism help us gauge the cultural politics of television's site-specificity in more general terms. What we discover in such rare moments of protest is a rhetoric of resistance that reflects, yet fails to play out, wider spatial politics of the medium and its spectator.

Corporate rhetorics of site-specific television are often directed toward the mollification of potential conflicts around the screen's entry into public places, a concern with media in context that explains why out-of-home television networks fall under a separate industry classification that borrows a "keyword" of cultural geography: "*place*-based media."[11] But is the "place" in "place-based media" the dynamic, politicized sense of "place" invoked in titles like Doreen Massey's *Space, Place, and Gender* or Nicholas Entriken's *The Betweenness of Place?* This corporate appropriation of the word *place*—a word heavily laden with connotations of specificity, materiality, cultural localism—certainly signals a close and careful attention to the distinctiveness of location and of the TV screen as a piece of signifying furniture within it. And place-based media professionals do demonstrate an almost ethnographic concern with context, seeking to understand how the screen speaks, marks time, attracts attention, and performs other interventions in its immediate social environment. Yet, as with larger scales of TV networking, this localism can mask wider, more standardizing logics, raising the question of whether the narrowcast networks of place-based media corporations merely replicate the space-binding tendencies of broad(er)cast networks on a smaller scale.

The practices of local networks mirror those of more global ones in part because, although they seek to enter their environments unobtrusively, they do so in order to position that environment within a broader network of consumer places. The value of the place-based TV network, as a tool for organizing people's behavior in space, is thus not confined to the immediate environment of the screen. Rather, institutional discourses on the space of the screen connect their particular site laterally to locations of exchange that are within walking, driving, or flying distance of the spectator. Although they are not located precisely at the point of purchase, the audiences of site-specific networks are "sold" to advertisers on the assumption that most place-based viewers will pass through a site of retail consumption in their travels outside the home. Presumably, the argument goes, advertising on place-based media networks can shape consumers' behavior once they enter these contiguous commercial spaces; like VideOcart, place-based media offer a fantastic image of the mobile TV spectator influenced by ads witnessed "on the fly." As this suggests, models of advertising effects for nondomestic TV are thus closer to those of "outdoor advertising" (billboards and the like) than to those of regular network television.[12] But although these networks share with billboards, transit advertising, and other forms of public signage an image of the spectator as a moving target in a particular environment, what distinguishes them from other outdoor media in marketing circles is the distinctive physical form of television as a medium — the changing, readily reprogrammed nature of its display, its use of sound, its associations with domestic space, and above all, its ability to integrate into the human processes of its environment. Time and again the trade literature of place-based media probes the specificity of the screen's relationship to its space, looking for clues to the commercial values that are bound up in this relationship.

Although I base my account of this network logic of TV as an integrative, localizing form on the professional literature, I must note here that as primary sources, trade journals should be handled with care. Peppered with promotional press releases and strategic speculations about future directions for corporate and industrial growth, they are not very reliable as empirical indicators of material and economic "truth." However, their status as arenas of speculation and idealization does make "the trades" a useful directory of commercial ideologies. A reader trained in cultural studies will immediately recognize place-based media's professional print culture as an arena for the construction of an ideal advertising spectator. And it does not take great acuity to note that this spectator has some peculiar characteristics, such as an apparently extreme receptivity to televised messages in the shopping mall, the waiting area, the truck stop, and other everyday places. Article after article on place-based media speculates about this imaginary subject's changing identities and divines the effect that site-specific commercial speech can have on his or her actions. These institutional images of the subject are often supported by complicated fields of data, quantifying the ineffable elements of everyday life via intricate hypotheses about the movements of subjects and bodies in space and synthesizing ideas about site-specific spectatorship from outdoor advertising and point-of-purchase display with more conventional discourses on commercial television's effects. This rhetoric of place-based media's spectator confirms Celia Lury's and Alan Warde's assertion that "adspeak" is not simply professional language but is also a corporate form of cultural theory.[13]

The consumer desire theorized in advertising rhetoric may be no more than a strategic set of beliefs, but it is a mythic force endowed with agency and power as it circulates in professional discourse. This power is clearest when the spectator becomes an economic object. This is what Marxist media theorists call "the audience commodity" — the quantified representation of viewers, based on ratings systems and samples, that networks sell to their sponsors. My exploration of the place-based media industry in this chapter is therefore largely an account of its audience commodity and the institutional context of broadcast advertising from which it emerged.

That site-specific commercial television emerged at all might, from some perspectives, seem surprising; how, when viewers of TV advertising already abound in the home, do place-based media justify their existence in the competitive economy of media sales? The answer is suggested in John Caldwell's description of professional media knowledge as a structure of problem solving. The institutional fictions and theories produced in the media industry are, he notes, best viewed as "cultural problem-solving operations" that "get to dramatize and enact the terms of the problem . . . [and] delimit potential solutions."[14] The audience commodity of place-based media, keying the body, identity, and desire of the consumer audience to its location in space, can similarly be seen as a response to particular institutional crises. Although a technological determinist might claim that the availability of new satellite-based technologies for closed-circuit programming delivery to particular sites prompted the rise of place-based media networks, such technological factors, predating the ascendancy of such networks by over a decade, do not by themselves explain the proliferation of site-specific commercial television at the beginning of the 1990s. Rather, an institutional and industrial crisis familiar to American broadcasting scholars precipitated the rise of place-based media in these years: the shifts in relations between sponsors and media corporations that occurred in the 1980s. As has been well documented, the growth of cable and the development of new audience measurement technologies and companies in this period inaugurated a crisis of confidence for the networks and the ratings systems on which their revenue framework was based, especially when new research allotted far larger audience shares to cable channels than previous studies had found.[15] In 1993, as one of several strategies for drumming up larger audience figures, the networks entered into an unprecedented partnership. Under the aegis of the National Television Association they joined together in sponsoring a Nielsen study of out-of-home viewers. The study aimed to prove that more people were watching the networks than new ratings systems had suggested; and in fact it showed, conveniently, that of the twenty-eight million weekly out-of-home viewers, nineteen million watch network programming.[16]

Despite the fact that this sudden concern with the out-of-home audience could only have stemmed from this ratings slide, professional commentators at the time endeavored to link the network interest in nondomestic viewers to an increased social and physical mobility on the part of the audience: NTA director of research Steve Singer claimed that "lifestyle changes in the 1990s . . . a rise in the number of working women, college students, and business travellers . . . indicates it is increasingly important for the industry to quantify all television viewing, regardless of viewing location, and to track the viewing behavior of these important demographic groups."[17] Although the evidence points in the opposite direction, in this view it was not the relations of TV institutions, but rather the viewers, that changed.

This perception of the *consumer* as changing, rather than the discursive relations of advertising, recalls postwar perceptions of the department store shopper as a being caught in new patterns of mobility, demanding new commercial techniques for reaching her, when it was in reality the position of department stores in the retail economy that was shifting. However, whereas in the postwar years retailers saw TV both at home and in the store as a new technique of consumer "education," consumers in retail and other spaces today are seen as "escapees" from advertising presented on television at home. This alerts us to the first of several characteristic attributes assigned to the out-of-home TV viewer, as distinct from the home viewer, in the place-based media industry. Broadly speaking, this first level of distinctiveness hinges on the apparently self-evident *fullness* of the out-of-home viewer's lifestyle—one that seems too crammed with productive activity to include TV viewing. When General Motors signed on as a sponsor for the Airport Network in 1991, hoping to reach an audience of upscale business travelers, the company's advertising director commented, "It's no longer good enough to expect your communication system to work after somebody gets home at 7:30 at night. You have to be able to go where they are." [18]

Such depictions of the ideal audience as a collectivity no longer located in the home can be interpreted as a devaluation of the home audience's commodity value, one based, circularly enough, on the fact that it is watching TV rather than pursuing other activities—working late at the office, traveling to a business meeting, shopping, or exercising. In 1998 Michael E. Kassen, a prominent media buyer, suggested as much when he told a *Los Angeles Times* interviewer, "You can no longer guarantee that you will reach everyone by putting an ad on Thursday night on NBC. Advertisers want to be wherever the consumer is going to be. Placing a product in a movie, putting an ad on a piece of fruit—advertisers are approaching the whole equation differently." [19] Instead of a stable, knowable, commodifiable mass, such perspectives on the home audience see it as disintegrating under the oft-cited forces of fragmentation and proliferation in expanding media markets; the only way to reach people, they suggest, is through nonmassified, highly contextual forms of commercial speech.

Note how, in the above descriptions of the home audience, viewers are construed as patently *un*receptive to advertising by virtue of their location in the home. This calls our attention to the second conventional characterization of out-of-home audiences in the rhetoric of place-based media. Out-of-home viewers are, from this perspective, more open to commercial appeals because such appeals are more closely matched to the environment in which they air. "How much good can that commercial for Tylenol be in the middle of a *Seinfeld* episode when the viewer has no headache?" asked Turner Private Networks president John McMenamin. Place-based media, he argued, present advertising in a far more timely fashion: "if you're sitting in a medical waiting room it has a much greater impact on your thought process and your staying power." [20] Such assertions suggest that the home audience was both too mobile to be reached and too hard to mobilize; advertising airing in the home would therefore have little effect on what consumers did in the store. Through such claims about the home audience, place-based media professionals exploited sponsors' fears about conventional TV networks as tools for effectively shaping consumer behavior, invoking the philosophy of immediate consumer motivation associated with the intense competition taking place among national brands at the point-of-purchase to sell their audiences to sponsors.

However, such vilification of the home audience commodity was not, by itself, much of a platform on which to make the case for out-of-home TV sponsorship in the early days of place-based media. After all, the retail sales floor already existed as an arena in which national advertisers could try to stimulate sales directly with conventional sales floor advertising. And a thriving outdoor advertising industry had been disparaging TV audiences for years; sponsors had no reason to believe that TV advertising outside the home would be any more effective than any other out-of-home advertising medium. Why would TV commercials at the airport gate, in the food court, or in the physician's waiting room ever seem like an essential item in a corporate advertising budget?

To make the case for out-of-home television's superior audience commodity, place-based media companies honed in on the distinctive physical and technological arrangements of home and public space as viewing environments. They argued that other places served as more "productive" sites for the display of TV advertisements because of the way people watched TV within them, touching on some existing sponsor anxieties about viewer behavior at home in the process. These sponsor anxieties were twofold. The first concerned what Friedberg has called the "virtual mobility" of the home audience within the total programming environment of television. This was the mobility made possible by the remote control, empowering the consumers to "zap" advertising by channel surfing and time-shifting. The second anxiety concerned what marketing professionals call "clutter"—the desensitizing excess of too many commercial messages clamoring for viewer attention. Place-based media professionals promoted their wares as a solution to both anxieties at once, delineating in the process a third distinctive feature of the out-of-home audience commodity: its captivity. As a CNN Airport Network brochure told potential sponsors, commercial display at the airport gate "allows your message to break through the barriers that reduce television advertising effectiveness: Zapping, Clutter, and Lack of Competitive Separation.

In many of the busier airport gate areas in the United States, the CNN Airport Network is the only channel to watch."[21]

Paradoxically, in such formulations, a "captive audience" was more likely to be receptive to advertising than one that had the option of choosing to view a sponsors' message. Whittle Communications extended this paradoxical principle even further in its now defunct health-based Special Reports network, supplying subscribing physicians with monitors resistant to channel switching and instructing receptionists to prevent the television set from being turned off.[22] This sense of captivity and immobility sparked public antagonisms to place-based media; one reluctant viewer of the Airport Network told an interviewer, "It's worse than the grocery stores . . . because you have to sit there for hours and there's no way to get away from it."[23] But this was precisely the point as far as the network was concerned. For like other place-based media, it promised its advertisers an audience for their messages, one immobilized by necessity within a particular place for a particular amount of time.

Both captive and mobile, both receptive and hostile, the out-of-home spectator constructed by place-based media professionals was doubtless a paradoxical and contradictory entity when it arrived on the advertising scene in the 1990s. What obscured these contradictions — although not entirely, as further discussion will presently reveal — was the way place-based media corporations presented their audience commodity as a "quality" rather than "quantity" product. Exploiting the spread of narrowcasting as a paradigm for advertising, place-based media corporations asserted, and continue to assert, a close correlation between audience demographic and environment. One advertising agency media director summed up this situation succinctly; place-based media, he explained, are defined by the fact that "the demographics of the reader, viewer, or listener are controlled by the location in which the message is delivered."[24] The verb *controlled* is crucial here because it points to the fact that what place-based media offered their potential sponsors was the idea of location as a tool for standardizing and predicting market composition. This sense of "geography as destiny" is the fourth characteristic of the out-of-home audience commodity and the one I want to dwell on at length as a way of teasing out place-based media's relation to wider network logics of location and localism that base profit-making media practices on the spatial position of the audience.

If demographics can be targeted by location, this economistic logic of place illustrates a key institutional understanding of the local as a fertile source of market knowledge. In foregrounding the site-specific qualities of the TV screen as an object in social space, place-based media professionals develop a deeply environmental view of television spectatorship, one in which the meaning of images is bound up with the rhythms of the screen's location, and in which the audience's *identity* is rooted, somehow, in its position in space. What we face in the place-based media industry, in other words, is a form of corporate cultural studies, in which a contextual approach to television's material culture and its locality is transformed into a profit-making discourse. A usefully extreme example is the newborn channel that airs in postpartum hospital rooms, safely guaranteeing its sponsors a very precise and narrowly targeted viewer for "an eight-hour program discussing infant care, family relationships, nutrition and related topics" in which ten minutes of each hour are advertisements from Procter and Gamble and other makers of parenting-related products.[25]

As this example suggests, the place-based media industry bases its value as a commercial sphere on an ability to guarantee correlations between space and identity. It is a guarantee that can furthermore apply to highly mobile audience commodities as well as captive ones, thus allowing place-based media corporations to claim their hold on wealthy viewers, often considered a difficult market to reach. Networks in places of transit, like the Airport Network, were presented as ways to ambush prime demographics too upscale to be affected by advertising on broadcast TV. Some place-based media companies went to extreme lengths to reach the rich this way, ending up in odd or unexpected locations as a result. A parking garage, for example, might seem a dingy and unwelcoming place for a spectator experience, and it does not immediately conjure up images of upscale consumers ready to purchase; indeed, in many cities parking garages are shelter for homeless people. However, proceeding from the assumption that only upscale consumers can afford to park in valet garages, a start-up place-based media company in 1996 announced its plans to place thirty-five-inch TV screens in such sites, targeting "consumers who have to wait from 5 to 15 minutes for attendants to handle their cars."[26]

This example is particularly instructive in that it reveals how *manufactured* the link between identity and space may be. This network's sense of localism has some rather noticeable shortcomings. It does not target the people who work in its immediate vicinity in eight-hour shifts; rather, it offers advertisers access to a subject who spends fewer than fifteen minutes in earshot of the screen over the course of an entire day.[27] But although the narrow and rarified blue-chip demographic is by no means the only one represented in the garage as a space, the network nevertheless produces a deeply embedded sense of location and temporality in the very precision of its image of the wealthy, waiting spectator (one imagines a businessman checking his Rolex and glancing at the screen as he waits for the Lexus to roll up). Its pseudoethnographic realism, presupposing an intimate knowledge of the rich person's everyday habits, helps to filter out other viewers in the space's total population.

Now by itself, the fact that place-based media classify consumer behavior and audience identity by location is not surprising; all marketing institutions rely on geographic models in their construction of audience demographics. Such models are usually maps of populations and economic activity keyed to particular units of measurement. The example most familiar to readers in the United States is probably the PRIZM system, which classifies the economic and behavioral characteristics of consumers by postal code.[28] However, place-based media construct their markets with a different spatial instrument, one that derives its imaginary consumer profiles not from the location of homes but from the physical location of the consumer's *body*, outside the home. This reflects the industry's close ties to the traffic-measuring, car-counting frameworks of knowability devised by billboard companies and transit advertising brokers to measure the "impressions" outdoor advertising forms make on their spectators as ratios of traffic flow. However, the geographical construction of the commodity audience of place-based media is distinct from these existing frameworks in that it can produce far more specific forms of "knowledge." For such corporations location not only reveals details about gender, or class, but it also conveys more transitory and contingent information about the viewer sitting in the vicinity of its screens. For example, Christopher Whittle, who developed several place-based media ventures in the mid-1990s, told an interviewer from *Advertising Age* that "if you walk into a gastroenterologist, I know something about you. I know that you have some kind of digestive problem. That's an important piece of data for some marketers."[29] Place-based media, in short, invite their sponsors to infer the state of the spectator's body from its location in space.

But such data are valuable to marketers for other reasons too; they can be transformed into information about consumers even more elaborate than the equation of location and identity or bodily health. Specifically, place-based media networks use market research to define the consumer's *movement* from place to place, as well as his or her reason for being in a particular location. Lifetime Medical Television, for example, was a short-lived venture of the Lifetime cable network, providing health information to female patients waiting in family practice, OB-GYN, and pediatrics offices in 1990. Describing the network's demographic and behavioral techniques for acquiring information about its audience, its president told a group of electronic media advertising professionals: "We can follow them out of the office. In our early research at pediatric sites we saw that many times the office visit was followed by a trip to a supermarket, drug store, or other retail venue." [30] This statement, noteworthy for its unnerving voyeurism, exploits the contiguities between spaces of everyday life — in this case the waiting room and the drug store — synchronizing the routines of the waiting room with the routines of the point of purchase. But such imaginary maps of people's errands outside the home are commonplace in the professional discourses of advertising, and they only indicate how far place-based media are able to go in their extraction of commercial value from TV's close association with the rhythms and itineraries of the everyday.

This close observation of public behavior allows place-based media companies to produce a highly ethnographic image of TV advertising as a form of commercial speech deeply integrated in the workaday world. The spurious character of the behavior claims that result from this image cannot pass unremarked — no evidence suggests that the women whom researchers followed to the pharmacy actually *bought* the products that hailed them from the waiting-room screen. However, as discursive constructions of audiences, such assertions reveal how the corporate cultural analysts of place-based media acquire authority on the basis of their ostentatiously contextual understanding of the everyday movements of the subjects who — on another level — they desire only to instrumentalize as numbers in a grid of exchange. Through such minute protocols of space-time management, tailoring the screen to its site, place-based media endeavor to make dwelling in, and passing through, particular places an imperceptibly sponsored experience. The Airport Network "brands" the entire time frame of a journey, playing at the gate as we wait to depart and greeting us again when we arrive at our destination. Flashing a quick reminder of the network (and, agency professionals optimistically avow, its sponsors), the screen at the gate marks our departure from, and reentry into, the terra firma world of consumption. In the exhausted travelers' final glances at the monitor as they head toward the baggage claim, a positive brand impression for CNN piggybacks on the relief of reaching the end of the journey.

There is a temporal component to the place-based media industry's claims to contextualism as well. Like printed transit advertising and other out-of-home displays, these networks target a viewer caught at a particular place and time in the cycles of daily life. When the makers of Thera-Flu reported a "successful" test of advertising on the transit-based Commuter Channel, one company spokesperson praised the network because "it's able to reach people who are suffering from cold symptoms just when they realize they might need a cold remedy — on their way to or from work."[31] This construction of the Commuter Channel's effects on its viewer thus envisions television advertising as a form of interpellation deeply bound up in the rhythms of the working week. If the broadcast schedule often serves to mark the transition between work life and leisure pursuits in the home,[32] place-based media companies like the Commuter Channel extend this structuring principle of the TV broadcast outside the home to other sites where the work-leisure distinction is particularly marked. Transit areas are a favored choice because they are a very literal and physical zone of transition between the two; advertising within transit locations, the Thera-Flu commercial on the Commuter Channel positions itself as a solution to problems that may arise as one negotiates this transition.[33] The predictable schedules of capitalism's spaces of transit and commerce, and the unremarkable ways commercial speech has come to mark and narrativize these schedules, are what allow place-based media corporations to commodify the individuals who move among them as an audience for advertisers.

Like the broadcast schedule in the home, place-based media also conform to the temporal characteristics of their locations. As one industry audience researcher explained, place-based media must respect the temporal integrity of their environments: "the media must reflect the length of time people spend at the site. If video is used where people are actively moving around, the program segments should be very short. . . . On the other hand, video in areas where people are in a waiting mode can use longer, more traditional television-length segments such as those shown in gatehold waiting areas and on planes."[34] Yet this even underestimates the flexibility of place-based media's customized temporality. The Airport Network changes its programming length with seasonal variations in waiting time at airports, and the now defunct Checkout Channel varied its programming in a familiarly gendered mix of "soft" and "hard" news for different dayparts: its daytime programming featured fashion tips, and evening programming consisted of "stock prices and economic news."[35]

It is important to note that the attention to context that defines the place-based media industry's market research has its drawbacks, as it is always threatened with the epistemological meltdown that Ien Ang calls "contextualization gone mad"—an endlessly expanding sense of context that threatens to engulf the texts that it surrounds, sapping all meaning in the process.[36] This possibility is readily discerned in the place-based media industry's negotiation of two continually vexed issues: the already sensitive question of audience measurement in such environments (an important one given that such data form the basis of advertising rates) and the inescapable fact that—no matter how hard Turner and other companies try to adapt the screen to its environment with "quiet zones" and deliberately blocked sightlines—the inhabitants of the screen's social context are often liable to complain. In both of these bumpy moments in place-based media's otherwise fairly smooth entry into public places, context translates into contest, becoming a thorny maze from which place-based media professionals strive to extricate their corporate images. Negotiating issues of audience becomes a matter of containing, as much as exploiting, television's powerful ability to embed itself in a social context.

As far as audience measurement goes, controversies over ratings methods in the place-based media industry stem, ironically, from the mobility that helped to define and add value to the out-of-home audience commodity in the first place. For this prized mobility made quantifying this audience a distinct challenge. As an Airport Network executive admitted in a letter to the editor of *Advertising Age* responding to charges that its audience was unmeasurable, "each place-based medium has its own unique characteristics that make a single, standardized methodology for audience measurement impossible."[37] Although it may have been justified, this sense of site-specific uniqueness was of little use to sponsors in search of a baseline measurement system for assessing the amount of exposure their commercials were receiving. What's more, place-based media researchers noted that the transitional nature of the places in which the networks were installed made surveys particularly difficult to carry out. Bemoaning the vicissitudes of on-site market research subjects, a Nielsen Corporation vice president advised fieldworkers researching responses of place-based audience members to "keep the questionnaire . . . no more than 10 minutes long. Remember, people reached by place-based media are often on a tight time schedule because they are travelling, on a lunch break, or heading for an appointment." [38] The site-specific nature of place-based media networks and their mobile, targeted spectators was thus also a threat to their survival, requiring in-depth fieldwork in the physical space of the screen — it made audience measurement an expensive, time-consuming, and unreliable form of market research.

In addition to the mobility of this audience, the fact that it might be engrossed in activities other than viewing raised even larger questions for skeptics. After all, if place-based media were really so embedded in the rhythms of daily life, then what, exactly, constituted "a viewer" or "an audience"? In other words, the perennial problem of the "knowability" of the audience for television was not erased but rather *amplified* by place-based media networks' invitingly specific demographic connections between location and audience activity. *Advertising Age* reported that agencies were criticizing Whittle's Special Reports Channel in doctors' offices because the network based its ratings on nontelevisual factors — "traffic figures instead of true audience counts" — and they similarly disputed Nielsen's claims about the Airport Network, including its assertion that 50 percent of people in the Atlanta airport were watching the Airport Network.[39] As a solution to these issues, Nielsen announced that it was considering a plan to publish a report listing measured ratings of similar types of place-based media in one group, giving ad executives the opportunity to compare the demographic values of different networks and places. In addition to this paradigmatic axis of audience evaluation, Nielsen also produced (at Turner's request) a "consolidated Nielsen Air report" that rated "all airport media, including the Airport Channel, in-flight services, and fixed airport media" against each other.[40] In short, the only way to *guarantee* the value of the place-based audience commodity was to take it out of the context that supposedly gave it value in the first place and to standardize it in relationship to other commodity viewers.

Although this seems to have worked for the now thriving Airport Network, such solutions were not so easily applied to TV networks located closer to the point of purchase, as this meant that sales figures became the exclusive means for assessing advertising's effects. In such environments researchers resorted to surveillance techniques to determine the value of the audience commodity. Turner's Food Court Entertainment Network used methods virtually identical to those of the disciplinary anti-theft systems already operating in the location. Market researchers were instructed to stop shoppers as they left the mall and examine the contents of their bags. This shockingly panoptic market research technique apparently paid off, as it resulted in Nielsen's pleased announcement that "some food court patrons bought 50% to 500% more of the brands advertised in the 30-second slots than did shoppers who had not visited the food court."[41] Like VideOcart, this research traces the movements of brands and consumers as they are interwoven in the narrative of the shopping trip. Although highly problematic from both ethical and market research standpoints, such surveillance techniques must have been the most effective ways that Turner, and Nielsen, could guarantee the effects of the network's advertising. They undoubtedly legitimized this research for sponsors by constructing the space of the shopping mall as a clinical environment, a closed loop of images and behaviors. By bringing advertising, consumer, and measurement together in one place, this research method placed all elements of consumer culture's chain of representations, actions, and transactions in a quantifiable relationship to each other. Locating viewing and consumption in the same closely watched context, this technique of on-site audience measurement is a device that, like the grocery savings-cards we pull from our wallets to be scanned at checkout, traces a digitized trail of behavior that can be analyzed for multiple commercial purposes. Indeed, the food court network's ability to monitor the space of the mall extends beyond consumer behavior to encompass brand behavior as well. The network also promotes itself as a tool for targeting particular, actual retail sites with brand-based commercials and for assessing the amount of business particular retailers get. This is because its address can be programmed digitally so that "from a central feed, it can run a Reebok commercial that tags any retailers that Reebok indicates in a particular mall" (22).[42]

This technological feat serves the economic purpose of allowing for a precise comparison of retail outlets' brand performance—spying on the local distributors, as well as the local consumers, in other words. As a customized mode of address it induces a sense of faux localism similar to that produced by national radio station chains in America today, many of which use digital technology to create the impression that call-ins and interviews exist within one space-time frame (rather than as stored data on a hard drive, which is what they actually are). It is a small-scale version of the capitalist logic Arif Dirlik calls "global localism"—a term that "implies, organizationally, that the corporation domesticate itself in various localities without forgetting its global aims and organization."[43] This parallel with larger network practices is not coincidental. Rather, it demonstrates the adaptability and flexibility of the concept of localism for network exploits on all scales. In many ways place-based networks apply the lessons learned from global media markets to the local scale of the screen's physical locale. The Food Court Entertainment Network's site-specific constructions of audience, tracking behavior in elaborate surveillance systems and concealing the viewer's generic unknowability under a mask of specificity, can be seen as a miniaturized version of a more global corporate logic of surveillant market research and customized, locally sensitive commercial address.[44] It is telling indeed that Ed Winter, CEO and founder of Whittle's Channel One, described the growth requirements of place-based media in language that could apply equally to the global expansion of U.S. television into foreign markets. The profitability of place-based networks, he suggested, depended on "the capital intensiveness of the place itself."[45]

If "global localism" is a network strategy that can be translated to fit media spaces on many different scales, can we perhaps learn something new about this logic when we examine its operations in the compressed, relatively local spaces inhabited by place-based media? It has often been noted that the global expansion of Turner's flagship Cable News Network (CNN) into different world regions required a flexible and adaptable local identity. As David Morley and Kevin Robins note, CNN's dystopian goals of global growth and control proved difficult to sustain as the network grew and encountered "the real world, the world of already existing and established markets and cultures."[46] As it increased its global reach, CNN thus found it necessary to increase collaborations with regional partners in an effort "to reconcile global ambitions with local complexities."[47] Turner Private Networks may be designed simply to sell audiences to advertisers without any pretense at news reporting, but they are nevertheless a low-stakes, small-scale materialization of this same logic. In each case corporate strategies for the commodification of space take place under the banner of the local. But if the local is "the site upon which the multifaceted contradictions of contemporary society play out," then this must be as true for the airport gate as it is for the nation state. And indeed, perhaps because they are so literally and physically concerned with inserting TV in personal space, these network discourses on the local make it clearer to see how the spatial politics of media are shaped by relations between institutional agents. "Space-binding," in short, is a social effect of electronic media that is produced not through the magic of technology and its phenomenological forms, but rather through the economic interests and

professional negotiations of organizational subjects in particular industries. Though the place-based media network's ersatz engagement with
particular sites reveals the dangers of romanticizing the local as a site of
resistance, it certainly does indicate that the local installation of TV is an
occasion for the exercise and transfer of power from one scale of the social
to another.

Broader social contradictions become visible in situations where the
presence of these networks in an environment prompts contests over the
norms and privileges that come with the use of public space, a symbolic
location in which ideals of democracy, norms for the protection of "public
property," and the defense of individual rights (including the right to privacy) find expression. Place-based media professionals might optimistically predict, in the words of one industry researcher, that "the activity
the viewer is doing is likely to make the message 'work' better," but they
must always acknowledge that locational factors might equally provoke
unfavorable reactions from viewers.[48] Indeed, this same researcher noted,
a toothpaste advertisement in a dentist's office might "be perceived nega-
tively, because the viewer is scared as they sit in the waiting room. . . . No
advertiser wants to be associated with a medium where hostile viewers are
writing letters to the editor asking for the televisions to be removed." [49]
As this suggests, corporate attempts to commodify location do not go un-
noticed or uncontested, although protest is perhaps less frequent than one
might expect.

However, it is interesting to note the terms in which this resistance is expressed because it also reveals the terms in which media activism is *rarely*
imagined — the blind spots and no-go areas of anti-television rhetorics.
Audience hostility generally centers on questions of rights and the control
of space, expressed as a debate over the boundary between ambient sound
and noise pollution. This concern with *formal,* or structural, properties
rather than programming content noticeably differentiates this backlash
from many other antimedia rhetorics, such as critiques of Hollywood TV's
cultural imperialism or violent media imagery's effects, but it also couches
the offense of place-based media very specifically as an offense against the
individual. A good example is the backlash against the Airport Network,
which reached a head in Atlanta (CNN's headquarters) in 1997, when airport officials responded to passenger complaints by reducing the volume
on almost half the Airport Network monitors.[50] This public rejection of the
network in CNN's corporate hometown was led by a newspaper columnist,
Colin Campbell, who claimed that the network infringed on the rights of

the individual: "In most . . . public places, minorities as well as majorities retain certain rights. And apparently a substantial minority considers it intrusive to have to listen to the blare of repetitive T V news and ads."[51] Later he phoned the mayor's office to ask "why passengers are not permitted to play radios on city buses and subways"; the answer, he reported, was "that it would probably be disturbing for others."[52]

Campbell's pointed question to the mayor was a good one. Foregrounding a discrepancy in the city's policy for public spaces, it called attention to the fact that the city had bestowed a power on a corporate "citizen" that it withheld from its human ones.[53] But his claims had a reactionary flavor, tinged with a hint of racial offense in the semiparodic adoption of the term *minority.* The appeal to a collective politics, one that recognizes the users of public places as a *class* with common interests, is a comic rhetorical flourish used to support a sense of outrage at the personal nature of the offense television performs. The argument against the (undeniably irritating) sonic presence of CNN locates the politics of place-based media in the relationship between the T V set and the body, or at least the sensorium. Because we can shut our eyes but we cannot avert our ears (or at least we cannot do so without the help of a portable stereo), the protest becomes a rally against the invasion of privacy by media.

These struggles for viewers' rights, or nonviewers' rights, activate only one aspect of the political relationship between bodies and social power. For by posing the politics of place-based media as a question of the individual's control over sonic space, activism over television's presence in public space rarely connects to the body politics of institutional economics—a politics in which the body of the waiting or shopping or eating person is offered for sale to advertisers as a captive audience. The personal *deflects* the political in this scenario because its activism does not extend to address questions of *whose* body, and *whose* free time, is being sold to the sponsor and *whose* objections to T v's presence get the attention of the network. Valet parking attendants must work within constant earshot of the start-up T V network for parking garages mentioned earlier, but it is doubtful whether their opinion of television's presence has been solicited. Workers are not the only press-ganged audiences in public space to be treated in an abject and disempowering manner, as a group of second-class citizens, within the place-based media industry. For example, when senior citizen "mallwalkers" protested the installation of the Food Court Entertainment Network, arguing that it disturbed their postexercise coffee sessions, the network's president countered with a surprisingly unalloyed response, pointing out that their efforts were wasted because seniors "represent less of an economic value" than other audiences in malls.[54]

The fact that activism avoids questions of the commodity status of the listeners who play a crucial and uncompensated role in the economy of advertising sales means that networks are free to present their commercials as a public service on a par with other sources of helpful institutional communication with the users of the space in question. When critics object to the screen's "intrusion," networks counter with an image of the TV as a free attraction, another dimension of a site's publicness. Responding to critics of the Airport Network, McMenamin proposed that the audio was not a nuisance at all: "Most people waiting for flights appreciate the news and information that CNN Airport Network offers. And others know they can read or converse without being disturbed. That's because the audio portion is controlled against ambient noise levels—lowering or raising the volume so that it never becomes disturbing. It also cuts off when gate announcements are made."[55] This image of the medium as a fully integrated part of its environment, adjusting to ambient sound levels, articulates the network's ideology of localism to an infinitesimal degree. The rise and fall of sound levels, based on "real time" monitoring, is a small-scale spatial calculus of "flexible specialization" akin to the just-in-time brand appeals of VideoOcart. It places commercial speech precisely at the threshold of consciousness, a fact that is presented not as evidence of the network's insidiousness but rather of its user-friendliness, no different from any other form of airport communications.

What this public service position fails to acknowledge is the fact that the waiting, working, eating populations targeted by place-based media serve an economic purpose regardless of whether they watch or not. Radical media economists often note that because ratings play such a key role in network profits, viewing should be a *paid* activity (to which the industry replies that viewers *are* paid, with free programming). But in place-based media one "counts" as a member of the commodity audience simply by moving through a space. We are not paid for donating our bodies to media corporations in this fashion, although they effectively rent out the time we spend waiting. Although calling for the rights of individuals to peace and quiet in public is an admirable liberal cause, it does not confront the economic power relations on which place-based media profits are based.

The same is true for solutions like Adam Hochschild's suggestion that airports combat Turner's noise pollution by constructing a special room for TV watchers similar to the small, cramped, smelly spaces where smokers gather.[56] In keeping with its Swiftian style, this solution is interesting precisely because of its inevitable failure. A CNN room at the airport gate would defeat the principles of captive audiencehood so important to the place-based media audience economy: viewers must *choose* to watch. In appealing to concerns about the pollution of space, Hochschild seems oblivious to what is surely a far larger offense to both individuals and the users of such spaces as a collectivity—the terms in which such networks define all air travelers as an audience commodity. The glaring nonrecognition of this *marketing* logic of place-based media among Hochschild and the few who resist TV's presence in public space is also an avoidance, on some level, of a politics based on collectivity. And in this respect, protest that advances on the basis of individual rights also risks complicity with the logic of individualization that underlies place-based media companies' customized programming, offering a "quality," targeted, advertising audience. Such protests can at best recommend a cultural policy aimed at restraining place-based media (similar to UNESCO's largely symbolic 1969 resolution banning Muzak).[57] They cannot call attention more radically to the ways public places become demographic laboratories that distill some anonymous users into quality market profiles, discarding and disregarding the others who spend time in the presence of the screen.

It may be small consolation, but it is helpful to return to the fact that the idealized institutional images of the out-of-home network and its putative effects don't have much hold on the actual ways that TV appears in different public places. As with larger-scale TV networks, forms of appropriation and unpredictability continue to define how TV's institutional power actually appears in the local world of its subjects. This idea of local appropriation is old hat in cultural studies; evidence of site-specific adaptations of cultural "content" in various cultures and innumerable parts of the globe abound in the scholarly literature of media reception. As Morley and Robins note, the wide range of regional appropriations of network imagery "should alert us to the complexity of the modes in which cultural power is both exercised and resisted."[58] But perhaps there are ways in which this complexity of local appropriation extends to the *form* of television, as well—as an object and a media technology. Perhaps, in other words, it is not only stories, images, and characters that get taken up and repositioned within other local contexts; it is also the temporal structure, the physical form, of the TV monitor. Now, this is a counterintuitive idea in many respects. As Morley and Robins note, drawing on the work of

Annabelle Sreberny-Mohammadi, Stanley Cavell, and Richard Wilk, the "facticity" of broadcasting's time structure is a more resilient element in television's ability to conquer and standardize localities. As Wilk suggests, "Satellite television has removed an essential element from the equation of colonial time. . . . TV time is now a single clock, ticking away a single rhythm, in every place it reaches."[59]

But in the small-scale world of the public airport lounge or the doctor's office, a broader range of engagements between local human processes and television's temporal "facticity" emerges. For example, the repetitive programming cycles and private modes of spectatorship produced in place-based media must always intersect with the unpredictability of user trajectories and local systems. Television may always be on time, but flights are often late, people working nearby may turn off the volume, monitors often malfunction. These local accidents may seem like random and irrelevant processes, but they are as much a part of the reality, and "facticity," of television as the global network ideologies that lie behind the screen. If it is difficult to mobilize collective politics around the audience commodity, it is certainly possible to note how these inevitable and commonplace facets of everyday localities always cross and complicate the institutional fictions of place-based media anyway. This is what Dirlik calls the "conjunctural situation" of the local, a situation in which the intersection of various material cultural elements and scales of action "strips" a site of its reification so that it "appears instead in the nakedness of its everyday practice."[60] And these practices themselves hold the key to the spatial operations of the screen, for they constitute a network of the type Latour has in mind when he points out that, "the two extremes, local and global, are much less interesting than the intermediary arrangements that we are calling networks."[61]

What I am suggesting here is that perhaps "place" can on occasion overwhelm the media that are "based" within it, and this might even be an inevitable by-product of the site-specificity of both discourses and practices of televisual media. But this idea requires some development, and it asks us to move in the direction of an even closer scrutiny of the screen's relationship to its immediate environment than this chapter's tour of the professional literature has allowed. The ineffable specificity of the relationship between site and screen is not something too infinitesimal for TV theory and criticism; it is something worth taking into account as best we can. For, as John Hartley has observed, the local meanings and statements that attach themselves to TV are easily visible in the medium's material culture.[62] To explore the significances of this cultural, spatial dimension of TV's facticity, its material and visual culture, requires a commitment to the act of close reading and a willingness to perform it on "actual" TV sets in the built environment. For only by asking what the particular installation practices of the TV set communicate in everyday spaces, as a kind of talking furniture that both blends in with and disrupts the human activities taking place around it, can we understand the kinds of networks, in a Latourian sense, in which it plays a role. Such readings take time to unfold. Indeed, they take up the entire second half of this book, which now offers a series of eye-level interpretations of what various TV installations are doing in diverse spaces of our daily lives.

PART II

PLACES AND PRACTICES: READING TV INSTALLATIONS IN DAILY LIFE

CHAPTER 4

SHAPING PUBLIC AND PRIVATE SPACE
WITH TV SCREENS

Television is just another appliance. It's a toaster with pictures.
—*Mark Fowler, Reagan-appointed* FCC *commissioner, 1981*

Fowler's notorious use of the toaster metaphor to justify the radical deregulation of TV advertising reduces the medium to the status of an object. Although one might easily see TV's object-status as the source of
its flexible, discursive relation to social space, Fowler characterizes television as an object in order to demonstrate its inertness and passivity. But
of course, his conservative logic has one fundamental flaw: the fact that,
when you think about it, a toaster with pictures would really be much
more interesting than a regular appliance. Like much Reagan era political speech, Fowler's metaphor is a science-fictional image deployed for
rhetorical effect. One can imagine potential product names—the GE Tele-
broil? The Sony Imagicrisp?

But Fowler's statement not only encapsulates the rhetoric of deregulation; it also, unwittingly, reminds us of the gendered history of the TV set as
a signifying machine.[1] This sci-fi image of a toaster TV recalls a rather older
ideological image of site-specific television spectatorship: the prototype
TV/stove publicized briefly in the immediate postwar years as a solution
to an imagined housewife's desire to work and watch TV at the same time.
The product of a web of midcentury spatial discourses on social roles, this
imaginative contraption, and others like it, embodies the gender-based
contradictions within the period's negotiations of postwar social change.[2]
These tensions are discernible in myriad debates and bits of advice con-
cerning where to put the TV in the home and how to integrate TV viewing
with domestic tasks. As Spigel has shown, TV's physical position was often
represented in pictorial space as isolating the laboring housewife from the

recreational viewing of the rest of the family or else integrating her into the collective space of viewing as a compliant servant.[3]

What such material cultural histories recover, and what conservative policy makers like Fowler disavow when they describe television as *nothing more than* a thing, is the fact that things do, in some sense, "talk." As anthropologist Janet Hoskins has shown, objects tell stories, shape social relationships, delineate boundaries between self and other, public and private, the absent and the enduring.[4] Television may indeed be "just an appliance," but appliances, like all commodities, are complicated discursive objects. In their design and placement, to say nothing of their sanctioned patterns of use, everyday machines, gadgets, and apparatuses speak volumes about the social structure, and power relations, of the environment they inhabit.[5] That television is a commodity that quite literally speaks to its owner is only one of many local uses of television that marks its complexity as a communicating object. As a number of studies document, complex social operations are assigned to, and appropriated by, the screen in the home at different times and in different national contexts.[6]

However, as part 1 of this book suggested, institutional treatments of the screen and its imagined spectator vary greatly from place to place, their variation reflecting the specific forms in which power circulates within a site, although all position the screen's immediate environment within wider discursive networks (think of the way television's presence in the tavern helped middle-class reformers focus their fears about juvenile delinquency and the corruption of the lower classes). The diversity of these institutional rhetorics of site-specific television makes a closer examination of its quantum relationship to its environment particularly valuable. It opens up the possibility of "reading" the social space of the screen, tracing how TV *as a distinctive kind of object* communicates in particular public contexts. By looking very carefully at individual screen installations and the public worlds in which they are embedded, we may grasp what happens when the generalizing institutional rhetorics that define places and their imagined, idealized spectators—the rhetorics outlined in the first half of this book—are materialized in the four-dimensional world of the social, through actual screen installations.

This is the task of this chapter and the three that follow. Each undertakes an illustrated, eye-level account of some conventional relationships between screen and space in diverse public settings. In this chapter I am concerned with one particular aspect of the screen's communicative functions as an object: the physical position it occupies within a space. I argue that examining *where* the T V set is located in a restaurant, or a retail store, or an airport, and tracing its physical relationship to other signs and objects, can tell us something about the parameters that are defined for public personhood in such spaces. In the process I also offer my reading of what these parameters are. As part of the public built environment, television operates through invisible and unremarkable conventions, inchoate forces of culture, control and habit that conspire to determine where the T V sits within its environment — behind a counter, or up high, or in an alcove. Such issues may seem dictated by transparent functionality, but they are simultaneously, like all architecture, *forms of social communication.* The position of the T V set, in short, helps to position people — not necessarily the empirical persons who work, wait, and relax within eye- and earshot of a particular screen but certainly the spectator positions these persons are encouraged to occupy within the social organization of the space and within larger networks of power, as well.

Of course, this demarcation of space and subjectivity is an ability shared by domestic and nondomestic T V sets alike. The T V is clearly an object through which people make local statements, regardless of where it may be.[7] But this commonality should not obscure one immediate difference between the domestic and the nondomestic, namely, that public spaces are televisual sites in which spectatorship can encompass a far broader range of physical scales, from the spectacular collective address of a huge screen in a basketball arena to the personal viewing position annexed by the small T V set placed behind the counter of an all-night gas station. Figure 8 exemplifies a technological assemblage of spectatorship that one can only encounter out of the home. It shows fans of the New York Yankees using a portable T V screen at the stadium. Although they are seated in the looming presence of giant T V images of the baseball players on the field below, they are instead concentrating intently on a "live" broadcast of a *basketball* game — the New York Knicks meeting the San Antonio Spurs in the final round of the National Basketball Association playoffs. Such bipolar spectator positionings are not only possible but *frequent* in public spaces, making the spectator a multimedia product of many different visual and spatial ideologies. This diversity of possible spectator positions reminds us that home and public space are asymmetrical spatial categories, and the latter incorporates a more diverse set of permutations of the televisual apparatus than domestic space: in addition to T V consoles identical to those found in the home, nondomestic spaces can contain multiple-screen video walls and video banks tuned to all manner of signal combinations,

FIG. 8

Portable TV sets allow multiple forms of spectatorship to coexist in public places, as in this scene at New York's Yankee Stadium, where baseball fans watch basketball playoffs. (Photograph by the author)

closed-circuit surveillance screens, touch-screen information kiosks, and illuminated, animated signage—all of which coexist with other portable electronic media (laptops, cellular telephones) in a dense web of electronic mediations of public space.

The bulk of the following analysis of positional conventions of the public screen concerns a very gross and basic discursive function of the various forms of visual media apparatus we routinely encounter in public —the capillary-level processes through which the screen sustains and/or reconfigures relations of public and private in particular environments. My analysis traces the constitution of private and public, as well as penumbral distinctions like personal and public, individual and collective, inside and outside, in three of the conventional positions assigned to television in public space: overhead screens, single-viewer structures, and screens in store windows. This multiple focus is important because it prevents us from simply assuming that television is automatically aligned with one or the other side of the public/private binary. The arrival of television in the postwar home did not simply bring public space into the private space of the home; rather, it reshaped the ways in which the boundary between public and private was conceived in domestic discourse, particularly its highly gendered ways of imagining the relationship between labor and leisure.[8] Similarly, the effects of television's presence in places other than the home are not reducible to "the privatization of public space," as some might argue. This is because public spaces are not purely and self-evidently public; they are, like every other cultural space, characterized by particular configurations of public and private.[9] Indeed, what makes the public/private division such a major category of social power is the fact that it is dynamic and flexible, varying from place to place. Taking this into account allows us to specify, with a great deal of precision, how the visual and bodily constitution of the subject as a citizen, or a consumer, or a trespasser occurs in quantum ways within the spaces of everyday life.

Let us begin with the most pervasive positional convention of the TV console in public places: its placement near the ceiling of a room, secured and immobilized above eye-level and out of reach of the casual user of the space. How does this positioning, in and of itself, make a statement about the space, its users, and its proprietors within a rubric of public and private? On the one hand, this overhead placement guarantees equal visual access for all viewers. It is a positioning that designates the screen as public address, perhaps even public service. Yet on the other hand, putting the screen out of reach like this marks it as private property. Indeed, one could argue that the most widespread difference between the physical treatment of domestic TV sets and public ones may be the fact that (for reasons of safety and security) the latter are often firmly fixed in place, requiring a ladder and screwdriver to move them from their locations.[10] In discouraging physical interference with the TV, overhead placement also prevents the users of a space from accessing its controls. In this respect the ceiling-mounted television even acquires some of the status of institutional speech; its inaccessibility communicates to the users of the space that the right to make a decision about what channel the screen is tuned to is reserved for its proprietor alone. Overhead placement is thus a physical positioning that addresses the viewer as an anonymous individual, physicalizing a modern conception of the subject in public space as a stranger—a subject whose motives are, to some extent, unpredictable and perhaps even counter to the collective ethos of the space through which he or she moves.[11]

The simultaneous production of a sense of publicness and of private property (and limited access) via the ceiling-mounted TV is compounded in locations with multiple screens, places where television forms a series of animated electronic windows visible from every point within a space. Often identical and synchronized with each other, the images on these screens tend to dominate the spaces they overlook, extending the principle of public visual access until it implodes in the fact that there is no way one can *not* watch TV. This proliferation of screens paradoxically makes public spectatorship a particular kind of private experience in which each viewer is provided with a personal sight line distinct from that of his or her companions, fulfilling a long-standing bourgeois ideology of spectatorship as "being alone in a crowd."[12] However, whereas the visual relations of the theater—the classical articulation of spectatorship's promise of a discursive zone of privacy in public—guarantee maximum access by positioning the bodies of the collective audience in ranks with unidirectional sight lines,[13] multiple monitors guarantee an unobstructed view through the opposite technique: fragmenting the audience into multiple physical viewing "stations."

This kind of arrangement is shown in figure 9, a drawing of a shopping mall food court with multiple TV monitors on which the Food Court Entertainment Network plays. It is a convention of screen-subject relations often found in bars and other social environments, with sometimes disconcerting results. Clustering TV viewers in individual eye-image apparatuses, this media architecture decentralizes spectatorship across an envi-

FIG. 9
Multiple overhead screens divide this shopping mall food court in
Bethesda, Md., into individualized viewing zones.

ronment. When two people sit at a table facing each other, with TV screens positioned behind each person's head, the arrangement affords an opportunity for easy switching between two roles—conversationalist and spectator—often requiring no more than a redirection of the gaze, not even a repositioning of the body. The effect of this impolite triangulation of conversation, making interlocutors compete with the image for each other's attention, is often a disconcerting split focus between distant spectacle and intimate talk in which neither experience is very satisfactory. We watch each other watching the screen as we converse, and we watch each other struggling not to watch; if the screens are in synch, then we are virtually mirror images of each other's spectatorship, participant-observers in the production and consumption of a spectacle of distraction.

A die-hard Habermasian might want to interpret this physical collapse of conversation and spectatorship via multiple overhead monitors as an apt spatial metaphor for the historical decline of the public sphere—the replacement of rational discourse with the commodified world of entertainment.[14] But such an interpretation seems insufficiently nuanced as an explanation of this particular form of TV spectatorship; I would argue that the capillary-level action of the screen in particular places is more complex. Serial spectacles on overhead screens both symbolically join spaces together in long-distance communication and fragment the social atmosphere of their immediate environments. The connotations of public address that come with the convention of overhead screen placement suture the conversing spectator into (at least) two places at once. We hesitate between two modes of spatiality—distance and proximity—so that mediated images can seem more "live" than the person with whom we are sitting.[15] As a result the intertwining of conversation and spectatorship in bars, restaurants, and other places with multiple monitors confuses and conflates the multiple meanings of individuality in Habermas's public sphere. On the one hand, the subject is interwoven with image-based networks of long-distance exchange and information transmission, on the other he or she is a rational, discursive, copresent citizen of a space, of a conversation, of a social relationship. If spectatorship is a subject position that offers a kind of "virtual mobility," then the paradoxical effect of the multiscreen apparatus is to anchor us in place, making us unable to take off. The triangulation of spectatorship and conversation produces a sense of distraction that stems less from the "privatization" of the space via the screen than from the incompleteness of this privatization process. Finding oneself caught between talking and watching is more likely to en-

courage reflection on the omnipresence of media in everyday public life than facilitate this process of media saturation.

If television's frequent presence in overhead space often seems to compete for visual attention with the rest of the environment, it may be because the overhead area of a public place so often turns out to be a dense symbolic zone. In the spaces we move through in everyday life, the ceiling is a location where, when one bothers to look, words, images, and optic devices like cameras and surveillance screens abound. Television, placed overhead for reasons of security or visibility, inevitably takes on diverse semiotic tasks within this elevated communicative space. In informal spaces of commerce and leisure, especially, the screen often participates in the construction of rich visual statements that are not always fully legible to cultural outsiders. A striking example of the sign-rich nature of overhead space may be found in the restaurant illustrated in figure 10, where a TV shelf constructed near the ceiling (presumably by a prior tenant of the space) is being used to house a shrine decorated with prayers and candles. This image suggests that such enclosed alcoves make ideal shrine locations for much the same reason they seem like good places to put TV sets: they are easily accessed visually but not tactilely, thus isolating their contents from the messy social world below. In this particular location the displaced TV screen sits in a more profane spot, within easy reach of the casual observer; no longer isolated from other objects in the space, it forms part of a visual sentence that also includes a good-luck kitty, a laughing Buddha, and a cash register.

One might choose to read this instance of TV demoted in favor of a religious object as culturally specific, a peculiarly *Chinese* spatial logic of the sacred and the profane. Indeed, this is how I might have interpreted this image when I first started photographing public television screens. But by the time I encountered this one I was accustomed to finding TV consoles in close visual proximity to religious images in a host of different spaces (from snack bars to hospital emergency rooms). It is a convention of TV's public placement observable across multiple religious, cultural, and diasporic-national contexts.[16] Indeed, I would venture that religious imagery and TV screens are two categories of signifying objects one sees most frequently in the overhead area of a public space. Consider the placement of the screen in figure 11, a TV set placed near sacred image material on the wall of a small Indian restaurant in Manhattan. Here the screen, displaying "Bollywood" movies, is located just below an electric clock bearing an iconic image of a Sikh saint; it sits atop a refrigeration unit along

FIG. 10

Although TV often sits in protected overhead space in public, other important objects can displace it from its perch. In this San Francisco restaurant a shrine occupies the shelf specially built for the TV set.

FIG. 11
The overhead placement of the public screen often brings it into close proximity with religious imagery. In this small restaurant in Manhattan, videotapes of Indian movies play next to a saint-clock. (Photograph by the author)

with an array of video recording and receiving equipment, including a surveillance monitor. These electronic apparatuses share an electrical source with the sacred icon. The tangle of wires links them together visually; indeed, the antenna line forms a suggestive pathway for the television signal, which must pass directly behind the saint's gesture of blessing before it enters the receiver.

Such schemas of wall decoration and protocols of TV adornment, both symbolic and practical, are much wider than a single culture's visual practice. As figures 12–14 illustrate, the TV set is a kind of semiotic magnet in social space, a place to put stickers, posters, plastic flowers, real flowers, and written signs that communicate something about the space to others. Often this communication is institutional, as in the conventional placement of informational materials on or near the TV set in medical waiting rooms (see chapter 6). In many cases the screen is plastered with signs telling viewers not to touch the controls. Such supplements to the institutional injunction already implied in the screen's overhead position foreground how much TV in public spaces serves as a site of interdiction— TV sets are often used to display no-smoking signs, for example. In other cases the statements made by the decoration of the screen are far more subtle. Decorative practices, for example, can be interpreted as evidence of television's status as a foreign object and a signature of class, as Ondina Fachel Leal suggests in her discussion of the recurrent placement of plastic flowers on top of TV sets in working-class homes in Brazil.[17] However, in American cultural spaces, where a TV set is affordable and omnipresent, we must seek other explanations. Perhaps the pervasive practice of decorating the TV screen expresses an impulse to anchor the TV set within its immediate environment, making it part and parcel of the space rather than a neutral conduit of images from the outside. Decorations help foil the mute ugliness of the console when it is turned off, softening its blank, faceless stare by turning it into a stand for displaying objects.

The conventional positioning of the overhead screen within a thicket of symbolic cultural images and decorative artifacts, concentrating the gazes of the space's users toward one particular area, has a complicated effect on the way public and private experiences are organized within a space. The decorative statement is at once a form of public address—an act of identity work directed toward a world that may or may not understand the significance of every element—and, simultaneously, a form of intensely personal meaning production. The two effects are not necessarily opposed; one need not completely understand the cultural codings being produced

FIG. 12
Written signs attached to TV sets in public are a form of managerial
communication, establishing protocols for TV viewing.

in a particular T V array to recognize and appreciate its status as an identity statement.[18] Figure 13, a paradigmatic example of the use of television to create a polysemic, mixed media cultural "shrine," illustrates this possibility, as well as the semantic complexity and heteroglossia such decorative arrangements of the screen can achieve. In a restaurant decorated in the *tricolore* theme of the Italian flag, the screen has been placed, overhead, in a corner where signs of all kinds are arranged for public display. These diverse visual, verbal, and sculptural forms are arranged so that they are easily perused by the waiting customer. It is easy to find a place to sit in this restaurant where the screen and its surrounding images and objects are not visible. However, if one does look at the screen, it is impossible not to notice all the paraphernalia beside it. From left to right the T V is surrounded by

A bowling trophy
A satellite dish receiver
An image of Patti Labelle
A bell
A red-and-white clock
A ceramic image of a man holding a downward-pointing horseshoe
   with a red pepper
An actual horseshoe, pointing downward, with a red pepper
   hanging between its prongs
A holy image of Padre Pio, a revered Italian priest
A souvenir plate from Italy
A surveillance camera
More souvenir plates
Restaurant and liquor licenses
Holy images of the pope and a monk
A bronze bull
Family photos, mostly of children, affixed to another framed
   municipal license.

The camera and the T V screen, two objects that require an unobstructed view, call attention to the fact that this wall is an important visual location within the space. However, the words and images it displays do not necessarily speak one language. Rather, this series of signs interweaves a sense of religious devotion, national pride, "folk" beliefs, hobbies, civic compliance, and surveillance together in one unique display. Some elements are public documents, such as the municipal licenses that all restaurants

FIG. 13
In a suburban Philadelphia pizza parlor the overhead TV screen is part
of a complicated statement made from images and things. (Photograph
by the author)

are required to display. Others are recognizably tourist souvenirs, used to convey an émigré sense of belonging. And others still are accessible only to persons familiar with particular Italian religious figures or Sicilian vernacular culture. One central motif, for example, is the dried red pepper known as *il corno* (or sometimes the "Italian Horn" in the United States) — an object that, depending on its physical orientation, can signify good luck, virility, or cuckoldry. Although it circulates widely in Sicilian and southern Italian culture, *il corno* is a symbol relatively unknown in the United States outside Italian-American communities. The TV set occupies a semiotic position somewhere between the arcane cultural resonance of such symbols and the institutional, regulatory speech of the liquor license.

But the polysemy of this arrangement does not prevent some of its elements from referencing each other across linguistic and material categories — Patti La Belle is paired with an actual bell, in a restaurant called Bella Italia; the horseshoe image on the ceramic plaque is juxtaposed with an actual horseshoe. A similar kind of material and symbolic cross-referentiality is activated by the TV screen at certain times of the week. On some Sunday mornings the pizzeria is crowded with soccer fans watching satellite Italian broadcasts of matches from Europe and Latin America. At such times the wall's dense semiotic interplay between images and things extends to encompass the material onscreen as well. The tricolor pattern that saturates the restaurant now appears in the designs of soccer uniforms, in corner-of-the-screen icons, and in commercials as well. Together with the Italian language, TV images become scenographic elements of the space that surrounds them, animating the sentiments expressed in its decor. However, this romance of Italianization is not a sustained effect of the TV screen at Bella Italia but rather an intermittent and flexible phenomenon. At other times in the week, depending on who is working behind the counter, the screen may be tuned to Spanish-language soap operas or local news, or it may not even be switched on. The screen thus cannot be described as dominating the environment of Bella Italia or as "privatizing" it with commercial or nationalist messages; rather, its overhead placement in a complex array of signs both public and personal illustrates how the symbolic elements of the screen's positioning are themselves subject to other everday processes that go on within the space.

Such uses of the TV screen in an assemblage of personal meanings and memories in public space can be thought of as an everyday practice through which individuals tactically fashion a sense of public and private within their workspaces. Compare the decorative treatment of the TV screen at Bella Italia with a similar use of the screen in another Italian-American establishment, illustrated in figure 14. There are certainly noticeable parallels between the images employed in this downtown New York pasta store and those in the Bella Italia wall — personal photos of loved ones (in this case a cat), tourist imagery, religious iconography. But here the screen is placed in a very different relationship to the customers. Positioned in a corner of the room, it is barely visible from the other side of the counter. This placement marks spectatorship as a private pleasure reserved for the employee or owner; to see the screen one must crane one's head and stare at the "backstage" area of the store, an impolite gesture, to say the least — I felt very awkward requesting permission to lean over and take a picture.

Such positionings reference the fact that many public spaces are also places of private employment, inhabited on a daily basis by the people who work there. They suggest that the TV screen can be a useful tool for territorializing the workspace and for carving a personal space within it. Figure 15 shows the work area of a concierge in a New York apartment building — a place where packages are stored, drycleaning and other deliveries picked up and dropped off, messages relayed, and other miscellaneous residential services coordinated. Building residents enter and leave this space all day, but the screen within it is not placed in such a way as to accommodate their vision. Instead, it helps to delineate the parts of the space that are off-limits to them, serving as a kind of physical barrier. Although this area of the mail room is part of the "public space" of the building's ground floor, this is not a public TV screen, and the chair that offers the best view is not a public chair. It would take an immense act of *chutzpah* to sit in it and claim the right to watch what's on the screen.

Such televisual constructions of a single viewing point and a zoned-off space are a positional convention of TV in public space that contrasts sharply with the overhead screen's institutionalizing arrangement of public and private. Instead of public access, these private arrangements are a far more tightly directed, architectonic opportunity for an immersive relationship to the screen. Accommodating one person at a time, such positionings are explicit in their invitation to use spectatorship to construct a zone of privacy in public, often referencing domestic space and domestic conventions of screen placement in the process. But they are not always the products of one individual's needs. Indeed, such private views are often part of the architectural scenography of the built environment. Figure 16 shows perhaps the most familiar example of this positional con-

FIG. 14

In this New York pasta store, as in many small commercial sites, TV viewing is incorporated into the routines of the workspace. Here the set is partly concealed from the customer's view. (Photograph by the author)

FIG. 15
In the concierge office of a large New York apartment building the placement of the TV set helps to separate public and private areas of the workspace. (Photograph by the author)

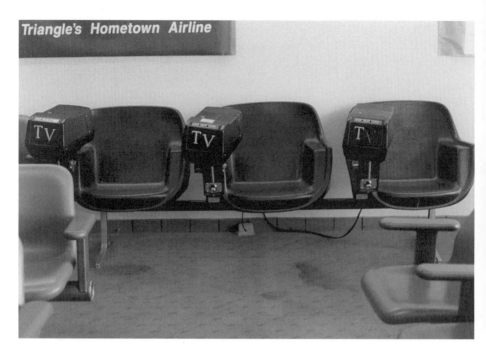

FIG. 16
At the Raleigh-Durham International Airport, coin-operated TV
spectatorship is a form of privacy in public. (Photograph by the author)

vention: coin-operated seat consoles in transit locations. These particular chairs, located as it happens at the Raleigh-Durham International Airport in North Carolina, are installed and operated by a company responsible for a number of different vending machines scattered throughout this airport; a twenty-five-cent piece buys the viewer fifteen minutes of access to black-and-white images broadcast from local stations.

What this vending machine model sells its user is not only the television signal but also a relationship to the rest of the space—the ability to separate oneself from others through spectatorship. The fact that one must pay for this privilege foregrounds the scarcity of full privacy in public locations; broadcast television makes the plastic veneer of the seat feel more like a dwelling place, if only because the fact that we have paid rent makes us more inclined to remain there. Located in places of travel and transit, places that are sites of trauma and dislocation, as well as routine, such TV seats equate the familiarity of the small screen with the calming focus of the hearth. Although reading a book might arguably produce the same effect, the TV screen offers a more literal representation of the private forms of transport that texts can offer. Viewing is not only a means of sensory isolation from one's immediate surroundings, but it is also a visually induced sense of travel to another place, if only the fictional national community of network TV programming. The gradual disappearance of these coin-operated apparatuses from air travel locations may stem from the competition provided by the CNN Airport Network, but the privatizing function they serve has by no means disappeared. Rather, it seems to have been supplanted by a host of other, more portable personal media experiences—the tinny buzzing of personal headsets, ringing cellular phones and their loud users, images on laptops, etc.—each of which serves as a way of isolating oneself from public space.

Private TV spectatorship in public space also produces a sense of being on display, paradoxically, of placing oneself under public scrutiny through a desire for privacy. This is an effect that retailers frequently exploit, as in figure 17, a chair demonstration/display I photographed in a branch of the gadget retail chain The Sharper Image in a suburban Washington, D.C., mall. Here a TV set showing a slick promotional video stands in front of the luxurious leather, electronically controlled recliner it demonstrates. (A child was sitting in the chair when I took this photograph, a fact I remark on because children often seem far more attracted than adults to private TV screens in public space—grown-ups generally seem to avoid them with a vague sense of embarrassment). This display, like

FIG. 17
Private viewing setups in retail spaces put TV viewing onstage. This TV is
part of a chair display at The Sharper Image in Bethesda, Md.
(Photograph by the author)

the coin-operated screens in the airport, also references the spatial relations of domestic TV viewing. However, it does so in even more literal,
although idealized, terms, showing the consumer a fantasy of home on the
screen. But more important, from the store's perspective, is the fact that
when customers sit in the chair and test its feel, they become part of the
display, demonstrating for others the attractiveness of this private viewing
position.

When I first encountered this particular display, I couldn't determine
whether it was the chair or the TV that was being sold. I felt that both
were offered to me as a source of physical and mental relaxation. My
confusion stemmed from the placard on top of the monitor, which told
seated viewer/consumers, "You deserve the ultimate massage every day."
It was initially difficult to figure out whether the word *massage* referred
to the chair or to TV spectatorship. This is because, in addition to simply
denoting the qualities of the chair, words like *massage* and *spin* (something which this chair also does) allude to the manipulability of the
image in public relations language, an allusion immortalized in Marshall
McLuhan's self-reflexive proclamation (with Quentin Fiore), that "The
Medium is the *Massage*."[19] The multiple connotations of the word *massage* in this installation were no doubt an intentional marketing irony,
given the fact that The Sharper Image is a store packed with "executive
toys" and other signifiers of hip, corporate sophistication. The executive
hipster association is certainly encoded in the image on the monitor: a
thirtysomething white man in business attire reclining in *his* version of
this chair, holding the remote control that operates its massage mechanism. Near him, in the dining area of what appears to be a large modern
loft, a woman sets the table.

The luxurious, padded TV chair, this video installation suggests, is a
leather throne. It exemplifies the association between the sitting position and authority[20] — not only because of the obvious signifiers of wealth
and privilege that populate the mise-en-scene of this video but because
it comes equipped with an object thoroughly associated with domestic
(male) authority: a remote control. This chair also empowers the spectator more materially and immediately in the space of the mall. Chairs are
few and far between in retail locations, and the sight of a place to sit is
a welcome interruption in the midst of the tiring itinerary of a shopping
trip. Indeed, the mere act of sitting down can provide an oasis of privacy
in the middle of a crowded store, regardless of whether spectatorship is
an option or not. In The Sharper Image this sense of the chair as an es-

cape from public space reinforces the promotional goals of the material onscreen. Superimposed on the image is the word *getaway,* a word that references not only a potential desire to "get away" from one's trouble through a relaxing massage, or a comfy chair, but also a familiar motif of film and television marketing—the idea of the theater seat or the home barcalounger as a mode of transport or escape.[21] In this and, I think, other screen and chair apparatuses, the viewer's gaze at the screen is material for the construction of a space within a space, enjoining a televisual ideology of a private window to another world that often supports the immediate consumer goals of point-of-purchase advertising.

Thus far I have discussed such privatizing and publicizing effects of overhead and individualized screen setups in relative isolation, concentrating on one or the other as particular projections of the subject's position within the spatial discourses that define a particular place. However, when we move within retail space and other kinds of public locations, we often encounter such single-viewer setups alongside other, more public opportunities for spectatorship. Many places exhibit more than one way of positioning the TV screen, and some contain a multitude of screen-subject configurations designed to increase the mobility of eye and body for commercial purposes. The result, often, is the exhausting feeling of navigating through interacting layers of televisual gazes and images, especially in large retail stores.

A good way to understand this kind of experience, and the different positions assigned to the viewer-shopper by these various televisual apparatuses within public places, is to visit Virgin Megastore in Manhattan's Times Square, arguably the most televisual public square in North America. The megastore, nominated store of the year by the trade journal *Chain Store Age* in 1997, is a three-floor, seventy-five-thousand-square-foot establishment that features in its blazing interior a "fifty-foot high, glistening, metal D.J. tower . . . floor-to-ceiling graphics and oversized video screens."[22] Within this highly visual interior landscape TV images are offered both to public collectivities and private individuals, creating different zones of visuality in each case. Figure 18 illustrates the more private end of this spectrum of televisual modes of address: the personal viewing stations, located in the store's video section, where the discriminating consumer can test audio and image quality with headphones. But the individual media spaces these viewing stations construct in the midst of a crowded store are also merchandise racks; facilitating both self-service and impulse buying, they support a mode of spectatorship in which view-

FIG. 18

At Virgin Megastore in Times Square the personal viewing station is an
individualized media apparatus and a sales rack, presenting the film as
both a visual and a tactile commodity.

ing need not be separate from shopping. The heft and gloss of the wrapped videotape as a physical object supplements the audiovisual and narrative experience of the film and offers the pleasure of tactility as a supplement to sight and hearing.[23]

It is important to note that, particularly in urban retail spaces, these viewing stations are accessible to broader constituencies than the monied consumer. Purchasing is not a requirement for viewing, and anyone who wishes may unobtrusively come into the store and watch a movie (or listen to a current CD); it is not uncommon to find homeless people listening to music in the Virgin megastore. However, only certain kinds of movies are available for private screenings. A vast number of these tapes are children's media, which isn't surprising given that the videotape retailing market is dominated by "kidvid" sales.[24] A rather more diverse selection of media products may be consumed on the large video screen set into the wall adjacent to the ranks of private viewing stations (fig. 19). In an interesting reversal of film studies' assumptions about screen size and narrativity, the smaller individualized monitors tend to feature narrative-based entertainment, whereas the large screen displays music video, setting the mood of televisual spectacle. Although its economic goal is still, presumably, to encourage the purchase of the image material (in this case an ABBA video-disk), the large screen does not feature self-service copies of tapes or disks alongside its display surface. Its role seems to be to secure the carnival scenography of the space, emphasizing the megastore's location within the larger consumer mise-en-scene of Times Square in the late 1990s.

However, the fact that titillating music videos are displayed on this large screen is worthy of closer attention given that Times Square is a place historically defined by sexual display and its repression.[25] Indeed, TV's creation and reshaping of categories of public and private within the megastore is a process that can be contextualized in the wider social histories of the store's particular location. In the wake of the highly publicized transformation of the district from sex zone to Disney-sponsored "urban entertainment destination," it is significant that such sexualized visual material is not offered for consumption in the small, private viewing stations. These peepshow-like apparatuses might, after all, forge an unwelcome association with the spectatorial arrangements of the neighborhood's pre-Disney years. The presence of titillating imagery on the "public" screen in the Virgin megastore, and its absence on the private listening stations, exposes the fact that the logic governing Times Square's relation to adult images is one not of repression but—in classic Foucauldian fashion—of reenun-

FIG. 19

Music videos conventionally appear on the large screen at the Virgin Megastore. Is this because their sexual content, viewed on the "peep-show" apparatus of the personal viewing station, might recall the adult film spectatorship associated with Times Square in previous years?

ciation. The older institutions of adult entertainment may have largely left, but sexy images have not been eradicated from the area; rather, they have been legitimized anew along a different axis of public and private. Masturbatory stigmas apparently disappear when such images circulate publicly and freely on large screens, while being simultaneously privatized via their association with national brands and consumerism. The paradigmatic instance of this "relegitimizing" logic, authorizing only the sex-commodities that come in branded packages, is the moment in 1995 when Victoria's Secret broadcast its first supermodel fashion show on the Sony Jumbotron, backing midtown traffic up for blocks.[26]

The widest gulf between private spectatorship apparatuses and more "passively" accessed forms of televisual address, directed toward a collective, public spectator, exists on the central, atrium-like main music sales floor of the megastore. It contains the most publicly available configuration of screens, as figure 20 illustrates: a grid of music videos lines the space above the sales floor with the repeated display of synchronized moving images. This video bank introduces a Warholian aesthetic of mass cultural seriality into the environment, mirroring the repetitious display of merchandise on the self-service racks in a carnivalesque sense of competing spectacles.

As decorative, video wallpaper the video array is a figure of mass production and consumption of spectacle. However, this sense of massification starts to break up when one considers that when I took the photograph on which this drawing was based, a Webcam installed in the lobby continually captured images of the people passing through the store's doors. The resulting digital pictures, updated every minute or so, appeared on the computer screens of visitors to the Virgin Web page; beside it was a text inviting Net surfers to "relax, sit back, drink a cup of coffee" and watch people entering and exiting the megastore. The presence of the Webcam and its invitation to voyeurism turned the entire store into a fishbowl spectacle on an isolated viewer's PC screen, rendering the relative public or private nature of any of the spectatorial views contained within the space almost irrelevant.[27]

The Webcam's anonymous, remote point of view is in some ways merely an extension of two kinds of mediated perspective offered within the physical space of the megastore: the view of the surveillance cameras, concealed in forbidding black orbs hanging from the ceiling around the store, and the view of the passerby on the street, who glimpses the dense array of video images, posters, and merchandise in the window as a compli-

FIG. 20

On Virgin Megastore's main floor the synchronized images on the music video monitors mirror the serialized commodity aesthetics of the merchandise on display.

cated visual palimpsest. Indeed, the Webcam materializes the retail visual strategy detailed in the first half of this book: one in which shopper surveillance and commercial display intertwine as visual elements of the sales floor via technologies like VideOcart. But if the presence of watchful aesthetics in public space is old news, the commercial modes of spectatorship offered by the Webcam are quite new. Its live, voyeuristic view in real time expands postwar visual merchandising's dreams of a technological fix for uncertain changes in the consumer landscape of retailing. Just like early retail visions of TV sponsorship, it extends the store window beyond its physical location, stretching across the placeless landscape of the Internet into the home or office. Like the store window it is both a portal to and an advertisement for the space of the store. The Webcam's conflation of private surveillance and public promotion, and its appearance as a window within a window, also reminds us of the enduring nature of the store window as a metaphor for spectatorship. It bears more than a passing resemblance to the commercial display convention of placing a TV screen in a store window.

However, the collapse of space enacted by this convention differs from that of the Webcam in several respects. The view the Webcam offers its solitary (in all likelihood) viewer is private and individualized; the store-window TV solicits the attention of every passerby. The flashing, serial monitors in the windows of the megastore compete with the signage and attractions of Times Square, whereas the visual context of the Webcam is less cluttered. The impact of the Webcam is measured in "hits," whereas store window TVs are judged by the amount of foot traffic they stimulate. Often the image on the store-window TV is a kind of symbolic annex to the physical space of the store, expanding existing display space, and serving as a compressed index of what one will find inside. To conclude this chapter's analysis of the formation, and deformation, of public and private relations via the position of the TV screen, we turn to a brief consideration of this conventional positioning practice, examining how the construction of an image space in the window delineates public and private realms of spectatorship and consumption. This conclusion is also a prelude because it introduces some of the concerns of the next chapter, specifically, the ways that video screens create new spaces of figurative and literal mobility within the physical space of the sales floor in retail stores. For TV screens, as we shall see, do more than simply demarcate zones of individuality and collectivity in a retail space, or at least, if they do so it is in the service of particular economic goals. The store-window TV, located at the interface of the public arena of the street and the more private arena of the sales floor, introduces this process and concludes my consideration of TV's role as a technology for enacting public and private boundaries within a site.

Like the kinds of vernacular television settings that people make in everyday life when they decorate their TV sets with personal objects and forms of local address, the TV screen in the store window is often part of a syntagmatic array of images and things, words and sounds. It differs from other conventional retail uses of TV in that, as we saw in an earlier chapter, the latter are often used to direct traffic and motivate shoppers in the interior environment of the sales floor. The store-window TV is not quite located at the point-of-purchase, although it often serves as a technology for extending private rhetorics of commerce into the street's public world. Although stores in malls and other kinds of enclosed public concourses certainly place TV screens in their windows and in places where they are highly visible to passersby, the most complicated tasks of interpellation seem to be assigned to the screens that appear in the store windows of high-density retail and real estate locations, such as cities. In downtown Manhattan, for example, a video monitor in a window can sometimes substitute for the entire space of the store. Figure 21 shows a tape playing in the window of a "mini-bike shop" that is an offshoot of a rather more mainstream establishment — the pet store, to which handwritten signs direct the window shopper to take his or her questions about minibikes. The videotape endeavors to make the public street into a private space of commerce and, in addition, to elevate this rather specialized and marginalized hobby by turning it into a TV sport ("don't just watch the fun, be part of it"). The screen, in short, fulfills the role of the store's proprietor and expands the store's sales area. It speaks to the passerby on behalf of both John and the minibikes it displays, part signage and part commodity itself.

The store-window TV does not become a kind of public stockroom and browsing area like this simply through its physical position. Rather, it accomplishes its designation of space through the particular textual material that appears on and around it as well, as in John's instruction to window shoppers to take their inquiries to the pet store. The symbiotic relation of image to text is illustrated most clearly in figure 22, where the image itself is the merchandise being sold. Here, in New York's Chinatown, a TV sits on a ledge to promote the movies sold in the basement video store (a popular Jet Li film appears on the screen in this picture). Handwritten signs in

FIG. 21
Hand-lettered signs extend a promotional video's direct address in the store window, broadcasting the commercial speech of this small, specialized store into the space of the street. (Photograph by the author)

FIG. 22

This outdoor TV set placement in New York's Chinatown serves as a
show window for a basement video store. It targets distinct audiences via
signs that say different things in Chinese and English. (Photograph by
the author)

Chinese and English surround the image and announce that movies are for sale. The one on top of the screen advertises in English "BUY 3 GET 1 Free." The Chinese lettering beside it says the same thing, although it adds that the sale celebrates a particular Taiwanese festival.[28]

As this slight difference suggests, several distinct spectator passersby are addressed in this one television installation. This is confirmed by signs on the side and the bottom of the screen, which are not translated into English. The vertical sign on the left invites customers to apply for discounted senior bus passes in the video store, and the sign on the bottom offers an even more attractive discount on tape purchases than the one advertised in the bilingual sign above: "pay $100 for 100 tapes." As point-of-purchase television, this TV setting produces a complex sense of cultural space not only in the way it addresses different subjects in English and Chinese respectively but also in the juxtaposition of onscreen image and text. The *image* is often described as a key component of the cultural space that Mayfair Mei-hui Yang calls "transnational China"—"the spatial and geographical extension of Chinese culture across national and political boundaries and . . . the persistent interconnectedness among these cultural offshoots with each other and with the 'motherland' . . . becoming more connected and integrated through the reception of an increasingly common body of cultural products by dispersed Chinese audiences and readers."[29] But in contrast to this ageographical transnational space of media, the Chinese language *signs* glued to and around the screen acknowledge the more localized and immediate conditions of life in urban immigrant social networks—the vertical one acknowledges the difficulties of navigating issues such as housing and transportation in a world in which one is considered a stranger; the other acknowledges the possibility of a spectator who is a habitual viewer of Chinese-language media and who has enough available cash to buy tapes in bulk. If the image's space-binding positions the spectator in an imaginary "elsewhere," the *texts* around it are reminders of the historical location of the subject in the here and now. Moreover, in their selective bilingualism these signs together register the transnational conditions of life in a large immigrant community that is also a tourist destination—like New York's Chinatown.

The idea that it is not just the TV image but also the TV object, and the other objects around it, that engage television's powers of direct address and create "markets" is a topic that takes up an entire chapter. I conclude this one with a brief example of a store-window video that exploits, in a suggestive way, TV's ability to redraw the public/private boundary for commercial purposes. The T V set in question, shown in figure 23, sits in the storefront window of a New York tattoo parlor called "Whatever." On its screen an image of a tattooing videotape plays, surrounded by a dense and heterogeneous syntagm of totem objects that together signify different elements of "alternative culture" or, rather, some pop culture icons that are often appropriated for personal identity work in the form of tattoos: an alien mask, martial arts images, the devil's head, Mickey Mouse, the grim reaper.

The picture onscreen here is more than just a representation of what has happened — or possibly is happening at this moment — inside the store. It is an image that seems determined to confound social conventions of public and private relations via an aesthetic of excessive, highly corporeal visibility — we see the needle go in and out, and we see the image being formed on the skin. But if this particular image placement transgresses any boundaries of taste through the public spectacle of bodily "mutilation," it is a transgression as mundane as the ubiquitous transgressions performed by tattooed and pierced bodies in urban streets, and suburban malls, across America. Indeed, examining this image one is struck by, simultaneously, its graphic, violating effect and its thoroughly commercial nature, supported by the assemblage of disparate occult and cult clichés around it. As an interpretive key to the image on the screen, this array of objects hails a particular target shopper: if the occult, Bruce Lee, drugs, aliens, "apocalypse culture" is your thing, then you know you're in the right place. Indeed, one could argue that the fact that what we are watching on the screen is a tattooing videotape suggests that participation in this market requires an extreme and *indelible* kind of commitment. The televisualization of the tattooing process, displayed within a commercial scenography of underground goods for sale, shows us how tattooing can be less of a personal, highly symbolic process of meaning production than an irreversible imprinting of the iconography of "alternative culture" at one particular historical moment onto the body itself.

This possibility implicates the material practices of positioning the T V screen within other cultural processes beyond the designation of public and private. Specifically it exposes the possibility of a link between these practices and the materialization of consumer markets through spatial and visual representation. From this perspective the store's use of human skin as a kind of advertising medium seems highly appropriate. The tattooed body and the T V screen in the window can be seen as analogies of one another. Each is a physical form with highly symbolic properties; each

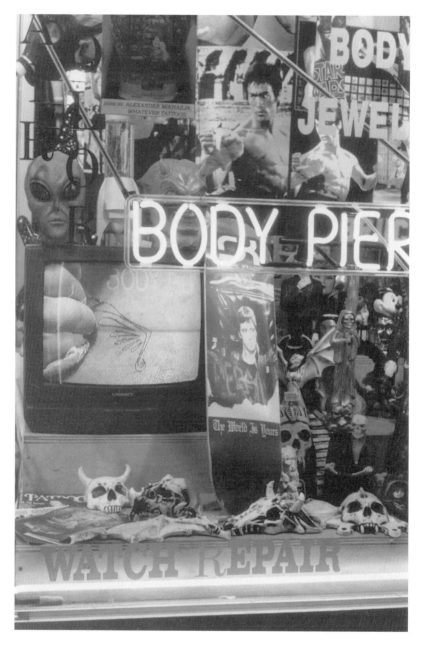

FIG. 23
This store window TV in New York publicizes a tattoo parlor with close-ups of the intimate art of tattooing displayed next to diverse icons of "alternative" taste culture. (Photograph by the author)

circulates, and makes statements, in public space. Perhaps this is a hyperbolic interpretation of the relationship between acts of consumption and practices of identity, but it certainly encapsulates certain marketing ideologies of how the advertising process works. The proximity of cult and occult cultural objects and the image of tattooing, either a homage to, or a parody of, "primitive" totemic assemblages, suggests a narrative of advertising's effects in which passersby who so much as glance at the screen and the cultural icons that surround it find themselves leaving the store an hour later with a *Star Wars* character etched on a shoulder. Whether or not this admittedly extremist scenario occurs, it nevertheless points to a wider utopian ideal in retail languages of television: the idea that the video screen is a representational space capable of moving its spectator both physically, and affectively, into the crosshairs of a commercial address that results in an immediate purchase. On the sales floor, in other words, consumer "positioning" is a screen practice even more precisely calibrated than the complicated designation of public and private zones traced in the foregoing examples. As we will see in the following chapter, the construction of the screen as a projective symbolic space within a physical consumer space is a semiotic operation of retail video that, when we examine it closely, reveals the screen's crucial role in embedding marketing assumptions about identity categories—age, race, class, gender— into the pragmatic, everyday, three-dimensional architecture of shopping.

CHAPTER 5

TELEVISION AT THE POINT OF PURCHASE

This chapter examines point-of-purchase video, one of the largest institutional uses of TV outside the home today. But although my goal is to parse the "grammar" of retail video and the assumptions about identity, consumer desire, and space it materializes in everyday life, the obstacle I face is the very pervasiveness, and hence banality, of my subject. For although readers who have spent any time in the contemporary landscape of North American consumer culture have surely been exposed to point-of-purchase video — if only of the sort described in the previous chapter's tour of the Virgin megastore — it is also quite likely that they have failed to notice it entirely. I think this is because TV assimilates so easily with the visual and plastic architecture of retail space, with its serial display of commodities, its use of glass, mirrors, and backlit signs. This sense of continuity is what spurs contemporary architecture critics to the metonymic characterization of consumer spaces as being, in some way or another, "like" television. Of course the problem with such analogies is that they are so quick, so intuitively fitting and rhetorically bold, that they tend to close rather than open up investigation and debate. They shorten the gap between production and consumption rather than elongating it, something Nick Couldry cogently argues we must do if we are to understand how media power is continually reproduced in the small, interactional spaces of everyday life.[1] But the analogy does get at the way TV seems *camouflaged* in retail space so that it takes a constant effort to stay focused on its discursive and physical tasks within a site.

These tasks are innumerable, but in general it is fair to say that what makes point-of-purchase video notable as a televisual form is this: it is installed not only in order to direct people's movements and attention in space, but also, often, to create a sense of actual, or "virtual," access to places that are distinct from the sales floor. Time and again, the screen is used to alter the store's physical and symbolic relations of consumption, sometimes generating private spectatorial worlds, as we saw in the previous chapter, and frequently supplementing the mundane world of retailing with various idealized representations of other spaces. These representations share with all forms of advertising imagery the promise of consumer identity transformation and realization — recall the construction of an idealized middle-class space in the massage chair installation shown in figure 17. Over the course of this chapter I will trace some of the display techniques that produce such distinctively spatialized uses of the commercial video image, relying heavily on visual documentation as I proceed.

It is impossible to offer an exhaustive account of all forms of point-of-purchase video in one go, but this does not mean that no points of commonality link different types of installations in different types of site, from megastores to minimarts. Because all point-of-purchase TV images are designed to shape the spatial paths, and material expenditures, of the consumer this means that retail TV images have more in common with other display forms on the sales floor — signs, coupons, live demonstrations — than with broadcast television images. For the latter are only rarely designed with such specific, short-term spatially precise goals in mind; "dialing the phone," Patricia Mellencamp points out, is "the only action [broadcast] TV requests."[2] In contrast, like other point-of-purchase media, video on the sales floor must intervene in the space and time of the shopping trip, increase our interaction with merchandise, and generally make customers' time in the store more "productive" (i.e., produce more purchases). In retailing textbooks the pages devoted to the spatial construction of the point-of-purchase are meticulous compendia of tips and advice for managing shopper behavior, presenting page after page of consumer "flightpaths" — balletic lines pirouetting and swirling across the floor plan of the store (fig. 24).

As this perennial concern with traffic flow illustrates, contemporary retail video installations continue the project postwar retailers envisioned for department store television. However, today's versions of the retail fantasy of the televisual sales floor, especially when documented in their immediate contexts, materialize more diversified understandings of the consumer subject than the stepfordist retail fantasies of the postwar period. They reveal both the more minute demographic ideas about identity in

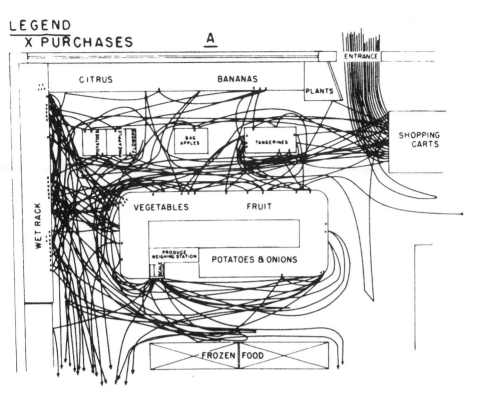

FIG. 24
Sales floor design is a kinetic art and science, materialized here in the balletic floor plans of a retailing handbook. (U.S. Department of Agriculture pamphlet)

which institutional visions of the subject are now based and, as I will argue, some of the contradictory relations of commerce and culture in which this subject is caught.

Another point of commonality between the diverse forms of commercial video art that appear on the sales floor is the way they often very directly and explicitly reference televisual properties as shorthand ways of expressing marketing notions of consumer desire. As in the early days of retail TV, the medium's powers of commodity representation and its space-binding ideologies of liveness, instantaneity, and telepresence serve as touchstones for the design of retail environments and a powerful model of retail motivation in general. One display consultant, for example, likened the 1990s sales floor to "a three-dimensional TV commercial. It's a walk-in container for words and thoughts and messages and ideas."[3] In this sentiment and others like it, an idealist, Orwellian TV spectator is a rhetorical figure of the ideal shopper: a subject not only seduced, and *influenced,* by images but also taken into other spaces for imaginative play and fantasy through the "window" of the screen.

Because such detailed forms of installation and address are highly ephemeral, eluding sustained attention, the camera was a particularly useful research tool for this chapter, even though the cluttered convoluted planes of retail space made reproducing these photographs in black and white a challenge. Exploring the material complexity of these installations after I photographed them provided a clear picture of the *range* of identity categories that are given a consumerist visibility, and marketability, by video screens in retailing. The camera extends the time of the moment of reception, and by fixing the details of the objects and images that together make up the commercial "television setting" it allows us to pay some attention to the production of spaces and demographic categories on the sales floor and to speculate about the wider contradictions in consumer culture they reference. My task in this chapter is to interpret these contradictions by calling attention to certain details in retail video use. We begin, therefore, with a reading, as it seems the best way to initiate the total immersion in retail visual culture, in the spectacular, and not so spectacular, scenes of shopping and browsing that guided my research for this chapter.

If you have ever walked into a branch of the athletic apparel chain called Champs, then you are likely to have passed a video installation similar, or even identical, to the installation shown in figure 25. I took the photograph on which this drawing is based in a North Carolina shopping mall, but

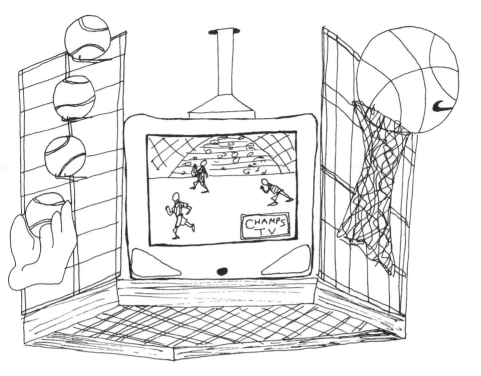

FIG. 25

In a North Carolina sporting apparel store an overhead retail video installation uses sculptural techniques to render televisual properties (slow motion, freeze-frame) in three dimensions.

I have seen these installations in other branches of the chain, too. What is this screen doing here? Placed within five feet of the entrance to the sales floor, it inhabits the threshold region known in retailing jargon as the "transition zone." Displays in this area are designed to invite the attention of passersby on the mall concourse and to serve as "bumpers"— fixtures that slow the entering shopper down, and perhaps provide him or her with a set of coordinates for navigating the space.[4] So the pragmatic answer to this question is easy to deduce: this particular screen placement, conveniently enough, stops the shopper directly in front of the new arrivals display rack. It shows replays of sports moments and music videos that might catch the momentary attention of the shopper, although after several years of visiting Champs stores I must confess that I am the only person who seems to pay any attention to these images. But if the TV screen is not for viewing, then what, exactly, is it doing here? What is it *saying* to the shoppers and passersby it greets? Like many athletic store TV monitors this one solicits the shopper's attention with sports imagery—in this case basketball highlights appear onscreen, and decorative sculptures made from store merchandise (baseballs, a glove, a basketball) flank the frame. Note that both of these sculptures represent a particularly *satisfying* kind of sports moment—making a catch or, in the case of the display on the other side of the screen, a "basket." This image of sports accomplishment, coupled with the screen's close proximity to the new arrivals shelf, seems to solicit the passing shopper with a visual pun, a play on the vernacular practice of calling a prized purchase a "score."

This is a very precise kind of consumer symbolism, and, indeed, it is difficult to generalize about point-of-purchase video installations because although they are pervasive, they are also incredibly site-specific in their detail. Although Champs is typical in some ways, as I will explain in a moment, it, along with the other six or seven installations toured in this chapter, is not so much a *representative* of a general subcategory of retail TV as it is a usefully explicit example of how particular sales floor display logics can be.

Champs's screen installation illustrates how properties of the video image, like slow-motion, get materialized in three dimensions, as figures for consumer desire, in retail display. It is positioned overhead, like a basketball hoop, and it is even decorated with a hoop and ball. This spatial, embodied reference to the experience of standing on the court seems designed to remove the spectator from the mundane world of retailing and to symbolically position him or her in a somehow more empowering space. It is a sculptural effect equivalent to the media ideology of "tele-presence." Like a network sports trailer, this installation offers the viewer a spectatorial experience that somehow encompasses the act of *playing,* rather than just observing, basketball. The ball falling into the (miniatur-ized) hoop even places the spectator in the bodily location of the athlete in the act of scoring—a scenographic treatment of the monitor that equates sports *viewing* and sports *achievement.*

But as with all TV, the production aesthetic of this sculptural TV in-stallation does not obey one singular stylistic program. Rather, Champs's motivational screen assemblage enacts a trickle-down model of postmod-ernism, collapsing subjectivities and media ontologies willy-nilly. Thus, just in case the basketball playing/viewing analogy is insufficient con-sumer motivation by itself, the sculpture also includes, to the left of the screen, four baseballs suspended in a line above a grasping mitt. The ar-rangement of the balls recalls the step motion of a videotaped image ad-vancing frame-by-frame. It is a material simulation of a video process, a reference to the act of viewing a slow-motion replay. But this simulation of slow-motion replay is an idealized extension of the televisual property it represents. This sculptural close-up, slowing down the moment of a per-fect catch, brings the spectator closer to the sight of a key baseball moment than most viewers of slow-motion sports get at home.[5] It thus reinforces the same sense of a connection among acts of viewing, shopping, and scor-ing suggested in the contiguous placement of screen and basketball hoop. In its use of an actual glove, with price tag still attached, this installation places the TV image on the "life-size" scale of the human body stand-ing below the screen in close proximity to products and cash registers. Together, then, the sculptures around the screen and the place where it hangs position the spectator as multiple subjects: a player, a viewer, and a shopper on the sales floor. Champs's video screen thus works hard to take the consumer out of the mass-market world of the chain store in the mall and into a more fulfilling fantasy world of sporty empowerment. Its col-lapse of spaces and subjectivities in sculptural representation physicalizes the oft-cited imploding spatiality of television—the proverbial "window onto another world." But like many TV screens in stores it exploits this ideology of spatial collapse in very *site-specific* terms, for reasons that have a lot to do with some very *local* merchandising goals—showcasing new arrivals, in this case.

The fact that it is charged with such specific goals makes point-of-purchase video an ideal tool for exploring how production theory (video production, production of consumer identity templates) transforms into practice, how marketing's theories of spectatorship appear in the everyday world of consumer culture.[6] If consumption is a microlevel cultural and economic process, then installations like this one at Champs allow us to see how the institutional strategies of images and space that aim to promote consumption manifest themselves on the small scale of the everyday. They do not tell us what actual shoppers "do" with their images. But they do reveal the techniques retailers and manufacturers use in their struggle for mastery over the rather unpredictable constellation of practices and tactics that make up the "forces" of consumption on the capillary scale of everyday life.

To convey the nuanced nature of retail video's representation of consumer identity and desire I will examine the mundane hails through which these installations signal their passersby across a range of store locations and implied demographics. Each of these screens offers its spectator a detailed, site-specific vision of shopping as a kind of identity work. Like Champs's overhead video monitor they not only work to shape the physical mobility of bodies in the store; they also visualize the figurative mobility of the shopper in consumer culture by referencing and displaying other, aspirational spaces. My analysis focuses on five different places: NikeTown, a produce market, the housewares chain Bed Bath and Beyond, a department store cosmetics counter, and a shopping mall athletic shoe store, with some brief comparisons to other installation sites along the way.

In all of these very different types of stores the spatiotemporal ideology of the screen as a kind of window, binding one place to another and bringing the spectator closer to another (real or imaginary) location, is materialized in retail techniques as diverse as the spaces themselves. Some of these installations use physical treatments of the screen to position the shopper in an alternative space to the cluttered environment of the actual store—a technique we already saw in Champs's gestural placing of the spectator-shopper on an imaginary basketball court. Others use TV imagery to make the sales floor seem like another place entirely, a place altogether distinct from the arena of commerce. NikeTown, the first space we examine, falls into this category; others not examined here include the faux movie set environments of Warner Bros. and Disney stores and the museum-like environment of the flagship Discovery Communications store in Washington, D.C.[7] In other instances the idealized space seen through the window of the TV screen becomes a stage on which the product is demonstrated and animated, as in Bed Bath and Beyond's cookware department. And in other places again the space onscreen is a fantasy scenography of a particular marketing demographic's putative habitat—the stage ghetto of mainstream music video, for instance. In outlining these specific spatial strategies, my goal is to show how point-of-purchase video uses television's powers of representation and its embedded relation to its environment as a figure and a ground for the transformative power of acts of consumption, for reasons that have everything to do with the institutional economics of contemporary retailing.

The institutional relations that underlie point-of-purchase video's techniques of display reflect the fact that many commodities on the sales floor today are assigned two distinct forms of identity work. On the one hand, they must produce a distinctive identity for the *brand*, on the other, they must assist the identity work enacted by the *consumer*. This complex kind of reification through branding animates capitalism's everyday visual culture. Critics and fans of the "theming of America," the "unreal America," and the "anaesthetics of architecture"—the entertainment architectures in which branded imagery proliferates—often neglect the institutional stakes that underlie the branded world of retail visuality. Taken together, eye-level close readings and research into retail and marketing discourse provide access points into these symbolic and economic relations in retail display, for they get at what TV images are, and what performative work they do, as elements of consumer architecture. In other words, rather than asking how and why shoppers are seduced by TV images at the point of purchase, we might learn more by wondering at the seductive appeal of these images for the retailers and manufacturers who rely on them so heavily.

What first seems striking about many point-of-purchase installations is the way they supplement the physical mobility of everyday spectatorship with a bigger promise: the promise of symbolic movement across identity categories, of inhabiting different *social positions,* as well as spaces, through the act of shopping. Yet this individualizing, aspirational rhetoric of consumer identity, of porous yet eminently definable boundaries between markets, can be read as a displacement of corporate anxieties about product differentiation in a competitive brand-driven economy onto the consumer. Why, we might ask, are TV screens such necessary elements of the retail environment?

The very *excess* of point-of-purchase video's commercial appeals communicates the intensity of contemporary brand-name manufacturers' struggle for a productive and predictable form of retail contact with the consumer on the microlevel, at the counter and among the racks, and reflects the particularly unstable positions consumption and retail occupy in capitalist processes of exchange and accumulation.[8] As part of the visual culture of consumption on the scale of everyday life, these screens call attention to the fact that the sales floor is a place that condenses consumer culture's chains of images and behavior into one location. The fact that advertising, product, and cash register coexist within its confines makes the retail store a microcosm of wider capitalist processes of distribution, exchange value, and reproduction. This proximity has both utopian and dystopian implications for retailers and brand-name manufacturers, the sectors that stand to gain or lose from the presentation of the commodity in the store. On the one hand, proximity makes it possible to measure the relationship between advertising and sales very directly. But on the other hand, this sense of certainty is heavily undermined by the vicissitudes of consumer behavior, perceived to be easily influenced by in-store appeals. The phrase "70-percent of all purchasing decisions are made in the store" dominates the institutional "script" of point-of-purchase advertising professionals.[9] This makes the sales floor the site of intense competition between brands, and retail display is believed to decide this competition, wielding immense power over microlevel free-market struggles. As an advertising industry writer specializing in retail promotions notes, "Stores are not simply places to buy anymore, but the last medium that can persuade people to buy."[10] Television advertising, considered a quintessential vehicle for "brand awareness," allows manufacturers to assert a modicum of control over the product's fate on the racks. Point-of-purchase video serves these final brand identification goals, creating miniature, branded environments on the sales floor.

Perhaps the most extreme example of the use of the video image in a logic of environmental branding may be found in flagship single-brand retail destinations like NikeTown—an establishment that has come to epitomize the journalistic term *shoppertainment*. NikeTown's highly publicized postmodern retail environment makes it a useful introduction to the scenography of point-of-purchase TV. But its overdetermined atmosphere of spectacle also makes it a limited space for exploring how retail screen practices suture spectatorship into everyday life, so we will visit NikeTown only briefly. To isolate NikeTown's excessive televisuality as a fetishistic example of the postmodern quality of everyday life is to obscure the role of more mundane and less fabulous point-of-purchase TV places like the supermarket. Indeed, I begin with NikeTown in the hope of demystifying its aura as a point-of-purchase brand temple and of providing the less-well-traveled examples of TV environments analyzed after it with a useful ground for comparison.

Brand Identity at NikeTown

It has become a commonplace in features journalism to describe Nike-Town as the architectural touchstone of postmodern "shoppertainment" — it is, after all, a mass-media architecture designed to simulate several structures at once—a museum, a gym, a temple, a theater.[11] However, having photographed so many televisual retail places, I find far more striking the vague and undirected nature of the screen's commercial solicitations within NikeTown. Also, these solicitations *feel* very different from the brand's regular TV ads. Although Nike broke new ground in the linguistic evolution of commercial speech with the intrusive second-person of its famous imperative slogan, "just do it," NikeTown deploys these and other commercials in an architectural form that seems to deliberately *minimize* any suggestion of a personal "message" to the shopper. Compared with installations like the one we saw in Champs, an installation that combined several visual, bodily, and rhetorical techniques for orienting and motivating a spectator individually, the screens at NikeTown seem to aim at a sense of *dis*orientation: the production of a collective Nike hallucination.

This unconventional approach to retail aesthetics first became clear to me when I visited the just-opened Chicago NikeTown in 1993. I stood with other viewers in a crowded, dark, and narrow hallway to watch reel after reel of old Nike commercials on a large screen while other shoppers trooped past, blocking the view. This deliberately awkward placement, creating a bottleneck between two areas of the store, violated many of the rules of store architecture—a professional arena governed at times by strict laws of traffic flow and floor plan. Now, in refusing to accommodate its viewers, this screen only made me try to concentrate even more intently on the images. It got my attention. But the motivation for this effect was unclear, for it did not bring me any closer to the merchandise for sale that day. Not only did the commercials feature old "product," but they were also presented in isolation, without any of the featured merchandise nearby or even signs saying where in the store one might pick up the particular products being advertised. This was a noticeable departure from conventional point-of-purchase video techniques. Whereas the latter generally pitch specific merchandise, located within the grasp of the shopper, the reverential, museological display techniques often noted by both critics and celebrants of NikeTown seemed to keep consumer and product at a distance from one another. The brand seemed purposefully out of reach, and NikeTown seemed a monumental and curiously *impersonal* commercial space.

It is striking that NikeTown should feel so different from Champs given the fact that both use TV to promote what is essentially the same retail category—athletic gear (the basketball for sale at Champs is a Nike-brand product, in fact)—and it is worth pursuing the comparison further, with more close reading. Figure 26 shows video monitors, along with some decorative alcoves, on the escalator wall in the San Francisco NikeTown. The cases that display the products are indistinguishable from the ones that house the video screens—a common "theme marketing" technique illustrated in the drawing of the Planet Hollywood gift shop in the following chapter. At NikeTown this visual technique, rendering image and thing indistinguishable, parallels the sculptural technique of Champs's installation. Both blend two-dimensional and three-dimensional forms and combine the *image* of sports with the tactile, material objects of sports participation. However, at NikeTown the objects are removed and set under glass, displayed as much for reverence as for vicarious identification. Here by the escalator and on the main sales floor (fig. 27) video screens display images of both famous and anonymous athletes. Monitors appear to be programmed separately, although their images occasionally synchronize; these synchronized sequences are followed immediately by the simultaneous appearance of the trademark Nike swoosh. Products and ads are thus made interchangeable; images flow in and out of synch, and anonymity flows into celebrity in this visual environment. The resulting wash of imagery feels like a metaphor for the sports experience of entering "the zone," a state in which all actions feel effortless and successful. However, at NikeTown, unlike Champs, this figuration takes place on the scale of the entire environment. We are always within eyeshot of the video image, and this image, rather than placing us in front of particular displays or asking us to focus on particular products, simply showcases one commodity: the Nike brand image that saturates the space. What is on display at NikeTown is not exchangeable things but the signifier, ownable but unsaleable, that constitutes the brand image itself.

This absence of personal interpellation—nothing, certainly, as personal as Champs's hoop/screen combination—in the display techniques

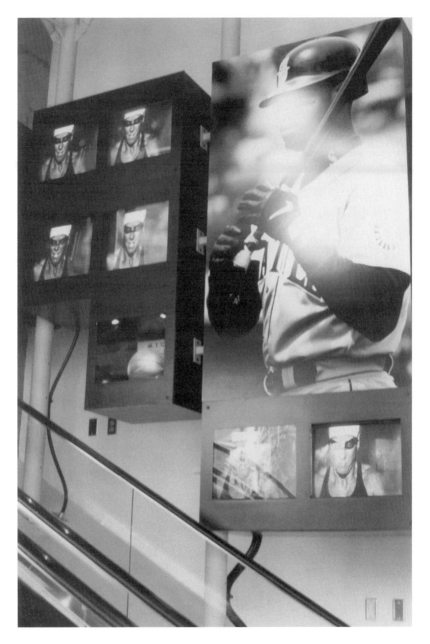

FIG. 26
At NikeTown in San Francisco merchandise and TV commercials are
presented in identical display cases to emphasize that the brand itself is a
precious artifact. (Photograph by the author)

FIG. 27
Celebrity and noncelebrity athletes are hard to tell apart on the
synchronized video banks of NikeTown's sales floor. (Photograph by the
author)

of NikeTown is noteworthy for several reasons. As an example of corporate visual culture on the retail level that seems to deemphasize merchandise while promoting the power of the brand, it conveys the seriousness of organizational anxiety about capitalism's quantum processes. By this I mean simply the indeterminacy of everyday retail practices, from the labor of the clerk displaying the product to the aimless browsing of the shopper. The monumental, elegiac quality of the video at NikeTown suggests that, in contrast to Champs's video, it is not so much the *consumer's* identity as it is the *brand* identity of Nike that must be empowered and rejuvenated in the animated spectacles of its retail flagship store. In this respect, NikeTown's swoosh-branded world tells us a great deal about the broader political economy of name-brand products at the point of purchase. Intense competition among brands on the retail level virtually *requires* that image-based corporations establish single-brand stores of this type. For Nike, as well as for Warner Bros., Reebok, Viacom, and Disney, such stores are sites for the ostentatious recuperation of brand equity in a competition-free and clutter-free environment.[12] The fifteen NikeTowns in North America do not generate particularly large sales figures—indeed, it is a commonplace in journalistic accounts of the store to note how hard it is to actually buy anything there—but they present Nike in an environment unsullied by the clutter of other manufacturer's brand images. Explaining the corporate purpose of NikeTown, one store's public relations executive pointed out that " 'mom and pop' stores . . . usually display all the different brands of shoes on the wall and all the clothes on a rail on the floor, and there's no clear connection between the Nike shoes and the Nike apparel."[13] As this suggests, the store's purpose is not so much the distribution of Nike goods as it is to continually reestablish and reinforce the idea of the brand image as a commodity itself.

To realize this goal the store at times assumes a rather absolutist, lecturing tone; at the New York branch, for example, "every 20 minutes the building's central atrium is transformed, with screens descending over the windows to dim the light so that visitors' attention is focused on videos about the brand."[14] This commercial address is a hyperbolic pedagogy, lampooning a mythical 1950s model of screen education, and an Orwellian vision of propaganda in which a faceless force compels all shoppers in range of the screen to give it their attention at precisely timed moments. This authoritarian use of video is perhaps only possible in NikeTown, considered the avant-garde of retail design precisely because of its daring use of such ironic techniques. The New York store's ostentatious pedagogical imposition of images might even be interpreted as a lampoon of what many point-of-purchase video installations do routinely—demonstrate products and call shoppers to attention. The joke is that instead of the conventional second-person, expository address that points out benefits of the product to a hypothetical attentive spectator, this screen fills the store's atrium with the elliptical, experimental visual slams that garnered Nike advertisements so much industry praise when they first appeared.

This intrusive imposition of one corporate image style on a space is a highly site-specific technique. It would not be permitted on a regular sales floor, where brand competition is fierce and where the screen's goal is a direct impact on the shopper's decision to make a purchase. In this respect NikeTown exemplifies TV's role in "theme retailing" as opposed to multi-brand retailing; it uses TV not to shape behavior in the marketplace but to create a space that, like the brand image in its most idealized representations, exists apart from the competition of the market, above the laws governing more routine relations and representations of commerce. Later, when we examine point-of-purchase video in one more athletic apparel store, we will see that a very different spatial logic governs the marketing of sneakers with television in the more mundane and low-rent location of the shopping mall fashion and athletic shoe chain.

Now, however, we move directly to the kind of store that the ironic brand absolutism of NikeTown New York's timed large-screen commercials seems to lampoon. Stores, that is, where brand competition is fierce —housewares stores, supermarkets, hardware stores, for example—and where pedantic and pedagogical modes of commercial address are a video mainstay. Unlike NikeTown these spaces embody a design aesthetic predicated on ideals of legibility, of comparison shopping, of discernment and judgment. Abstract and stylized video images like the branded displays of NikeTown would seem quite useless, or even counterproductive, in the warehouse-like halls of wholesale "buyers clubs" or in housewares super-stores. But these are nevertheless sites for point-of-purchase video. As the next section details, video installations in such places weave an educational narrative of self-fashioning that proceeds by a very particular display technique: the video demonstration. But demonstrations themselves are product displays that take on particular institutional strategies in different places. Comparing two video demonstrations in retail institutions devoted to "necessities" like foodstuffs and housewares, we can see how in each, video becomes a figure for distinct forms of economic aspiration. And we can also see how it comes to embody some of the contradictions and crises that characterize consumption as a tactical act, one which situates the consumer in an overall system of cultural capital.

Middle-Class Cultural Capital and the Video Demonstration

The video demonstration is both a popular and an enduring commercial form in point-of-purchase display. Its seductively didactic mode of address is a sales technique that has been around since the very first experiments with point-of-purchase video in the 1940s, detailed earlier in this book. Like other forms of department store display, the demonstration harnesses what cultural historian Neil Harris calls the "operational aesthetic." This is a technique of visual display that exploits a spectatorial fascination with the hidden operations of machines; intricate techniques of construction, manufacture, and display; and assorted marvels of all kinds.[15] P. T. Barnum's museum exemplified this display aesthetic with its exhibition of objects that one might marvel at *both* as fantastic artifacts and as well-constructed hoaxes. A sense of television as a technology of operational aesthetics pervades contemporary retailing, as figure 28, an image taken in a Costco "warehouse club" store, illustrates.[16] In this photograph a point-of-purchase video demonstrates a portable heater designed to operate like a fan. Beside the T V monitor on the steel-framed, no-nonsense display shelf sits a floor model of the appliance, accompanied by a placard explaining its benefits in some detail. Now surely a video image can hardly convey heating properties very effectively, but it is nonetheless asked to do so in this installation. This incongruity only emphasizes the strength of video's appeal as a technology of *showing;* respect for its demonstrational effectiveness must be great indeed if the image is allowed to communicate a quality so physical—and indexical—as heat.

This installation is notable as an example of an "aspirational" address to the consumer in the way it negotiates the particular balance between thrift and taste that characterizes class-coded "budget" stores. The text on the placard behind the fan contains the curious phrase, "COMPUTER DESIGNED PARABOLIC REFLECTOR! Focuses heat like a satellite dish concentrates T V signals." This metaphorical reference to the T V apparatus foregrounds the value of television as a flexible cultural signifier. Satellite dishes are not objects of household economy like the heater; rather, they are very visible signifiers of domestic expenditure and of conspicuous T V consumption.[17] The reference to the satellite dish thus conveys both a sense of thrift (the economical "focusing" of heat) and an aura of ex-

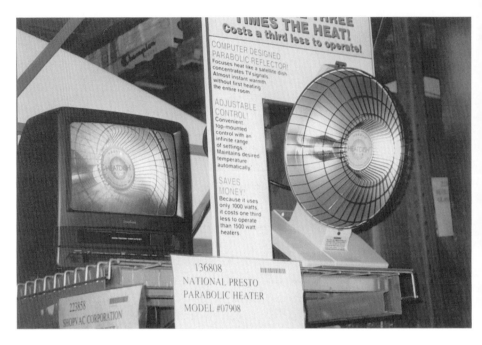

FIG. 28

This merchandise display at a Costco store in Queens, N.Y. uses both video imagery and a video analogy (the satellite dish) to promote the benefits of a heating fan. (Photograph by Rachel Harrison)

travagance (satellite dish ownership), extending the cultural capital implied in the purchase of the heating fan in multiple directions. Moreover, this use of a pseudoscientific analogy is typical of television demonstrations—a memorable example from the annals of television history is the classic Remington advertisement that demonstrates the finely calibrated blade of an electric shaver by using it on a ripe peach (the commercial is lampooned in the credit sequence of *Will Success Spoil Rock Hunter?*). The appearance of a pedagogical and analogical consumer address via video at Costco foregrounds the enduring retail romance with the demonstration as an educational tool.

Often this educational address is used to engage shoppers who might not take a "natural" interest in the merchandise onscreen. One researcher described instructional videos in Home Depot hardware stores as tools for "educating" female shoppers in the techniques of home improvement: "these stores realize that the woman who is taught to hang a picture today will spackle tomorrow and install crown molding next month."[18] Of course, such attempts to sell women on the peculiar conglomeration of labor and leisure that constitutes "home improvement" conveniently forget that women routinely do a great deal of non-"recreational" domestic maintenance already. But it is nevertheless a useful marker of how acts of leisure and consumption can be figured in retail rhetoric as a kind of labor as well—the labor of learning, the labor of home improvement. If, as Marianne Conroy suggests, consumption is treated as a form of work in discount retail locations, then the demonstrational videos at Costco, or other megastores like Home Depot or Wal-Mart, might be thought of as forms of job education.[19]

In presenting itself as a kind of pedagogy, teaching the spectator how to combine discernment, taste, and economy in consumption, video advertising in the household-oriented store enacts a more traditional narrative associated with schooling as well: a narrative of class mobility. In such categories as fruit and vegetable retailing, or housewares, the video demonstration brings expanded connections between class and consumption into everyday retail contexts. Indeed, as the next two installations I examine suggest, demonstration videos on the sales floor are often site-specific materializations of some of the crises that shape middle-class identity in the United States, concisely enumerated by Conroy as "ongoing crises of overproduction and restructuring; straitened business environments that find many major retailers in the United States operating under bankruptcy protection; pervasive consumer cynicism about the levels of service and price provided by retailers; and declines in real income and consumer debt."[20] And what must here be emphasized is the fact that, as in the case of NikeTown, the forms and techniques of point-of-purchase video in these everyday retail locations also reflect the status of the store and its wares within broader institutional relations of retailing.

First, consider the produce department of the supermarket, an every-day mise-en-scene of consumption where video demonstrations are fairly common. According to one retail industry source, 82 percent of all TV screens in supermarkets are located in the produce department.[21] Figure 29 shows one of these videos in action, not in a supermarket but in a suburban Philadelphia produce market I photographed in 1997. Usually distributed by agricultural corporations and growers associations, these demonstrations are intended to promote products on the exotic end of the vegetable spectrum; in addition to nutrition information and recipes, they offer some (often hurriedly glossed) information on the country or region of origin. The United Fruit and Vegetable Association "Fresh Tip" videotape shown in this image introduces its product (fennel) as an affordable "gourmet" item. In positioning the vegetable in question within a reasonable price range and a connoisseurial disposition, produce videos generate a visual representation of a particular intersection of class and cultural status at the point of sale. As the title of one retail report on produce video proclaimed: "Exotic Produce Shouldn't Be a Mystery."[22] Video, in short, is intended to offer the produce shopper a series of instructional opportunities for class mobility via culinary experimentation.

If we attach political meanings to vegetables in supermarkets at all, it is in geopolitical terms, as the end product of a class-conflict of immense proportions, waged on the scale of the global labor pool in which large agricultural corporations are key actors. But these advertising videotapes dramatize a different set of economic battles enacted via the sale of commercial produce on the microlevel. On the sales floor these videos serve a distinct purpose for the supermarket within the competitive local economy of food retailing. Perceptions of video's selling power may at first seem great indeed if produce managers willingly sacrifice valuable display space to in-store TV demonstrations, ones that, moreover, promote vegetable categories that aren't even on most people's shopping lists. However, when we look closely at the terms in which this effectiveness is figured within the professional discourse of the supermarket trade press, we find

FIG. 29
In a small produce market in suburban Philadelphia, "Fresh Tip Tapes"
demonstrate exotic produce recipes and elevate the store's retail status.
(Photograph by the author)

that the opposite is the case. Retail managers are rather more anxious than certain about video's relationship to fresh-produce sales. One trade writer, for example, proposes that "to achieve maximum effect, video must be accompanied by: a massive display of the featured product . . . product literature or recipe brochures, product samplings and demonstrations, [and] featured prices to cement the sale." [23] What this barrage of educational material in the marketplace communicates is not so much a sense of certainty about video's "effect" but quite the opposite — that video installations only work when surrounded by a plethora of economic and audiovisual incitements to purchase. How could one *not* buy the product under such highly promotional conditions? One must assume, therefore, that the video's middle-class cultural pedagogy in the produce section is not so much a means for retailers to achieve vast increases in sales of the item demonstrated but something else entirely, perhaps linked to the institutional conditions of the retail food trade.

A better explanation of the prevalence of vegetable video is the possibility that it increases the status and prestige of the store by signaling the presence of "gourmet" items in its aisles. This idea of the video installation as an indirect language of institutional upward mobility, strengthening the store's position on the battlefield of the local foodstuff economy, was clearly evident in the market where I took this picture. When I interviewed the owner, who acquired these tapes when he worked as a produce manager for a large supermarket chain, he described video as "good publicity," fostering the impression that the store was "interested in trying new things." And indeed, the video's slick commercial address in his small, quiet store did feel like an elevation in status. More specifically, the screen seemed like a pocket of space borrowed from the kind of suburban megamarket where the Saturday-morning shopper is hailed by countless human demonstrators hawking free bite-size samples. The generic pedagogical address of the professional-quality videotape had a pseudospatial effect, locating the store within a more prestigious institutional category, if only symbolically. In the end, however, this strategy proved sadly ineffective. Although its use of video was somewhat unique for a store of its size, this small market's fate was the result of an utterly typical set of economic circumstances. Like several other independently owned produce marts in the area, it closed a few years after the arrival of several branches of an upscale, wholefoods-oriented national supermarket chain in the area. Video's symbolic magnification of the scale of the produce market was no match for the actual economics of scale that have made superstores and megamarts into consumer institutions known in retail investment circles as "category killers." [24]

The fact that video demonstrations are part of these retail spaces too — spaces that hardly need to elevate their positions as aspiring retail leaders given the fact that they are an embodiment of competition-quenching strategies — underscores the site-specific and adaptable properties of TV in diverse institutional settings. Nevertheless, in these stores as in the produce aisle, the use of TV is a key to the larger economic uncertainties that haunt retail institutions. To understand TV's uses in the superstore, one need look no further than the phrase "category killer." The term acknowledges the monopolistic tendency of such stores to eliminate competition from other retail outlets in their class. One category killer CEO concisely summarizes the ideology that justifies this strategy: "offering more products than anyone else . . . transmitting to the customer the sense that there [is] no other place to buy [them]." [25] Consumer choice is thus both eliminated and overproduced in the concept of the category killer — one has no choice but to patronize the establishment that offers the most choice. With their promise of a comprehensive selection, inviting shoppers on all budget levels, category killers are retail utopias of a "classless" consumer culture premised on the fact that everyone, rich or poor, loves a bargain. And the idea, if not the reality, of a bargain is crucial here, for one of the central conceits of the megastore is that a retail economy of scale guarantees not only the widest amount of consumer choice but also the lowest markups. (Often, though, the latter promise is grounded more in strategically deployed "loss leader" merchandise than in the overall pricing of regular store stock.)

The video demonstrations that we encounter as we prowl the wide aisles of superstores like Bed Bath and Beyond, armed with our oversized shopping carts, support this sense of massive selection and economy with a product-based pedagogy designed to guide an overwhelmed shopping public. Bed Bath and Beyond tapes use a didactic address similar to that of the "Fresh-Tip" tape in the supermarket, although perhaps more grounded in idealized and aspirational representations of the well-appointed household interior. Arresting the frenetic physical mobility prompted by the design of this particular sales floor, shown in figure 30, the representational space of the video image offers symbolic mobility within middle-class identity. This utopian domestic space appears in this particular photograph as a well-equipped kitchen, one that bears a strong resemblance to the cookware department in which the video plays.

Bed Bath and Beyond, filled from floor to ceiling with gridded rows and squares of identical merchandise, could be described as a densely cluttered archive of middle-class taste.

But this impression of completeness serves rather more prosaic goals too. As in many superstores, Bed Bath and Beyond's sales floor is also its stockroom. This is to say, its design follows the "open stock" plan in which most of its merchandise is on the sales floor rather than stored in a separate, behind-the-scenes space. Products are organized by brand name (e.g., Calphalon) rather than type (e.g., sauté pan) in a warehouse-style display strategy that seems very direct and "no-nonsense."[26] The managerial goal of this design is to eliminate the labor costs associated with restocking and the general movement of merchandise around the store. Yet this design has a purpose within the persuasive mechanisms of point-of-purchase advertising strategies. It actually requires a lot of moving, searching, and reading on the part of the shopper; to compare prices on a particular item one must wander back and forth from one brand area to another. The disorienting effect of this brand-oriented layout is unquestionably deliberate. Increasing the amount of close interaction between the shopper and the merchandise is a perennial goal in most chain store design because, from the behaviorist perspective of retail science, the chance that a shopper will make a purchase (the store's "conversion rate," in professional jargon) increases with this kind of interaction.[27] At Bed Bath and Beyond departments are not connected by orderly aisles; rather, obliquely placed bays introduce dead ends and deviations into the shopper's travel path, which leads from one place to another in a haphazard, nonuniform fashion. Within this chaotic forest of consumer categories, watching TV demonstrations feels like a lot less work than reading boxes and signs; indeed, when one stumbles across an infomercial for a hi-tech mop in a hidden alcove, the screen can be a kind of ocular oasis. Its focused educational address provides a sense of continuity that links the disparate areas of the store, and a unique and constantly changing image space that seems restful next to the visually repetitive brand images that characterize the open-stock floor plan.

In ideal terms, when we position ourselves in front of one of the rotating roster of instructional tapes, we are transported, along with the commodity, out of the marketplace and into the screen's simulated domestic middle-class context. But not all kinds of merchandise make it to the small screen. Like many infomercials in the home, video advertising in Bed Bath and Beyond highlights merchandise in one of two distinct categories: cheaper versions of high-end brands (as in fig. 30, where a chef and spokesmodel in a studio kitchen demonstrate the advantage of an anodyzed aluminum cookware set priced lower than the top-of-the-line Calphalon brand) and nonessential gadgets (e.g., plastic bag-resealers, hi-tech mops, juicers).[28] In other words, they alert customers either to items that are not on their shopping lists or to product lines with a highly aspirational value (anodyzed aluminum cookware is marketed as equipment for serious home chefs) but that may be one notch higher than they can afford. What links these two categories is the fact that they are both oriented toward impulse buying, toward in-store purchase decisions rather than predetermined purchase plans. In this respect television shopping in Bed Bath and Beyond replicates the commercial strategies of home-shopping networks on broadcast and cable TV, networks that also target impulse shoppers rather than "presold" ones. However, Bed Bath and Beyond makes products even more instantly available than home shopping networks can, as the latter depend on the combination of phone, credit card, and shipping service for their purchase and delivery systems.

The fact that home shopping and shopping at Bed Bath and Beyond have something in common clues us in to the class-coded architecture of identity on which its video displays are based. The store's detailed exposition of products recalls the style of the Home Shopping Network's closely focused and continuous demonstrations, characterized by White as a pedagogical spectacle of connoisseurship, presenting a potent lure of upward mobility to the spectator.[29] The presence of similar televisual techniques for registering class and taste in Bed Bath and Beyond casts the store and home as equivalent aspirational spaces. (Indeed, the fact that free demonstration videos are often packaged with the merchandise in the box at Bed Bath and Beyond makes the store's idealistic TV images of the perfect home seem portable. In such instances consumer spaces collapse, as the feeling of home shopping in the mall is an experience one can then take home with the product). But the store exceeds the home as a scenography of class mobility in one crucial way: its TV screen is not an interface to an outside world, a world beyond the domestic setting. Rather, its figurative window links the sales floor's domestic utopia to other, equally idealized domestic spaces where products inertly packaged on shelves are suddenly shown in use. In fact, one could say that video at Bed Bath and Beyond helps construct the sales floor as an interior without an exterior, a vertiginous closed loop of images in which middle-class taste is constructed and affirmed.

FIG. 30

Demonstration videos at Bed Bath and Beyond are set in studio kitchens that look a lot like the interior of the store. (Photograph by the author)

This sense of interiority without exteriority is suggested in the idiosyncratic real estate strategy of Bed Bath and Beyond, one which distinguishes it from other "category killers." Whereas many discount superstores are located—for semiotic as much as practical reasons—in physically remote locations, closer to highway interchanges than to settlements, Bed Bath and Beyond, notes a textile industry magazine, opens stores in "nearly every conceivable type of retail real estate," from strip malls to Sixth Avenue in Manhattan.[30] It is as if the state of the world outside the store does not matter when one is inside it, surrounded by video images that affirm the stability of middle-class aspiration via consumption. This sensibility is the product of a far longer lineage of representations of domestic space as a seedbed of bourgeois consumer identity. Since at least the nineteenth century, representations of home in literature and art have served, in Jean-Christophe Agnew's words, as "a ready-made laboratory (quite literally, a drawing room) in which . . . recombinant visions of personhood could be experimentally refined, safe from the ordinary claims of daily life yet indissolubly connected to them."[31] Television's idealized representation of home in Bed Bath and Beyond supports such ideas of the home as a site of class mobility, a site of *control* over the raw materials of cultural capital. And it does so even though the home—especially in its quantified form as a zip code from which demographic information is extracted, a code we are often asked to divulge when we get to the cash register—is what marks one more than anything else as a member of a particular class strata.

Just as the video image playing in the small produce market of figure 29 helped bolster the authority and credibility of the store in a competitive local market, this construction of an idealized domestic space in Bed Bath and Beyond serves some very pragmatic goals as well, ones that reflect the store's position in the political economy of retailing. Whereas in the produce market video helped open lines of communication between the store owner and the customer, TV advertisements at Bed Bath and Beyond substitute for the communicative presence of trained floor personnel. This reflects some of the changes in the geography and structure of housewares retailing that have taken place over the course of the past few decades. Starting in the 1960s, long-anticipated changes in the labor relations and profit structures of the department store industry spread rapidly. More and more stores consolidated into national chains, organizing the industry increasingly around an economy of scale. The transition to a national level of competition increased pressures to lower labor expenditures, and the result was a gradual replacement of a knowledgeable and extensively trained sales personnel with a part-time, minimum-wage labor force—a labor shift predicted, as we saw in chapter 2, quite soon after the war. According to one study, this transformation in labor relations led to a transformation in the commercial techniques of the sales floor. Along with an increase in self-service, "the department store chain [now] relies on advertising to sell the product, leaving the 'sales staff' to process orders. . . . Advertising has become the chief means of reducing the skills required of the retail sales force."[32] In effect, advertising helped to *automate* the sales pitch. Bed Bath and Beyond, like the department store housewares floor that it supercedes, is a competitor in a low-wage, mass-market retail economy.[33] And to be competitive it turns to television as a form of mechanical demonstration in the store.

The aspirational consumer aesthetics of the middle-class home encoded in the demonstrational videos at both Bed Bath and Beyond and in the produce market are thus site-specific in that although their content is generally a pedagogical display of the commodity's use value (e.g., nutrition or labor-saving and energy-conserving properties), they are deployed to meet distinct institutional needs for the store within a particular local or national retail economy. They are also narrowly targeted at one particular consumer demographic—the middle-class household purchaser. Although this paradigmatic consumer subject is generally figured as female because of closely watched statistics on family-based consumption, point-of-purchase video is an opportunity for these stores to signal their progressive view of domestic gender relations to their presumed-female audience. Gender-specific modes of commercial address are rare in Bed Bath and Beyond's video appeals; the product demonstrators and impressed consumers that appear in their onscreen kitchens are both men and women, and time-saving devices are often presented in gender-neutral language as aids for working *people* or *parents* rather than "women" or "moms." But in other kinds of retail space, where gender plays a more central marketing role, we have the opportunity to observe how particular televisual conventions at the point-of-purchase become site-specific articulations of shopping as a process of gender identity work. Now, then, we turn to two spaces where TV's spatial operations are harnessed very specifically in a process of gendering, and racializing, the commodity and the act of consumption: the department store cosmetics counter and the athletic shoe chain.

Screen Space and the Visual Architecture of Identity Marketing

Of all modern retail institutions, the department store is the one that, unquestionably, embodies in its architecture and its history the complex gender politics of consumption and spectatorship. As a contemporary department store technology for linking female spectatorship and consumption, video screens serve as a continuation of the historical practice of spatial management through store design detailed in chapter 2. The fragrance-oriented video installation shown in figure 31 is a clear example, although it is also one that reveals historical changes in the store as a space since the national transformation of department store retailing in the 1960s. At the Clinique counter in a small suburban Philadelphia department store, this small video screen substitutes for the staff person in greeting the shopper who approaches the counter on the ground floor of the store. This installation is here to provide shoppers with a space in which to pursue the much-shepherded process of identity production through consumption. Like the NikeTown interior discussed earlier, it endeavors to cordon off a pure, immersive brand-image space for the passing shopper, a space of self-fashioning in which everything one sees is Clinique. Placed next to a fragrance tester and a credit card display, the screen is one of several direct textual addresses to the shopper within this space. These framed and glowing images and inscriptions are fully integrated with each other.

Except for the small charge-card display placed there by the department store, everything in visual range of the shopper who passes this counter is branded with the company's distinctive design and color palette. On the monitor, black-and-white images of supermodels appear and disappear in the void of an all-white TV studio. The image behind the tester display is a life-size still from the video advertisement: a white, blond woman, apparently naked, head thrown back and eyes closed in a pose of relaxation and laughter. This image is positioned as if it is a mirror, and its strong continuity with the image on the monitor suggests that perhaps the latter is, like a mirror, a projective and reflective identity space. This possibility certainly conforms with the corporate image of Clinique as a kind of blank simplicity. Moreover, the adjective *Happy* designates a particular kind of affect—not a grand, engulfing emotion (compare it with Obsession) but, like all of Clinique's products, an ineffable mood of pureness, simplicity, and balance—an unfragranced fragrance.

What is curious about this image, however, is the fact that the TV console's contribution to the branding of the space and the address to the

FIG. 31
In this suburban Philadelphia department store the TV set helps define a
semiprivate space, a "catchment basin," for female shoppers.
(Photograph by the author)

consumer is by no means seamless. Indeed, this squat, mushroom-beige TV/VCR *fractures* the sense of trademarked continuity between onscreen and offscreen space. Marked by a distinctive brand name (Panasonic), although it is clearly not for sale, the screen seems to exist in a wholly other dimension than the feminine bliss of Clinique's imagery. Like a graceless audiovisual technician at a fashion show, it intrudes on Clinique's pristine vision of "perfect" white, thin femininity. Why, then, if the video monitor's lumpen materiality undermines the idealist image of tasteful, middle-class feminine confidence promoted by Clinique, is it there?

The answer lies undoubtedly in the pragmatics of department store retailing. In addition to substituting for absent staff, the screen supplements the store's architectural imperatives of traffic control expressed in a floor plan that guides shoppers invisibly through the store. More specifically, it is positioned to attract shoppers' attention and to reinforce a design element closely associated with the department store fragrance counter: the "catchment basin"—a kind of cul-de-sac constructed by placing the counter at an angle to the larger flow of traffic to siphon shoppers off the open sales floor. The goal of the catchment basin is to provide female shoppers with a sense of privacy while they try on different products. Set off and obscured by other parts of the store, catchment basins offer shoppers an isolated "backstage" area (a *clinic,* perhaps) for testing out cosmetics.[34] They are, in other words, recessed alcoves designed to shelter and nurture practices of feminine identity work via consumption (or, more precisely, given the competitive nature of brand visibility at the point of purchase, the consumption of one particular brand).

It is a deep irony that department stores offer women shoppers this architectural invitation to step *outside of* social surveillance, given that the stores themselves are institutional spaces paralleled only by casinos and banks in the number of closed-circuit cameras they train on staff and clientele. A rather more tangible irony, however, is the fact that this supposedly private design can easily work to make female spectatorship a spectacle in itself. Figure 32 shows the particularly elaborate catchment basin of an upscale Montreal emporium's Christian Dior counter. This image is difficult to read, but its illegibility is itself significant. Television screens are so fully incorporated into the expensive fixtures of the store that they are very hard to distinguish from the mirrors and illuminated signs around them, and shoppers are constantly framed and lit by the screen and other image planes as they move between counters. Like the theater box, an architectural design element that Beatriz Colomina describes neatly as a

FIG. 32
The TV screen is hard to pick out among the cluttered images and backlit signs that frame acts of feminine self-fashioning in an upscale Montreal department store. (Photograph by the author)

"device which both provides protection and draws attention to itself,"[35] this visual maze treats female consumers as participants in an interactive, highly sensory drama of self-construction that others may witness if they choose. As at the Clinique counter, the video here is a simple, evocative series of images (in this case a minimalist beach scene accompanied by a plaintive soundscape). Like the scents wafting past my nose, this sound from the video stayed with me as I walked through the space with my camera, offering a counterpoint to the reflective, cluttered theme park scenography of this Christian Dior zone. To become a window to a feminine elsewhere, and to produce an architecturally secluded space for female self-construction on the sales floor, the point-of-purchase perfume advertisement uses visual forms that have served traditionally as planes of pure projection—landscapes, open windows, the borderless white space of the TV studio.[36] The TV screen thus provides a space of contemplation more private than the sales floor, transforming the perfume counter into an idealized version of the bathroom at home, complete with a view of the ocean and an evocative soundtrack.[37] Whether integrated as an architectural element or simply perched incongruously atop the counter, the video monitor thus helps materialize retailing's most enduring (and needless to say, misogynist) fantasies about what women want in shopping: a branded, private zone for narcissistic contemplation and exhibitionist display.

Such highly designed commercial environments, in which stylized and evocative video images demarcate a space for self-construction, are characteristic of point-of-purchase display in fashion and beauty retailing—a sales sector that spends far more money on marketing and consumer research than on manufacturing.[38] For certain analysts such image-based industries have recently come to dominate the market as a whole, in a process one economist dubbed the "sneakerization of the economy."[39] Tom Vanderbilt, author of *The Sneaker Book,* describes the latter phenomenon as an economic trend in which "once simple, inexpensive goods such as sunglasses have multiplied—just as sneakers did before them—into highly segmented, rapid-turnover markets with endless product extensions playing on the power of brand equity and image building."[40] The periodization of this trend in manufacture and exchange is open to debate. One could argue that the retail and manufacture of luxury goods, a sector of the economy supported and promoted by the department store, has always been subject to this logic. However, the term is apt enough, given that the industry sector that most notoriously embodies the geopolitical inequities, and capitalist rewards, of this form of commodity production is the sneaker industry.

For this reason this chapter's exploration of the point of purchase closes with a third and final visit to athletic retailing, specifically, to the shopping mall chain called Footaction USA which, like Champs, specializes in sneaker sales. Footaction is acclaimed in the shoe sales trade press because its store design is based on extensive, in-depth interviews with young male consumers, to whom it aggressively markets its products as fashion — as well as sports — apparel.[41] My purpose in visiting it now is to trace how the store's professed design strategy and its physical plant enact market-coded representations of physical and symbolic space via TV. Television's discursive presence at Champs sets up suggestive parallels among watching sports, participating in sports, and shopping, and it replenishes the symbolic capital of the Nike brand at NikeTown. But at Footaction the TV images that line the walls, and the posters that accompany them, imprint what could be termed a modern "spatial-racial" unconscious in the visual architecture of the sales floor itself.

The sneaker is preeminently a political commodity. Not only is it perhaps the most condensed symbol of the global expansion of Western capitalism's cheap labor pool, but it also serves as a potent sign of avarice and excess in white American demonologies of black consumption. Dress codes prohibiting sneakers in various kinds of public space are class- and race-coded forms of spatial management, aligned with the intricate systems of racist knowledge that position black consumers as "a nation of thieves" and that spin endless variations of urban legends about black teenagers being killed for their sneakers.[42] Sneakers are also frequently evoked in cultural conversations about how white suburban teen-style practices borrow from "the hood," conversations that index the skyrocketing transformation of the athletic shoe as a commodity from a utility-based product to one of the hottest fashion items within the youth market.[43]

These fraught representational and cultural politics are not absent from the point of purchase by any means. Images of black athletes and hip-hop artists punctuate Footaction USA's fractured, repetitious, cluttered array of visual spectacles and frames. Within this environment, onscreen images work with posters, glass surfaces, mirrors, packaging, signage, branded merchandise, and highly "targeted" pop and alternative musics to transform the store into an illuminated vitrine that buzzes and pulses with racialized commercial images. Inside the space the monitor's changing

display—music videos and (less frequently) interviews with athletes—
breaks up the monotony of the ranks of shoes marching in place on the
shelves below and beside it. The plethora of shoe categories on the shelves
are labeled with posters whose text—"cross training," "casual," "basketball"—is accompanied by images of athletes engaged in a particular sports
activity.

The sounds that can be heard on the screen and over the speakers
are themselves for sale—on a CD compilation of music from the Bad
Boy record label entitled "Nothin' but the Hotness in '98." As a cross-
promotion tool the CD is itself a kind of point-of-purchase advertising,
designed to shape the itinerary of its buyer within the mall. Each one contains a $2 coupon for a Bad Boy CD that may be redeemed at one of several
popular mall music chains.[44] Ads for Bad Boy records play four times an
hour on the TV sets, and the label receives extensive promotion in Footaction's free in-store promotional magazine. The chain's decision to concentrate so much energy on the sale of an ancillary product rather than its
main stock, sneakers, may seem surprising, but it plays an important purpose within the store's architecture of teen identity. As a marketing vice
president explained, "Music and fashion are two very important things in
a teen's life. [Association with Bad Boy] makes us credible, and I think it
makes us relevant with teens."[45]

Although its programming differs greatly from that of the department
store screen, the video screen in Footaction USA is assigned rhetorical and
spatial tasks quite similar to those of the screen at the cosmetic counter.
In both places the screen is the site for the representation of a projective
"elsewhere space." In the shoe store, however, the goal of this representation is not in any sense to shepherd the shopper toward an alcove of
private, inward reflection. Instead, the world on the screen is, more often
than not, the ghetto—as imaged in music videos by Sean "Puffy" Combs
and Coolio. And although, like the cosmetic counter's private, contem-
plative video views, the screens in Footaction USA are also windows to
another space, that space is recognizably televisual: the popular image of
black urban style that the pop hip-hop artists onscreen have come to embody. The hip-hop celebrity, a figure of conspicuous black consumption,
mimes authenticity for the imaginary white teen spectator targeted by the
store. It cannot go unremarked that although these *images* of black consumers circulate prominently onscreen, the circulation of "actual" black
consumers in shopping mall retail stores is not so easy. As Regina Austin
notes in "A Nation of Thieves," black shoppers frequently get "the treat-

FIG. 33

In the Footaction USA store, TV's serial images of hip-hop stars tell the store's target demographic—white, male, middle-class teens—that they are in the right place.

ment" from a suspicious sales staff when they enter the sales floor.[46] Regardless of whether Bad Boy's pop music video actually reflects ghetto style, its site-specific deployment of black cultural references in the store is clearly crucial to the mimetic cultural logic of *white* teen marketing.

The idea that the Footaction video spectator is assumed to be a white teenager is expressed not racially but geographically by its industry professionals. Note how Jayson Jackson, marketing vice president for the youth-oriented hip-hop record label Bad Boy, explained the goal of the label's CD cross-promotion with Footaction: "In the suburbs they know about Puffy and Mase. . . . But there's a whole slew of Bad Boy artists who they need to be introduced to. This is the perfect way to do it."[47] Such characterizations of the store's target demographic depict video not as a kind of narcissistic mirror of the self, as one might read the idealized image of femininity at the Clinique counter, but as a form of pedagogy that trains the "suburban" (white) consumer to recognize new forms of "urban" (black) popular culture. This racialized, spatialized pedagogy can be discerned in public statements about Footaction's business plan, statements that use spatial categories to explain style trends. The company's CEO, Ralph Parks, explained that the store's decision to stock FUBU (a fashion, rather than athletic, brand) stemmed from the fact that "FUBU's exposure on MTV has gone from urban to suburban."[48] And another store executive communicated the "authenticity" of its promotional magazine by explaining that it had feedback from focus groups of teenage boys: "They said it was not quite real, that the look was too posed. That the models weren't wearing their pants right. That the pants should be lower."[49] In such depictions video enacts racial identification along a behaviorist, rather than psychodynamic, model of the subject, training the white shopper—and the store executive—to recognize the correct signifiers of "authentic" black style.

Such attempts to evoke the "urban" for white teen consumers in the suburban mall might seem at first like a simple case of minstrelsy. But the images of consumer desire produced in these snippets of marketing-speak bear little resemblance to the complex class dynamics of "love and theft" that Eric Lott traces in his study of minstrelsy's cultural forms.[50] The difference lies in the object of identification. Key terms like *urban* and *suburban* (rather than *black* or *white*) are more than just *euphemisms* for race; they are terms that encourage identification with racially coded market categories—not people. Modeling brand-name styles, video images of black performers help to facilitate a white teen spectator's identification with a consumer *profile* that is mnemonically represented by black consumption's most visible embodiment on the national stage: the hip-hop star. The point-of-purchase music video's "urban"-styled images, a fashion look that is "edgy, dark, a little threatening,"[51] thus encourages a fantasy of virtual movement across identity categories or rather across marketing categories based on race. It mobilizes the spectator with a virtual trip to the culture of "the ghetto" on a path marked out, one could say, by the "soles" of black folk.

At Footaction, as in the other spaces we have examined here, TV is a rhetorical figure for a utopian ideology of retailing. This is the promise of identarian mobility encoded in the "virtual mobility" of TV spectatorship. Television's spatial operations in the design of particular stores, from Bed Bath and Beyond to NikeTown, construct an idealized space that seems to be outside the sales floor's language of commerce, although it nevertheless reflects site-specific institutional concerns and economic goals. As we saw in an earlier chapter, the use of TV to shape spatial relations at the point of purchase derived from a long-standing set of gendered institutional practices linking spectatorship to economic exchange and equating acts of looking with acts of buying. Now, however, it should be clear that when these practices take shape in particular retail contexts, they are not simply instances of the "televisualization" (awful word) of public space; rather, in each case television's representation and reorganization of space reflects very particular problems in retailing. The point of purchase is a terrain of practices marked by distinct institutional uncertainties about the consumer and consumer desire. And it is also a space where the infinite world of possibility conventionally evoked in advertising imagery narrows dramatically, where fantasy and projection drain away, leaving it all up to the consumer. The latter's relation to the commodity is no longer curled up in anticipation and potential but rather consists of a simple and prosaic question of choice — do I, or do I not, buy this product or brand?

Video's role in this space of decision making is to dramatize the point of sale in endlessly new ways.[52] But it does so through a deeper television ideology, the "virtual mobility" that makes another space figuratively present in the screen's immediate environment. Televisual attempts at spatial manipulation physicalize diverse advertising rhetorics of consumer motivation. As I have tried to show here, point-of-purchase video can externalize in three-dimensional space any number of institutional theories of identification, whether they be the mimetic logic of the female cosmetics shopper as an introspective narcissist, the ideology of class transcendence that underlies the idealized TV kitchens of the housewares superstore, or the behaviorist racial positioning practices of the shoe-store screen. As we saw in the latter's case, certain aspects of contemporary cultural politics come into view when consumer institutions attempt to create symbolic spaces of identity with video installations. We explore this possibility further in the next chapter and the conclusion that follows it, examining the temporal relationship of the screen to its environment. As we'll see, though, TV's presence may serve as a means of commercialized space-binding—the annihilation of space with time—it can also, in some very different ways, call attention to moments of ambivalence, asynchrony, and even rupture in electronic capital's geographical project of linking places of different scales.

CHAPTER 6

TELEVISION WHILE YOU WAIT

Waiting casts one's life into a little dungeon of time.
— *William James*

As the emergence of corporate entities like the CNN Airport Network and the Commuter Channel indicates, one of television's central institutional tasks in spaces outside the home is to accompany—and, in the case of place-based media, commodify—the act of waiting. This foregrounds the centrality of time, and environmental rhythms, in the processes through which television and TV images interweave with the habitual atmospheres of social space. Many critics have pointed out that the passage of time in home life is measured through the repetitive, segmented structure of the TV schedule, intertwining viewing with other domestic habits and practices.[1] Questions of when, and for how long, we watch TV at home are also questions about how the relationship between time of work and time of leisure in domestic space is demarcated. Marking the familial division of labor in temporal terms, TV plays a crucial role in the (highly gendered) relations of power within the home.[2] Similarly, site-specific relations of time and space shape televisual places outside the home as well. The temporal structures of TV programming interweave with, and sometimes warp, the patterns of time, duration, and repetition in different ways from place to place. The duration of a program or sports game can set a time frame for socializing in a bar or specify times to avoid going there. In the shopping mall the Food Court Entertainment Network aspires to make time spent eating less a retreat from shopping than a "productive" form of consumer leisure—the viewing of commercials.

Now these small-scale processes of time coexist with rather more large-scale temporal mediations, too. Time-based TV processes like live transmission serve to link places — particular homes, particular regions — together in spectacular ways. The technoideology of liveness situates the home within the fictional simultaneity of the nation as an "imagined community," even when the image in question is not literally "live."[3] Such myths of national participation through liveness are not confined to the home screen by any means. Popular representations of live media events often seem to rely heavily on shots of crowds gathering to watch TV *outside* the home, in bars, restaurants, and store windows — think of key scenes in movies like *The Truman Show, Quiz Show, It's Always Fair Weather,* and *It Could Happen to You.* Live broadcast reception in public places, such Hollywood moments imply, is a metaphor for the nation's collective interest. This idea recurs in the journalistic practice of gauging public opinion of large-scale media events, including sports, by surveying the diverse collectivities of strangers and acquaintances who gather in public locales equipped with TV sets. Such moments of group engagement with live spectacle, guaranteeing the "realness" of public reactions, can constitute a potent image of national *communitas* in journalistic narratives. However, liveness is a temporal ideology of television that can acquire a specific cultural and symbolic resonance in certain public sites and cultural contexts. As a mode of festive viewing it has become closely associated with one particular place — the bar, where sports spectatorship allows fans a sense of virtual copresence on national and international scales. And indeed, as we saw in chapter 1, these site-specific experiences of television liveness in places like the tavern can politicize the act of spectatorship along class lines.

This chapter asks how TV sets regulate the flow and experience of time in public spaces. As a temporal stricture of TV, liveness is associated with crisis; it interrupts. But here I am concerned with a related, though opposed, organization of televisual time, namely, forms of *deadness:* routine, boredom, and repetition, the unremarkable, taken-for-granted continuousness of the TV schedule. These are the temporal modes against which the shock of live broadcasting is often defined.[4] Outside the home as well as within it the rhythms of reception produced by the cycles and patterns of broadcasting overlap with the rhythms of social life, although not necessarily in the same ways.[5] Certain temporal effects are *limited* to the public screen and its often site-specific programming because they mesh with the flow of time associated with particular institutions. Just as the social organization of time is structured differently from place to place, so too are the ways in which television blurs distinctions between time of work and time of leisure in various locations. As I will suggest, television shapes time flexibly and adaptively, in consort with other institutional and personal elements, and according to site-specific cultural norms and protocols.[6] Moving between very different kinds of space—from the physician's waiting room to Planet Hollywood, a tourist-oriented "theme restaurant"— I analyze in words and images the consistent presence and invisible conventions of TV time in public places of waiting.

To be sure, the waiting area is not the only place where we use TV sets to pass time. Default, time-passing viewing is an activity we can pursue anywhere—we wile away hours at home with TV, as much if not more than we find ourselves watching TV while we wait in the bank lobby or the lounge of the auto-parts store. But waiting areas are particular kinds of places, and the TV sets installed in public zones of transit, work, and service— places where waiting often predominates over other activities—become meshed with the features of their environments in particular ways. There is something very distinctive in the fact that waiting rooms are often serialized environments. When we travel, or when we visit places like hospitals, we are often moved from one waiting area to another. It is a testament to the mobility of the spectator in contemporary life that the screens in such places can, on occasion, track the action of a sporting event for passengers moving from one transit waiting area, one airport bar or snack area, to the next. In Tokyo, where many places of transit are equipped with monitors for watching sumo wrestling, this phenomenon is a routine part of municipal life. In the United States a similarly serial address to the spectator moving at jet speed emanates from the monitors of the CNN Airport Network at the gate. As a promotional mailing tells its potential advertisers and subscriber airlines, the network is a service "designed . . . to keep passengers informed while travelling."[7]

This CNN brochure also listed a number of other passenger benefits that offer a useful index of how site-specific media corporations envision the screen's environmental effects on the spectator. According to this mailing, a "passenger research study" had also discovered the network's ability "to make waiting time more productive, to shorten perceived waiting time, to entertain, to alleviate boredom, to reduce stress caused by delays and travel hassles." This is an image of television as a time-warping companion within the waiting area, an environmental distraction that somehow changes the overall affective experience of being there. Yet these "effects" are surely not so easily measured. Even under the rigid quality-control guidelines of corporations like Turner, TV's environmental address is always embedded in other kinds of noise, within other forms of inter-action, and modified by additional site-specific factors like, for example, the particular position the screen occupies within the room. Its relation to the space is different depending on whether it blurts its cycles of news above one's head or sits silently in the corner, an incongruously mobile and brightly colored square set against the beige sameness of an institutional décor. If different waiting environments have distinctive features, then any attempt to understand the role of the television screen within them must isolate these features. We must ask how the presence of the screen shapes the experience of waiting as an activity — one often contained within other activities (going to the doctor, traveling) — and pay close attention to the workings of power that are set in motion in places where people, for whatever reason, are required to wait. For waiting is something we generally take for granted, rarely stopping to pay much attention to the specifics of the relationships it establishes in space.

So what, exactly, is at stake in the commodification of an activity so routine, so unmarked, as waiting? Although it is a banal and omnipresent facet of everyday life, waiting is a surprisingly complicated form of human (in)action. In *Queuing and Waiting,* perhaps the most famous study of waiting as a particular set of social relations, sociologist Barry Schwartz approaches waiting as a temporal modality that materializes larger power structures; as he puts it, modern society might easily be divided into two classes: those who have to wait and those who don't.[8] Yet, as he also points out, waiting is most often treated in institutional practices as a purely instrumental problem in the flow of goods and services; environments designed for waiting materialize a set of ergonomic directives and compromises that are more reflective of ideas about efficiency than comfort or habitability.[9] Waiting areas are not places where we dwell; they are places we occupy temporarily, on the way to somewhere else. However, for many people — women, the poor, and others who occupy particularly disadvantaged positions within systems of social administration — the long wait is a time-consuming and inevitable requirement of basic access to goods and services in modern life. Because of this sense of instrumentality and passage, the experience of waiting is associated with low-intensity affects like boredom, which, precisely because of their apparent simplicity, remain inscrutable and inaccessible to others.[10] The vagueness of boredom, waiting, and other "moods and feelings that resist analysis" makes waiting an emblematic instance of the unmarked universality of everyday experience that can all too easily slip through the conceptual nets that surround it.[11]

At the same time, however, waiting is a form of experience that necessarily anticipates change in, and even *destruction* of, predictable temporal flow. After all, although it might be described as a state of inactivity, waiting—along with the queues and traffic jams it engenders—is a situation we often find ourselves in at times of urgency, emergency, and crisis.[12] It would be wrong, therefore, to associate waiting solely with passivity and implicate television in this passivity, despite the fact that it is a medium persistently associated with passivity in certain kinds of cultural criticism. Such prefabricated interpretations neglect the possibility that television might also make the waiting room a place where one wants to remain— making it more like a place of dwelling and attachment. (I can recall waiting situations in which I've found myself hoping that my name would not be called before the end of the TV program onscreen.)[13] If the presence of a screen in a public space is a clue, on entering, that delayed access is a normal, natural, and inevitable fact of social life therein, then it is also a license for the waiting person to indulge in a little TV-viewing. Often associated with *wasting* time, watching television is a way of passing time suddenly *legitimized* when it takes place in waiting environments.

This possibility for multiple relations between TV and waiting means that, rather than insist categorically that television has one dominant effect on waiting spaces, it is wiser to approach the screen's role as highly indicative of the temporal tensions that define the act of waiting—tensions between the here and now and the anticipated future, between boredom and the expectation of its release. My goal in the following is to trace such tensions in the particular discourses and practices associated with television and the act of waiting in a few carefully chosen sites—focusing sometimes on TV screens that are placed within waiting rooms per se and TV screens in multiuse environments that serve to designate a space of waiting. I must note, however, that the most immediate obstacle to this task is the fact that waiting rooms are anonymous spaces not meant for dwelling—it is hard to register their distinctive features in light of their overwhelmingly functional and institutionalized design. Take, for example, the TV screen in figure 34. This screen is clearly located in some kind of waiting area, but where? Is it a doctor's office, an employment agency, a car dealership? (It is, in fact, the last one.) The conventions of televisual waiting here, as in many places, are so familiar as to be invisible to the observer. What does one say about the gumball machine on its wooden support, about the no-smoking sign on top of the TV set? Similarly, who has not spent some time waiting in the presence of the cluttered, shelf-like console of an

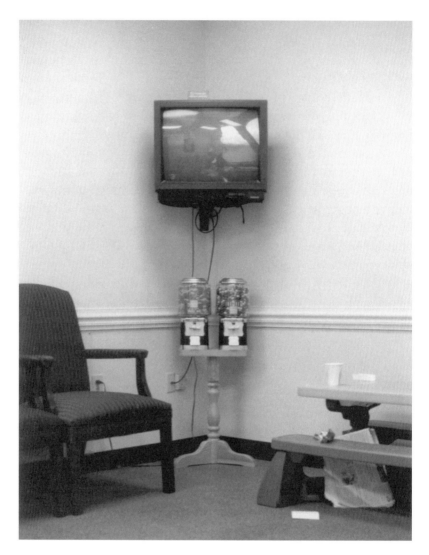

FIG. 34

The presence of T V can call attention to the fact that waiting spaces are generic: is this a medical center, a car dealership, or an insurance agent's office? (Photograph by the author)

older model TV set like the one in figure 35? And is there anything to say, really, about this particular television set either? In its generic blankness, its banal recognizability, this image encapsulates the familiarity of TV's role in spaces of waiting. *Because of,* not in spite of, its blankness, it will be our gateway to understanding the social production of space and time that occurs through television's unremarkable, often unremarked, presence in the waiting room. We begin, then, in this small doctor's waiting room in a suburban area of the northeastern United States, moving from this space to others in order to chart the spatial dialectics that crystallize around the presence of the TV screen.

This TV set is located in a general practitioner's office, housed in what was recognizably once a residence, although the space has been remodeled and rendered "institutional" through the addition of a number of functional and decorative elements: drop ceilings, fluorescent lights, framed pastel-toned posters, magazines, no-smoking signs, pamphlets, coat pegs, and more vinyl-cushioned chairs than would ever be found in a real living room. The placement of the screen here provides good material documentation of the space's transformation from domestic living room to institutional waiting room. Located in the most visible spot in the room, the screen has been bleached of all signifiers of domesticity; like many TVs in waiting rooms, it is surrounded by booklets and brochures stacked almost to the ceiling. Its display of a local news broadcast sits at the center of a large informational matrix, a densely packed area of pamphlets, health-education materials, and commercial forms of publicity from drug company literature to credit card applications. This positioning makes the console an instrument of public address rather than private entertainment; to look in its direction is to be reminded, simultaneously, of the medical orientation of the space and of the availability of alternative, and perhaps more health-related, texts with which to spend time waiting.

Through its physical alignment with information, the screen attaches specific meanings to the passage of time and the act of waiting in this space. As part of a syntagm of information dissemination composed of magazines and other paraeducational print matter, it links the activity of passing time to the enduring, institutional goals of education and information Michel Foucault defined in the final chapter of *Discipline and Punish* as a central function of clinical space. Historically, institutional spaces like hospitals and almshouses anchored networks of information dissemination that, in teaching habits of self-discipline and monitoring, enjoined the production of what Foucault calls the "great carceral continuum" of

FIG. 35

This family practice office in suburban Philadelphia demonstrates a convention of the TV set in doctors' waiting rooms: its frequent alignment with informational and institutional modes of address, from no-smoking signs to STD prevention booklets.

modern society.[14] An extreme example of the waiting room TV's position in this continuum of self-regulation is vividly portrayed in figure 36. In this hospital emergency room waiting area a large religious statue hangs on one wall, and a TV screen hangs on another; the placement of the TV screen duplicates, in a secular sphere, the ideas of solace and self-discipline associated with the religious icon.

More commonly, though, the meaning of the waiting room TV derives from a more secular disciplinary informatics. In medical settings where patients await procedures that have larger social, emotional, or epidemiological consequences (e.g., HIV testing and pregnancy testing), the video screen serves as an outreach tool, targeting particular populations by screening tapes that may—depending on the context—advocate behavior modification (videos that depict safe sex and needle-cleaning procedures), present legally mandated information leading to informed consent (available "choices" for pregnant teens), or explain complex internal physiological events (the mechanisms by which HIV infects cells).[15]

Television's normative alignment with information and self-discipline in the waiting room, whether through its position within a general informational matrix as in figure 35 or as a more aggressive outreach tool in patient education, is reflected on an institutional level in medical professional concerns about what patients do with the time they spend in health-care settings. A 1998 article in the journal *Medical Economics* reports that certain physicians are dismayed by the fact that their waiting patients watch "soap-opera couples in heat, and often bizarre daytime talkshow fare (e.g., left-handed vegetarian transvestites baring their souls)."[16] The article extols the virtues of informational television as an alternative way to pass the time in medical contexts: "patient education is the bright side of television in the waiting room. . . . By taking an active, creative approach towards television instead of just abandoning it, you can turn the small screen into a practice builder" (141). Surveying physicians, the article notes the widespread phenomenon of waiting-room screens tuned to informational and educational cable channels or to health-related videocassettes to keep patients occupied. It also suggests that doctors might use the TV set to promote their practices, citing the example of a New Orleans urologist who "transform[ed] the waiting-room television into a marketing tool by producing—and starring in—simple videotaped programs" (141).

Like many articles about on-site television, this report emphasizes the importance of minimizing the intrusiveness of the screen through low

FIG. 36
This New York hospital emergency room offers waiting patients a choice
of secular or religious solace by placing the TV screen and a religious
icon on adjacent walls. (Photograph by the author)

audio and strategic placement in "a corner or alcove where it won't dominate the waiting room; you don't want to force it on someone who'd
rather read a magazine" (141). However, it contradicts its own plea for
moderation in its praise for the rather more intrusive presence of the
CNN-produced Accent Health Network (AH)—a package of health-related
programming, presumably modeled after Whittle's now defunct "Special
Reports" network, distributed via laser disc to high-volume physicians'
offices. This once local system of on-site TV programming in Florida went
national when it signed a production agreement with Turner Private Networks in 1997, subsequently becoming the national standard of health-
related television.[17] In 1998 AH could be seen in six thousand health-care
facilities nationwide. Its forty-four-minute roster of health-related programming is interspersed with eighteen minutes of advertising designed
for each particular office's medical focus (OB-GYN, pediatricians, or general practitioners). Although all place-based TV networks offer us a chance
to explore the power relations that emerge around the rise of televisual
waiting as a corporate strategy, AH is a particularly interesting case study
because the relationship among broadcasting, advertising, and medicine
is fraught with long-standing tensions, from policy debates over false
medical advertising to current concerns over the "commercialization" of
medicine and the American Medical Association. Compared to, say, the
Airport Network, AH's presence in spaces of waiting is weighted with a
high degree of ethical negotiation.[18]

To explore how AH construes the phenomenon of televisual waiting, I
made several visits to a facility in which it was installed: an ambulatory
care center attached to an urban hospital in the northeast United States
with a large array of office suites devoted to general and specialized medicine. Figures 37 and 38 are images of AH screens in two of the thirty or
so waiting rooms in this multistory atrium building. I spent my time in
this place photographing the screens, observing interactions that occurred
around them, and tracking the amount of time people seemed to be waiting.[19] Serving Medicaid clients, members of several different managed care
"networks," and, presumably, some percentage of the fortunate few who
still have freestanding health insurance, this facility is populated by a large,
highly diverse patient base. Patients and staff move constantly among the
suites on each floor—from the office of a specialist to the radiology department to the examining table of a "primary care" physician—with much
waiting, in the patient's case, along the way. In each suite a video monitor,
nestled in its beige casing and occasionally supplemented with magazines

FIG. 37
The Accent Health Network in this New York outpatient care center offers brand-name pharmaceutical ads and health-related news and trivia to waiting patients. (Photograph by the author)

"borrowed" from American Airlines (perhaps by one of the staff), helps pass the time between consultations.

Like all place-based media, AH appears to equate location and identity and to attempt an alteration in the itinerary of the viewer on that particular day. As an earlier chapter details, a 1990 audience study performed by Lifetime Medical Television, a physician TV network owned by cable's Lifetime Television, claimed—not surprisingly given Lifetime's demographic—that the majority of the medical waiting-room population is female.[20] Informational advertising on AH suggested a similar demographic target. The prevalence of ads for cough syrup and children's over-the-counter medications suggests that AH commercial programming also, undoubtedly, drew on another market research "fact" discovered by Lifetime, namely, that women in medical waiting rooms (especially women in the waiting rooms of pediatricians) are likely to visit the pharmacy after their visit.[21]

Knowing this, it was very difficult to conduct this on-site research at first. I could not get past the initial dismay at seeing all of my worst fears about exploitation through advertising confirmed. As the slogan "information for healthy living" plastered to the screen's housing indicates, the network promotes itself as a source of information to peruse as one whiles away one's time, although the information it offers—often presented as trivia quizzes and recipes (see fig. 38)—seems to equate health education and the promotion of consumption. I gritted my teeth as I sat through commercial testimonies for brand-name health and lifestyle products of questionable therapeutic value in room after room. The sense that the on-screen advertising is a personalized address is reinforced by a bright, first-person, laser-printed sign affixed to the console in each waiting room, inviting the viewer to interact more closely with AH's news and advertisements: "Can't hear me? Turn me up!" (The opposite invitation would be unthinkable: "Am I too loud? Turn me off!")

If the sociological axiom that "the distribution of waiting time coincides with the distribution of power" is correct, then AccentHealth presents us with a persuasive corollary, namely, that these differential power relations are reflected in the question of who has the option to not watch television and which persons are able to isolate themselves from television advertising in a waiting environment—not the staff and certainly not the patients.[22] Freedom from television advertising is apparently a prerogative of the doctors alone. Yet although such an assertion tells us a great deal about the way power is organized within the waiting room,

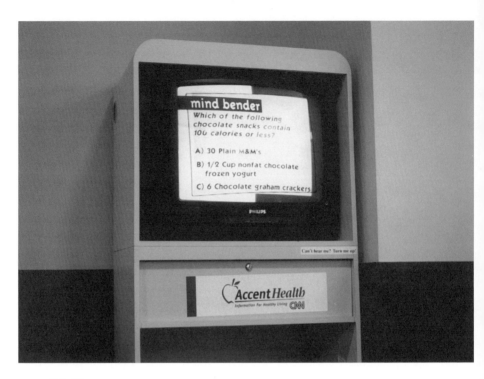

FIG. 38

Trivia questions are a programming convention of networks for waiting areas; note also the signs encouraging viewer interaction that are posted next to the screen. (Photograph by the author)

it would be a mistake to assume from this that the people who must sit and wait with the TV screen are passive "dupes" of this process. My righteous indignation at the hegemonic practices of AH was tempered, after a while, by the realization that the people waiting for their appointments approached the screen's promotional conceits with a healthy skepticism. Because there was little to do other than watch TV, people tended to observe me with interest as I photographed. When they saw that my subject was the screen, they would often communicate—verbally or with a wry expression and a shake of the head—their amusement at the irritatingly cheery discourse emanating from the screen. The only thing that really seemed to make waiting patients sit up and take notice of the screen was the sudden realization that they were watching a particular piece of trivia or news segment for the second or even third time. At that moment, knowing I was paying attention to the screen (I think I may have been misrecognized, in some cases, as a representative of either the hospital or AH or perhaps both), a patient might sigh in frustration and look in my direction with a weary expression. One woman held up three fingers as she did so, implying, I think, that this was her third viewing. In light of this obvious annoyance, it is intolerably ironic to note that the network promotes itself to physicians by suggesting that the presence of AH can ameliorate the increasingly inevitable long wait patients must endure: one physician's testimony claims that patients "really like it. . . . Some even take notes. Best of all, they don't complain about their wait as much."[23]

This kind of proposition about television's relation to waiting—the idea that it transforms the experience by providing an edifying distraction—ignores the possibility that the program's perpetual cycle introduces a jarring sense of conflicting temporalities into the waiting room. This temporal dissonance seems far more specifically *televisual* than AH's ability to distract the waiting patient, a job that magazines and pamphlets had been doing all along. Indeed, the network's cyclical, rhythmic programming can be seen as a compressed and speeded up analog of the cyclical returns and repetitions that make up the broadcast day or week. A bubble of machine-like, unvarying time, it foregrounds the structure of access, duration, and delay in the waiting environment, *heightening,* rather than diminishing, awareness of the duration of the wait for those who sit in its presence.

As an alternative to the ideological image of the TV screen as a soothing palliative, I would suggest that AH's articulation of a parallel, although asymmetrical, temporality in the waiting room might best be understood in the context of other, diffuse social anxieties, specifically, those articulated around the kinds of rupture in access to information, goods, and services that constitute *crisis* in modernity.[24] As Schwartz proposes, waiting is an activity that plays an indicative role in social conflict. Detailing the range of norms and challenges to normativity that define the social relations of waiting, he characterizes the everyday phenomenon of the queue as a masked arena of economic exchange and social contest. The long wait thus calls attention to the potential for disrupting flows of supply and demand and exposes the structural fault lines in modern forms of economic exchange, welfare, and leisure.[25] The photographs of New York photographer Anna Norris document these fault lines, showing how the walls of welfare waiting rooms today are plastered with posters telling the waiting person that "your time on welfare is running out" or simply that "the clock is ticking." Such exhortations further infuse the act of waiting with the temporal urgency of impending crisis.

Although situations of waiting and live television coverage of natural and technological catastrophes seem like antithetical entities, both are haunted by the specter of social breakdown and economic disorder, exposing the fragile artifice of the capitalist system as a whole.[26] The congruity is perhaps not so surprising, given that—as several critics have noted—the habitual regularity of the TV schedule and the irregularity of the "live" televised catastrophe are not separate televisual phenomena but rather intertwined modes of temporal demarcation, dependent on each other for their ideological effects. Interruption, in other words, is not outside the regular mechanisms of televisual discourse; it is a genre of TV programming. In Mary Anne Doane's words, interruption is "crucial to television because it . . . corroborates television's access to the momentary, the discontinuous, the real." The potentially radical dialectic of banality and shock produced—as Walter Benjamin has most famously argued—in a spectrum of modern systems of representation and social exchange is, she notes, the deepest cultural meaning of catastrophe coverage's role in broadcast television.[27]

One could argue, initially, that AH disarms the dialectics of shock—if a large-scale catastrophe were to happen while I wait for my doctor's appointment, I might only find out on leaving the building. Isolating televisual routine from televisual interruption and instantaneity, AH can be seen as the final evacuation of the cultural specter of crisis that Doane sees haunting network TV, replacing unpredictability with the semipermanent and endlessly repeating technology of the laser disc. From this perspective

TV's ideological image as a news technology of urgency and immediacy recedes in favor of the image of television as the ultimate ossification of habit; AH's comforting bedside manner reassures the viewer that nothing will interrupt its flow.

However, there is one obstacle to such an interpretation: the fact that the chipper commercial address of AH is entering the medical environment at a moment when, in fact, there actually *is* a crisis going on — a crisis in health care, not only health insurance but basic access — and it seems as if there is not much one can do about it. Rather than evacuating crisis from the experience of waiting, AH marks its existence. It calls attention to the probabilistic "just-in-time" economy of scale that leads many facilities to double book and overschedule rooms. For managed care "clients" the wait in the physical premises of the medical facility is often merely the end point of a far longer waiting period. In many companies one must pass the dual gatekeeping examination of the primary care physician and the managed care corporation's case managers before seeing a specialist.[28] Given this advanced institutional network of waiting, I suggest that crisis is still attached to the television screen. But it is not through the spectacular, interruptive iterations of shock that punctuate the boring flow, qualities of the network broadcasting Doane describes. Rather, it is through the resolute, unchanging banality of programming cycles unable to adjust to the cycles of the health care institutions in which they play. It is apparently easier for a place-based network to synchronize its programming with high-volume aviation networks moving millions of people across the globe every day than with health care "networks" on the ground.

To combat this problem, Accent Health now provides its programming solely to doctors' offices that have an average waiting time of under an hour.[29] It also recently entered into a partnership to develop a broadband satellite communications network, on which it now plans to deliver its programming. This network will help Accent Health consolidate profits from the doctor's office as a space of medical communication; the company plans to use it as the basis for a subscription two-way clinical messaging service. If implemented as planned, the Internet-based system will be used by doctors to communicate with consultants, labs, hospitals, and health agencies.[30]

Though it was unadopted, it is worth noting the network's initial response to its timing problems, formulated before these corporate acquisitions took place. It was an attempt to make the medical waiting room TV more integrated with the rhythms of the space while also — as I will explain—bringing the network in line with wider conventions of televisual waiting. In 1998, according to the company president, plans were underway to extend the length of programming significantly: "By the end of 1999, we hope to lengthen the program to *two hours.*"[31] Given the significant increase in production costs that come with adding news and other live-action program forms (especially in light of the research requirements, and legal restrictions on content, that all medical marketing faces), the new material added in 1999 would likely have consisted of the kinds of trivia texts—quizzes, recipe substitutions, and "did-you-know" segments—that already make up a large proportion of the programming on A H. Yet although this change would have made A H's program duration correspond more closely to the rhythms and routines of its environment, it would undoubtedly have led to a different kind of relationship between screen and space; in audio terms, for instance, the introduction of more text-based programming would replace the intrusive direct address of the network's "news and views" segments with the kind of benign contemporary Muzak associated with soft-core porn videos or the local forecasts on the Weather Channel. This no doubt explains why the network ultimately sought other solutions.

But this should not obscure the fact that such low-bandwidth, minimal-affect televisual address, closer to signage than broadcasting, is becoming more and more prevalent in television, via the numerous text-based cable channels that air in the wired home, as well as via programs designed for public spaces. Textual screens bearing advertising, trivia questions, top-ten lists, pop cultural quizzes, and other small bits of light information can be found in many sites that fit the latter category: on the (recently bankrupt) Commuter Channel T V screens in regional rail stations, on the Food Court Entertainment Network screens in the shopping mall, and in travel hubs where the screens of Bloomberg TV (a financial network) barrage the passerby with a frenetic, overloaded "info-aesthetic" (fig. 39). Affectively and economically, trivia of this kind are an ideally flexible kind of content for site-specific T V networks, easily adapted to the larger purposes of a space. They are cheap to produce, requiring nothing more complicated than an electronic character generator, and the minimal cognitive and emotional investments they solicit are easily integrated into the comings and goings of public space.

Yet the fact that broadcast television can contain similar "teaser" questions (posed, for example, just before entertainment news programs break for commercials) calls our attention to the fact that trivia, despite the pejo-

FIG. 39
On the public screens of the Bloomberg financial news network in New York's Pennsylvania Station, textual "factoids" support an aesthetic of information barrage. (Photograph by the author)

rative connotations of the term, have a recognized commercial value. Regardless of their program context or spatial location, these routine and unremarkable deployments of the hermeneutic code have a key structural role in the flow economy of television, working to direct attention toward a commercial address during a period of waiting. This possibility is borne out in numerous places of televisual waiting. An obvious example is illustrated in figure 40, the gift shop at Planet Hollywood, where fan-oriented trivia questions on the in-house network — like the tutelary quiz of Accent Health — work to reinforce the institutional identity of the space (here, the consumer-leisure environment of the theme restaurant gift shop).

The use of TV in this Planet Hollywood waiting area demonstrates how the mode of address, and physical location, of trivia screens in waiting areas work to position the waiting person as a particular kind of consuming subject. The informal slang of the title "Merch shop" addresses the Planet Hollywood customer as a knowing consumer, well aware of the store's commercial purpose. The trivia quiz on the screen tests one's "inside" knowledge of the movie business, asking the waiting spectator to name the actor originally cast as Indiana Jones.[32] It curries the favor of those who have waited in line by extending the thematic conceit of the restaurant's overall environment: that its diner is a movie fan, presumably a member of a group, perhaps even interested in showing off his/her knowledge to others. The questions recall those one sees projected on the movie theater screen (along with advertisements) before the previews — questions themselves clearly intended to distract from the experience of waiting by facilitating social interaction while promoting consumption. This *textual* contiguity with conventions of theater space is one of several ways Planet Hollywood reinforces its market image as an experiential and thematic crossover (born out of larger industrial convergences) between dining and moviegoing. Its "theme," indeed, might be described as the assertion of a metaphorical relationship between restaurant space and movie space — the set, the theater, the home of the star. Indeed, television seems to serve as a means of disguising the deficits and limits of the comparison — without video imagery, the "eatertainment" feel of Planet Hollywood would be severely impoverished.[33] Moreover, although the TV screens liberally deployed for scenographic purposes in high-volume, large-party locations like Planet Hollywood may help to secure the spectacle of eatertainment, their spatial function is the rather more prosaic task of accompanying the inevitable wait in such locations. In places like theme parks, where lines for rides can last over an hour,

FIG. 40

The televised trivia questions at Planet Hollywood's gift shop in San Francisco resemble the commercially sponsored trivia questions on the screen in movie theaters, addressing the waiting viewer as a film buff or movie industry "insider."

the very existence of a queue can generate revenue, providing the kind of captive audience for television advertising that is highly valued in the economy of the place-based media industry.[34]

This commercial function is not, however, the only purpose of televisual waiting in themed commercial environments. The presence of the screen can also serve a variety of disciplinary agendas, demonstrating the institutional conception of TV as a highly flexible instrument for the management of the public and its time. Consider, for example, a video-saturated midtown Manhattan theme restaurant called Television City (now defunct). The restaurant was located across the street from NBC's Rockefeller Center, where television shows like *The Today Show* and *The Rosie O'Donnell Show* are staged. Its location near TV tapings, a popular entertainment option for both tourists and metro-area people in certain U.S. cities, was undoubtedly the motivation for the restaurant's theme (it was originally conceived as a mock TV studio).[35] Television City was a place to grab a meal after attending one of these tapings—one might describe it as a budget version of dinner and a Broadway show. However, the comparison between seeing a TV show being taped and eating in Television City is perhaps a little too apt; in the entry area the presence of a velvet rope (the premier signifier of exclusivity in New York nightlife) marked the fact that one had to stand in line to get into the restaurant. And waiting, along with being herded in a group, are prominent components of the experience of participating in a live studio audience. On the day I went to see a taping of *Sally,* the Sally Jessy Rafael show, I and the other members of the audience waited more than ninety minutes in a bleak, barracks-like room with a pay phone and an automatic coffee vending machine. Tape after tape of the Jerry Springer show (with commercials) played on the screen. Like the audience line in the studio, the line at Television City linked TV spectatorship with the "dead time" of waiting, as if the mere presence of TV monitors authorized the treatment of the consumer-diner as a member of a mass. At Television City, the TV screen also performed tasks of behavioral management with a closed-circuit camera. As figure 41 illustrates, the restaurant's lobby featured a matrix of multiple TV monitors in a wooden frame, near which stood a mannequin dressed in clothes bearing the restaurant's logo—a color-bars image. These monitors and the mannequin demarcated the entry to the restaurant's gift shop, located, as in Planet Hollywood, on the way to and from the dining area. On Television City's waiting area screens, however, unlike those at Planet Hollywood, the waiting diner did not see in-house TV programming nor trivia ques-

FIG. 41
Closed-circuit surveillance images on a vido wall combine
incongruously with the velvet rope in this waiting area at Television City,
a now defunct New York theme restaurant.

tions but rather the hidden camera image of herself and the others waiting in line.

Putting the closed-circuit image of the queue on the screen, making it a spectacle, seems to serve two distinct purposes within this context. One can read it, on the one hand, as an attempt to distract attention from the length of the wait by making waiting people part of the scenography of the space, in this case by positioning them as "stars" on the screen. Along with the velvet rope, the fashion merchandise, and the close proximity of "real" TV production studios across the street, the hidden camera participated in the space's iconography of stardom, narcissism, and national celebrity. On the other hand, though, the display of closed-circuit imagery at the entryway to the gift shop offered a subtle alert very similar to the message conveyed by the surveillant images that are often prominently displayed at the entrances of retail spaces: when you enter here, you will be on TV. In combining these two signifying functions, the televisual waiting area at Television City offered a solution to some long-standing problems in the evolution of point-of-purchase display within commercial space — not only the enduring retail anxieties historically associated with self-service, as a practice that might easily translate into theft, but also the contradiction between the need to control traffic flow through the space, on the one hand, and to arrest and focus the consumer's attention on the other. This closed-circuit apparatus at the entry to the gift shop did both. As in the other sites of televisual waiting explored here, the placement of TV sets was far from random or accidental; rather, it articulated particular meanings for the act of waiting within the larger temporal rhythms and spatial flows of its environment.

To think so deeply about television as an apparatus of waiting, and the waiting spectator as a subject position deeply imbricated in the social organization of public space, invites consideration of the possibility that waiting is an affective state bound up, on a deeper level, with television viewing in general. If TV, as Paddy Scannell argues, blurs the distinctions between work and leisure, then this ambiguity can make the completion of routine tasks and activities more tolerable, at home as well as in places where we work, places where we are often waiting to leave.[36] The prevalence of TV sets in work spaces calls attention to the fact that work is an activity often suffused with a feeling of waiting for time to pass — something signified in the references to time in the titles of films about the experience of the corporate work space: *Nine to Five* or *Clockwatchers*. On a speculative level this opens up a space for asking, How much is the experience of waiting built into the format of TV programming and images in general—waiting for an upcoming program, a better music video, the resumption of a narrative interrupted by commercials? In other words, is waiting a "deep structure" of television spectatorship regardless of where we watch TV? This structural possibility is certainly suggested in theories of TV viewing like Scannell's, which draw on orthodox Marxist analyses of the functional position of leisure in capitalist relations of production to suggest that TV viewing is, at base, a way of managing the passage of time from one workday to the next.[37]

This proposition can help us understand spectatorship as a commodity experience within the temporal organization of capitalism, although it certainly does not exhaust the analytic possibilities in this area. It offers one way of explaining screen-based places like the growing genre of the mediatized eatery—illustrated in figure 42—that caters to the working lives of urban single professionals by providing magazines, television, video, and the Internet as accompaniments to solitary dining.[38] Such places, it could be argued, combat anxieties about time spent eating as a kind of wasted time, similar to waiting in its low-affect vagueness. They make eating a labor from which we must be distracted by news programming, or topical reading, or Web browsing, or all three. Moreover, given the pervasiveness of cultural obsessions with eating and diet, one could compare the discursive task performed by the video screens of the mediatized restaurant to that of the video screens in commercial aircraft (fig. 43). Both help to transform a space potentially fraught with anxiety into nothing more scary than a waiting room. This is an explicit rationale behind certain uses of television out of the home. One Beverly Hills dentist who offers his patients a headset and movies like *Die Hard* and *Braveheart* while he drills makes precisely this claim: "watching television relieves a tremendous amount of anxiety for them."[39] The warding off of difficult bodily sensations is certainly the logic that underlies health-club TV networks. Such networks often broadcast the sound over separate AM frequencies for exercisers with portable radios, allowing one to retreat from the there and then of the gym to another audio zone.

But although such general equations of spectatorship and waiting may access the reasons why some of us like to watch TV while we eat or fly or visit the dentist, I am wary of explanations that package themselves as master tropes for "decoding" televisual space. Specifically, they are of little use for exploring the differences between spaces and the variety of spatial and temporal relations of screen and place that are clearly observable

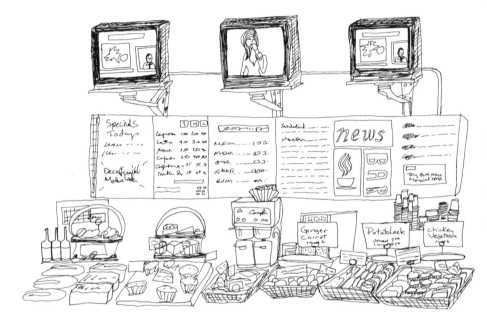

FIG. 42

Television links waiting and eating in New York's News Bar, where a selection of TV channels, magazines, and Internet stations provide media accompaniment to solitary diners.

FIG. 43
Video in commercial jets helps make travel something routine and
unremarkable, like waiting.

on the microlevel. They lead us instead back toward the heuristically exhausted idea of television as the absence of space and the eradication of spatial difference or, more simply — as the health-club TV example might seem to suggest — "escapism." This perspective can be very narrowing. It makes it difficult to see how places that offer customers a chance to use TV to pass the time while eating might do so in very different ways, serving quite distinct social or economic purposes.

Compare, for example, two quite different places that offer television while-you-eat. The first, the Video Diner, located in the Manhattan hinterlands of the busy West Side Highway, has little in common with the experience of televisual eating in news-oriented spaces like the News Bar. Both offer a dining experience suffused with televisual entertainment, but in each the television screen's relationship to its environment and its viewing — or nonviewing — subjects goes beyond the equation of viewing and waiting. The Video Diner screens, located in private booths, help create miniature "homes" that make the space seem like an oasis of privacy, an escape and retreat from the pace and crowd of city life. Many lunchtime "regulars" (a number of whom work at the nearby Saatchi and Saatchi advertising agency) watch a movie in small portions, day after day, much as they might read a few pages of a book on the train on the way to work or to home.[40] In the News Bar, on the other hand, televisual eating means an aesthetic of "information overload," produced through the multiple video screens that add a fashionable, futuristic sensibility of media bombardment to what would otherwise be a rather unassuming coffee shop in an area of the city already overpopulated with coffee shops. Although waiting is certainly part of the experience of television viewing in such spaces, to understand it as the basic, underlying condition of the viewing process is to ignore the distinctive uses marked out very visibly in its physical position within its location.

The fact that the difference between these two places, the Video Diner and the News Bar, is clearly annotated in the physical positions of the TV screens within them is also a reminder of how important it is to look for these tangible, material conventions of the screen as an object, to engage in "eye-level" readings of televisual places, in order to understand TV's presence in the visual culture of public space. As we saw in chapter 4, the screen organizes and compartmentalizes space by its physical position, and it comes to occupy that place because of an archive of formal and informal placement protocols — some of which I have traced in the foregoing chapters. The questions that remain will occupy this book's next, concluding chapter: how do oppositional, or critical, practices interact with the conventional site-specific operations of the public screen? When do they upset the routine ways in which the T V set "fits" as an *object* and as a *subject* of institutional and commercial communications within public places? And how, finally, do we evaluate the political effects of these practices; on what scale of everyday experience do people's actions reorganize television's politics?

CHAPTER 7

TERMINAL THOUGHTS ON ART, ACTIVISM, AND VIDEO FOR PUBLIC PLACES

This book has adopted a contextual approach to the TV set, seeking to understand it as an object around which a number of everyday human activities are focused: not only viewing but also eating, drinking, exercising, waiting, reading, and many other routine aspects of daily life besides. It may at first have seemed that the *location* of the screen would be irrelevant to such a task—many of these everyday acts are associated with TV in domestic and nondomestic spaces alike. But I have tried to show the many ways—some subtle, some not so subtle—that location does in fact "count." Place, the immediate place of the screen, is a key factor in the meanings we attribute to television and the uses to which we put it. This is because all places, even the most generic, featureless, mass-produced ones, are distinctive *discursive,* as well as physical, sites. They are endowed with a historical specificity that derives as much, if not more, from localized, and localizing, systems of knowledge and belief as from empirical or functional characteristics. When television enters a place, whether public or private, whether the home or the sales floor, the bar, or the waiting area, it simultaneously enters the webs of signification and material practice that define each as an environment.

Yet at the same time this relationship between television and its various environments is profoundly dialectical. Institutional rhetorics and material practices of the TV screen in different places reveal that TV does not simply *adapt* to preexisting rhythms and habits in its environment. Rather, as I've aimed to demonstrate, its presence also *activates and embodies* a variety of heterogeneous forces within and around a space. These span both the shared pleasures of collective spectatorship and the isolationist privilege of private viewing, both the economic conditions for extracting audience values from public space and the local contingencies that make measuring such audiences impossible, and they can encompass quite apparent and literal performances of resistance to TV as well as its unquestioned acceptance.

This must be seen as a deeply political process. When the screen brings external forces of commerce and control to bear on a particular location, it aligns this location's various populations with these forces as well — sometimes with unexpected results. The screen's location, in short, is anything *but* irrelevant to the varying dynamics of television as an object integrated into anonymous practices of everyday life; rather, location plays a central role in the way institutional actors and everyday subjects interpret screen images and imagine their effects on various types of spectators.

Throughout this book I have looked to existing studies of TV's relation to domestic spaces for insight on the politics of screen location. Such studies clearly demonstrate the deeply environmental quality of screen practices on the microlevel, within a single, and central, site. Expanding this contextual approach to other sites both places the specificity of the home in sharp relief and shows us how particular domestic discourses of the TV set "travel" to other sites — most notably, those discourses that position TV advertising within the household labors of female consumers. Whether on the sales floor or sitting in the waiting room of the doctor's office, women routinely find their itineraries through public space "branded" by the presence of commercial video images. This multisite approach has also broadened my sense of the spatial dynamics of the medium and its technological forms. I have learned a great deal about TV's ability to organize social space and shift social scales from looking *comparatively* at the local processes that are supported, and sometimes warped, by site-specific, quantum operations of the screen. The spatiotemporal conventions of TV's physical installation, the censorial and consumerist discourses of the image, the institutional constructions of place-based audiences outlined in the foregoing chapters are microlevel operations that suture the screen, and the networks that terminate on it, into a place.

So what do we conclude, then, about the ways in which the relationship among screens, spaces, and subjects changes from place to place? The analytical danger, of course, is that focusing on the *variety* of TV's forms in public places can become a simple celebration of localism, especially if it is uncoupled from larger structural issues. This is what Stuart Hall cautions against when he proposes that a respect for the tensions between "two paradigms," the culturalist and the structuralist, must be the crucial epistemological turn of cultural studies.[1] But the site-specificity of the relationship between screen and space that we discover when we examine TV's dissemination outside the home is in some ways a dramatization of this tension. The fact that notions of what television is, and of what its subjects are perceived to feel and do, can vary so greatly according to location conveys the power politics of TV technology in very material terms. For the quite different notions of what TV *is* that emerge from site to site offer strong evidence of the ideological *flexibility* of television, as an apparatus capable of linking everyday locations and their subjects to wider, abstracted realms of commerce, culture, and control in any number of ways.

The divergent meanings of TV screens in public places, as terminal points of the medium's "global" networks, exemplify how the "big issues" of geographically oriented media and cultural studies get localized in material practices. I have focused on some of these issues, tracing, for instance, how televisual ideologies of spatial collapse helped 1940s retailers resolve contradictions in their institutional visions of the female consumer, and provided a framework for integrating televisuality into an architecture of consumption that endures to this day. I have not attempted an exhaustive survey of the local processes that are activated, and networked, by the presence of the screen. Nevertheless, I hope that what I *have* said about TV's role in certain categories of space will be relevant to research on the televisual sites overlooked in my analysis. There is clearly a great deal to say about screen locations like the racetrack, for example, where TV screens displaying images and numerical information correlate live events and their economic value for both the spectator and the institution. Similarly, there is no doubt more work to be done on the collective play of media personality forms, the amateur theatrics of charisma and celebrity, that TV helps construct in the karaoke bar. And (in part because of a reluctance to retread some well-charted routes of Foucauldian analysis) I have said virtually nothing about closed-circuit TV's surveillance systems and the architectural ideologies of the image they materialize. I hope that the foregoing analyses can contribute to these and other areas of new research. All sites where TV screens appear provide us with rich material for assessing how electronic media connect places, intersecting with the diverse itineraries of their anonymous, mobile subjects. If I have neglected some of the complexities of media and public space in this study, it has been in order to probe others more deeply.

For this reason, instead of accounting for these "leftovers" now, what I want to explore by way of conclusion is an issue raised and provisionally addressed at different points in the previous chapters but that deserves closer treatment. It is the question of what kinds of critical and activist practices can arise from the way television interweaves with habitual webs of lived experience and activity on many different levels. The difficulty of answering such a question stems from the fact that, if the screen is really so deeply embedded in everyday, local processes, then aren't accepted scholarly analytical schemas like de Certeau's binary model of "tactics" and "strategies" somewhat inadequate for the task of assessing television's relation to its cultural context?[2] Although a binarized approach may be necessary for methodological purposes, isn't it true that to see screen practices, or any kind of microlevel practice, as *either* managerial or oppositional is to carve everyday life into categories that are not so clearly recognizable in the midst of the immersive intricacy, the continuity, the *flow* of experience? Television's status as a flexible, site-specific apparatus around which complex ideological negotiations are waged is, in short, a reminder of the need to avoid the pitfalls of an either/or approach to culture, and to cultural studies' "two paradigms."

In the preceding chapters I have noted at points some of the diverse ways the TV set's environmental role confounds distinct categories of social practice and makes the relationship between authoritative public voices and private, localizable meanings seem more like a movable threshold than a binary determination. They range, to recap familiar examples, from the heterogeneity and illegibility of localized display practices— such as those proprietary positionings of television sets within syntactic arrays that may include liquor licenses, religious imagery, folk artifacts, and tourist posters—to larger-scale reconfigurations of audienceship, as in television's arrival in the tavern—an arrival that at once enhanced the autonomous pursuit of leisure in working-class culture and enabled, on another level, the reformist supervision of working-class leisure activities. But by and large my analysis of this simultaneity of meanings and effects has concentrated on practices of site-specific television imagery that are not presented as oppositional, as *challenges* to the forces of institutional and governmental strategy, which, in de Certeau's words, "assumes a place that can be circumscribed as proper . . . and [can] thus serve as the basis for generating relations with an exterior distinct from it (competitors, adversaries, 'clienteles,' 'targets,' or objects of research) . . . a spatial or institutional localization."[3]

What therefore remains to be examined are two distinct but intertwined issues: first, the possibility that the TV screen may be used for location-based forms of contest and critique, "bottom-up" practices of screen and space; and second, the possibility that these practices, like the institutional strategies that they opportunistically engage for tactical purposes, might also travel across the political categories of everyday life — the tactical and the strategic, to borrow de Certeau's terms once more. Given the complexity and the contingency of cultural politics as they unfold in the discontinuous sphere of everyday life, it is unlikely that site-specific screen practices will always clearly signify as cooptation *or* resistance. I want to explore the dilemmas of both activist politics and critical analysis that arise from this condition and from the screen's promiscuous availability and adaptability as a communicative object in social space. I proceed from the possibility that the politics of everyday practices, in whatever form, might be better described through a logic of threshold and continuum than a clear-cut opposition between control and contest. This changes the kinds of questions we ask when we think about the politics of media in everyday life. On the microlevel, the concept of a threshold allows us to look at how practices "cross over" and take on particular political meanings from the continuum of possibilities in certain contexts. Instead of inquiring, "Is this screen practice hegemonic or subversive," we stand to learn from more closely situated questions like, Under what conditions does this or that screen practice take on more or less regulated or regulatory meanings? And what precipitates such changes in state?

This possibility is suggested already in new geographical work on the concept of place, work that has provided much of the theoretical grounding for this book. Place is a geographical sign of "betweenness," endowed with both specificity and generality, and always understood in terms of past and future, change and permanence. For geographers like Harvey, Entriken, and Massey it is therefore an inherently dialectical concept, exemplifying how material, experienced things are carved out of dynamic, ongoing processes. In Harvey's words, the specificity of place "gets constructed through the working out in that place of interventions and influences from outside."[4] Because it is so flexible, so enmeshed in, and constitutive of, the ambient flow of the everyday, television is a central force in the dialectical construction of a place, often providing a central link between that site and the "outside world." But although television's presence certainly helps to draw lines between forces of social control and the subjects who, for various reasons, these forces seek to govern, ongoing screen practices also intermingle with both "sides" and in fact, enable their interpenetration.

I do not pretend to exhaust the analytical possibilities of this state of affairs in my conclusion, but I hope to tease out some of its implications via two narratives of public video art practices, each of which centers on the everyday public presence of the TV screen. I choose them because together, they outline some of the rewards, and some of the administrative and conceptual problems, that artists and activists encounter when they attempt to turn TV's omnipresence in anonymous locations of everyday life into an arena for critical reflection and social change. Both installations take advantage of commercial transmissions, attempting to transform them and their contexts and foregrounding the politics of TV's presence in public places. The first project, a quasi-guerilla action by a public activist art group called Together We Can Defeat Capitalism, involved the commuter channel monitors in one Bay Area Rapid Transit System (BART) station in San Francisco. The second project is an interactive video installation, designed by video artist Dara Birnbaum for a shopping mall in Atlanta, that was based in part on the repositioning of CNN broadcasts.

I must stress at the outset that comparing the two projects does not yield a clear sense of either one as necessarily more "effective" than the other as a politicized use of the TV screen to critique institutions. Indeed, I am not interested in making simple political-aesthetic judgments, in declaring one piece or the other to be a better piece of socially critical art. Rather, I see the stories of these two projects as parables that delineate, in their significant differences and similarities, how activist art can become what Lucy Lippard calls "an art of contact."[5] I take this provocative label to mean art that, in its attempt to connect disparate constituencies and value systems, has an agonistic relation to both "theory" and "practice" as they are currently conceived. The activist insights of both of these pieces shed light on larger problems in the way we conceive of institutional strategies and oppositional tactics, by showing their points of contact in particular places. Both of these artworks harness and embody the contingent, "threshold logic" of everyday practices. They tap into the capillary flow of power as it passes between institutions and subjects in particular places, and they therefore require from the observer a mutable and deeply contextual reading practice. Each of the two installations I trace here is thus a useful reminder of both the difficulties and the potential of television screens as material tools for grassroots refashionings of the built environment.

Together We Can Defeat Capitalism

In 1998, Together We Can Defeat Capitalism (TWCDC) became a place-based media sponsor for one month. Its founder, Andy Cox, purchased advertising time on the Commuter Channel screens in two stations of the BART system — the train system connecting the city to Oakland, Berkeley, and outlying suburbs. The organization's "video insertion" was a simple message, broadcast silently to waiting passengers several times per hour: the short, direct phrase "Capitalism stops at nothing." The slogan was graphically designed to look identical to the BART announcements that provided passengers with travel information (figs. 44 and 45). When I interviewed Cox about this project via e-mail, he explained that the piece was interwoven with the everyday visual space of the station and with the routine of waiting for a train:

> I was standing in a BART station one day staring at a Commuter Chan-
> nel screen when a colorful ad appeared encouraging people to place
> ads: "Advertise *Your* Business," it pleaded. That planted a seed. I'd
> noticed that passengers either checked the screens frequently for train
> destination information, or stared at them blankly and continuously,
> like me. People wanted to catch their trains. They *needed* to look at
> the screens. The screens needed to be subverted. People don't have
> the same reason to look at billboards. There was never any question
> that I had to do something on the Commuter Channel.[6]

What seems striking about TWCDC's "video insertion" is the fact that it called attention to something very abstract — capital, the driving force of the materialist dialectic — a force that "stops at nothing" because it is not a *thing* but rather an economic relation manifested in things. TWCDC materialized the abstraction of capital within the material and temporal experience of the train station. But the form in which the message ap-peared achieved something else, too: it brought the commodity relations of advertising and public service messages in the transit station into sharp relief. It replicated the visual style of the BART announcements about up-coming trains, but it only coincided with the arrival and departure of a train by accident. Appearing at the same rate as an advertisement, it would

FIG. 44

The Commuter Channel screens in San Francisco provided travelers with information about arriving trains. (Photograph by Andy Cox)

FIG. 45
Together We Can Defeat Capitalism designed its advertisement to look
identical to a train announcement. (Photograph by Andy Cox)

have solicited a sense of irony in attentive observers, who would discover that the cycle of advertisements is faster than that of train arrival. The piece's effect on the space was thus transformative not disruptive, though it was discreetly camouflaged. Moreover, as an advertisement "against" capitalism, it used a place-based logic for correlating the receptivity of the audience to the functions of its institutional location. The ad got the attention of waiting customers at a moment when they might be frustrated and bored, tired of the cycle of work and leisure, perhaps impatient and disgruntled, too.

But although TWCDC exploited TV's ability to interweave with the rhythms of its location, the group did change the social environment of the BART station for a limited duration. The station became an art gallery for an afternoon, when Cox held an "opening" for the piece and invited the people on his mailing list to visit the Montgomery station platform during commute hours to watch the announcement. Twenty-five viewers attended this *envernissage* (or more appropriately, perhaps, *de-vernissage*, "unvarnishing") on Thursday, July 2. The group took advantage of this "opening reception" by handing out July Fourth survival kits: "patriotic cookie, flag toothpick, flag napkin, red white and blue balloons, a commentary on freedom of speech, and extracts from the US laws on desecration of the flag." As this playful didacticism might suggest, the "culture jamming" methodology of TWCDC was like that of other contemporary interventionist agents, from the rather more "preachy" fake commercials of Adbusters to the aphorisms of Jenny Holzer.

But from a longer view, TWCDC's work embodies the critique of everyday life that arose from a nexus of aesthetic-activist-intellectual techniques formed in the early-twentieth-century emergence of the "historical avant-garde" and extending at least to the situationist movement of the 1950s and 1960s.[7] Cox in fact described the artist/activist work of TWCDC in situationist terms: "I like to create situations that might reveal something about the power structure in which the situation occurs." An activist art practice, an intellectual movement, and a "phenomenology of urban life," situationism was, in Edward Ball's words, "the conscious construction of 'situations,' or theatrical environments inside the urban environment — acts of cultural sabotage or diversions that might strengthen the growing bohemian subculture."[8] The object of situationist acts was to expose what Guy Debord called "psychogeography": "the precise laws and specific effects of the geographical environment, consciously organized or not, on the emotions and behaviour of individuals."[9] Although its own interventions were primarily textual, the movement advocated a broader range of tactical and opportunistic interventions in everyday life, most notably the practice of attentively moving through and paying attention to everyday spaces that situationists called the *dérive,* or "drift."[10] In its emphasis on the everyday, TWCDC's video insertion exemplifies the contemporary legacy of the *dérive* and what Ball calls situationism's "delinquent play." The video seemed to follow situationist instructions on "how to recycle the detritus of official learning; how to reinscribe texts, figure and artifacts so as to empower them with new meanings; and, despite their precautions, how to make new products out of the leftovers of the commodity economy" (25). It intertwined political speech with the familiar grind of the everyday — in this case the suspended moment of transit between work and free time that "televisual waiting" so often accompanies in transit locations.

Yet there are also some differences between situationist theory and TWCDC's video practice, and they are important insofar as they mark the latter's more complex understanding of the television set than situationist theories would probably have allowed. At least in its later incarnations, situationism's tactics of detournement, plagiarism, and subversion targeted the society of the spectacle — Debord's famous term for the reifying process of late capitalist visual culture, often metonymically represented in TV. How situationists would have used video for actions in public space is unclear. Conceivably, though, they would compare to the TV interventions performed by members of the Fluxus movement in the same period. The two movements evolved relatively autonomously, although John Hanhardt's account of how Fluxus participants used video in their "happenings" suggests some points of convergence between the two; video, he notes, was the basis of "a major effort to demolish both the boundaries between art forms and practices and [acknowledge] the quotidian ebb and flow of life."[11] This characterization makes Fluxus seem like situationism's less explicitly and less rigorously Marxist American corollary; indeed, as Hanhardt describes them, some early Fluxus video art interventions in public space are textbook attacks on the Society of the Spectacle, targeting television as a degraded artifact of consumerism. Fluxus artist Wolf Vostell, for example, planned to scramble the images on the screens in a Parisian department store in order "to subvert the ordinary frame of reference . . . to comment on programming within the very marketplace that television serves" (89). Even Nam June Paik's affirmative embrace of television consistently presents a conception of TV as an all-powerful apparatus that tends to proliferate across spaces of everyday life in a relentlessly globalizing movement.

Cox's TWCDC embodied a more complex understanding of the relationship between image and environment than work like Vostell's "TV decollage," which treated television only as "something to be confronted and transformed through art" (90). In contrast, TWCDC was not really interested in attacking television at all. The group's departure from a situationist, or Fluxus, orthodoxy is indicated in the way Cox sought to distance the didactic address of his slogan from the judgmental didacticism of activist modes of address to the public:

> In general, the project seemed to be viewed very positively by both the art and activist communities, and this, for me, was one of the biggest successes of the project. I would like to think that my art can somehow bridge the gap between the often dogmatic rhetoric of the activist community and the questioning and uncertainty that is inherent in most contemporary art-world art. People should have the tools to think, not be led like sheep, and for this reason I'd much rather be called an artist than an activist.

When Cox outlined the kinds of "refusal" that he valued, they were refusals of strict distinctions between, say, art and activism or art and advertising. This seemed to him to be a more productive kind of refusal than wholesale damnation of public-image culture, no matter how commercial it may be. Cox proposed an inclusive definition of the membership of TWCDC: "For the BART project, I would include as members of TWCDC people who viewed the piece, friends who discussed it with me, BART officials who let it happen, and definitely John Winter of Metro Channel, who was such a good sport."

In addition to refusing dogmatism TWCDC did not aim to expose false consciousness by disrupting the experience of the space itself. When I asked Cox how much he saw this piece engaging with — and exploiting or perhaps even undermining — the temporal and spatial processes of modern capitalism, he replied, "I think the capitalism ad, by placing itself midway between advertising and the train information, caused a rupture in the normal train of events; an interruption in the schedule"; but he was ambivalent about how this might be interpreted: "perhaps undermining capitalistic processes, perhaps underlining them." In the end it seemed that the piece served mainly as an environmental disruption during its "opening," at which a crowd gathered to watch the screen: "This event, in some small way, destabilized the BART station space by holding a public event that was outside of its normal use as a regulated transportation system. People seemed bemused that we were just hanging out there fooling around and cheering from time to time when the Capitalism ad appeared. Several people asked for more information about what was going on, and a few were very appreciative of our efforts (and received survival kits)." In general Cox's attitude toward traditional configurations of domination and resistance maintained a situationist irreverence while simultaneously insisting on a more pragmatic approach to mass culture. This sense of irony and also of the limits of art's effects as a "serious discourse" is apparent in the group's mission statement: "The mission of TWCDC is to encourage discussion of the contradictions of late 20th Century capitalism and have some fun too."

Exemplifying the media savvy of post–Act Up activist art works, the group succeeded in this mission in that it generated controversy that secured publicity for the project and its critical aims for the duration of the ad's one-month run. This publicity was both local and national; on the latter end National Public Radio featured an interview with Cox on its financial program, *Marketplace,* and it was covered in the magazine *The Progressive.* For Cox what was most surprising about his encounters with the media was the fact that representatives of the Metro Channel, the (now defunct) company that operated the Commuter Channel, had been unfazed by the project. It was, rather, the BART system authorities who took action against the piece, after some riders complained about the message to the BART system authorities. Indeed, the manner in which BART officials were mystified by the advertisement only confirms the illegibility of categories like the strategic and the tactical, the hegemonic imposition and the subversive gesture, as approaches to the techniques of everyday spatial practice. According to Cox, "the theories circulating in BART were that it was . . . an ad for *Forbes* magazine with a missing second page." Because of this kind of confusion, BART officials pulled the advertisement temporarily from the roster of Commuter Channel messages. However, after some phone calls from Cox and some internal debate, the ad was reinserted, now preceded by a disclaimer that read: "The following paid advertisement does not necessarily reflect the views of BART, Metrochannel, or their employees."

The success of "Capitalism Stops at Nothing" in achieving its goals of promoting discussion and "having fun" is instructive in that it tells us something about the parameters to which media-savvy activist public art must conform. To begin with, it suggests that even though such work exists quite deliberately *apart from* the commercialized relations of the gallery-based art world, it is an art that must still proceed via an economic decision-making process that weighs the price of aesthetic activity in commercial terms. At some point Cox had to decide whether the piece was worth its $800 price tag, and this decision-making process oriented TWCDC within the reifying logic of the market. The fact that the advertisement only ran for one month conveys how expensive it can be to use actual television systems for art making—it is interesting to note that artist Chris Burden could only afford to purchase *ten seconds* of network airtime to broadcast images of himself crawling through broken glass in the 1970s.

Second, TWCDC's action suggests that the institutional legitimacy of particular media systems, their relationships to larger power structures, is an important factor in activist media artwork. Metro Channel was teetering on the brink of collapse at the time of the action, and cash flow problems may have made company representatives more receptive to Cox's proposal. It is difficult to imagine getting away with this piece on the lucrative and highly corporate CNN Airport Network (to say nothing of the more heavily policed environment of the airport in which it airs). "Capitalism Stops at Nothing" was thus conceived and executed as a local intervention for a limited time, on a low-bandwidth network, and it succeeded precisely *because* of these limits. It was no doubt aided by a third limit, namely, the fact that the message it sought to disseminate was very simple and nonspecific. Although it was carefully planned as a site-specific engagement with the motifs and cycles of its environment, the slogan "capitalism stops at nothing" was neither ad hominem nor institution specific. Its message was not a direct, nor even an indirect, indictment of consumer desire or of the BART system or any other more localized version of capitalism's spatial processes. It seems likely that Cox and TWCDC would have faced a much harder battle had they somehow raised the money to run the advertisement for a longer duration. No doubt Cox's previous encounters with censorship of his public art projects (bus shelter advertisements) taught him that activists' public engagements with advertising must fall within certain parameters if they are to reach a broad audience. The piece tells us, in turn, that quite dramatic and explicit contestatory speech must be produced on public television screens with careful and canny planning.

Another important lesson of TWCDC is the way it conveys some of the determining roles that temporal and physical scale and institutional structures play in activist public art. Once an artwork moves beyond a certain size, institutional collaborations are necessary. Cox's unauthorized collaboration with the institution of the transit system took an "authorized" form — commercial sponsorship — and in this respect it avoided the complex and unpredictable issues raised in other forms of artistic partnerships with institutions, partnerships that often require active attempts on both sides to construct terms of consensus out of institutional rules. The difficulty in the latter endeavor, as public artist Krzysztof Wodiczko notes, is that "art in public places" can become "liberal urban decoration" if it finds itself unable to engage in "a critical dialogue with state and real estate architecture." [12]

Wodiczko's work is an interesting illustration of the issues involved in large-scale institutional collaborations. Known for his gigantic slide projections on urban monuments, Wodiczko often situates his work at the interface between authorized and unauthorized forms of institutional collaboration; in one instance, during the height of Apartheid, Wodiczko temporarily repositioned a slide projector from one of his legitimate works — images of hands projected onto Nelson's Column in London's Trafalgar Square — to project a swastika onto the South African embassy. The piece existed for only two hours, although it was a highly publicized covert action, immortalized in postcards printed after the event.[13] Such opportunities are rare, however, and when questioned about how to reconcile "interventions that are almost guerilla acts [with] the necessity of working with bureaucracies," Wodiczko ultimately argues for political public art strategies that "engage bureaucracy and still retain flexibility . . . work with people who also want to act in the public domain . . . [and] coordinate different negotiations with institutions and agencies." [14] TWCDC was able to accomplish such negotiations through the creative use of existing channels of collaboration, entering into a temporary and tactical relationship with Metro Channel as an advertiser.

The implications of the reliance on small-scale actions and institutional support are fully extended in the second parable of public video art I want to relate, a public video installation designed, unlike TWCDC's "insertion," as a *permanent* architectural feature of a particular urban environment. This one might be seen, by most accounts, as having "failed" in its attempt to politicize its environment. It rarely ever "aired" within the space for which it was designed, and the artist who made it has subsequently disowned the work entirely, refusing to discuss it publicly. I want to revisit this well-known "folly" in the history of public video art because failure has such a high heuristic value. Indeed, in many ways it teaches us more about the political challenges than TWCDC's sponsorship-based institutional work. As I will explain, Birnbaum's installation allows us to look very closely at how the production of space, time, and imagery in a televisual environment derives from dynamic and often unpredictable processes of place. The piece provides rich material for expanding how we think about video art and video-based architecture as public art. But to do so we must focus not so much on what its makers *wanted* it to do, as we did with TWCDC, and more on what it actually *did*. For the history of this particular TV screen and its environment tells us a great deal about the social geography of media. Even in its failure, I want to suggest, activist video art can, under specific local circumstances, serve larger goals of social change and critical practice in everyday spaces.

A Screen, a Mall, a Place: Rio Videowall

In 1989 an Atlanta real estate developer named Charles Ackerman sponsored a national competition to find a video artist to design and construct a video sculpture for a shopping mall. The jury, composed of local arts administrators and representatives of nonprofit art groups, selected as its finalist Dara Birnbaum, a well-known New York artist.[15] The mall was a highly publicized attempt to "vitalize" a poor, undeveloped area of the city located immediately adjacent to the downtown areas. It was scheduled for construction on an empty piece of land that had been razed during processes of urban renewal in the 1970s. Ackerman bought the land from a development firm called Central Atlanta Progress (CAP), which owned a large portion of this poor inner-city neighborhood called "midtown." Because of its proximity to downtown, this neighborhood represented a prime opportunity for profitable development. CAP's long-term goal for midtown was to transform it into both a corporate business district and a location for "much-needed upper- and middle-income housing,"[16] and several major corporate and residential construction projects with this goal in mind were underway in the area during this period.[17] Ackerman visualized the shopping mall, which he named Rio (perhaps in reference to the hit Duran Duran song), as a "postmodern town square" that could help make midtown development goals a reality.[18] This visionary image was embodied in the mall's futuristic aesthetic; designed by the Miami firm Arquitectonica (a firm responsible for many of the buildings in the opening credits of *Miami Vice*), the site was conceived as a festive, entertainment environment for the hordes of young urban professionals predicted to move into the area at any moment.

Rio was planned as an open, atrium-like structure, although it was crammed with at least one too many idiosyncratic design elements. In addition to the video, these included a perisphere, a glass elevator linking the mall's two levels, and a reflecting pool dotted with brass frogs. Birnbaum's work was to be the visual centerpiece of the mall's spectacular space. The installation she proposed was a video wall consisting of twenty-five monitors arranged in a square matrix. For Ackerman this massive structure was ideal because it could replace the anchor department store as an "attraction" that would draw visitors to the mall.[19] But for Birnbaum, the piece was a complex system of interactive, "live" image manipulation that made a political statement about the geographic instability and multiplicity of everyday experience in consumerism's visual culture.

What Ackerman may not have been aware of was the fact that the video wall's complex production of space was in some sense a subtle *critique* of the land-use politics of shopping mall development and, more generally, of the televisual idea of malls as vanguard, mediatized spaces. The twenty-five screens used sophisticated computer circuitry to display layers of imagery from two sources: live news from the Atlanta-based Cable News Network (CNN) and footage showing the site before the mall was built (a grass slope sparsely dotted with trees). These image sources would be made to interact with each other through a random process determined by the movement of shoppers throughout the mall. Whenever a shopper entered the visual field of one of several surveillance cameras dotted about the space, a computer-based keying system would digitize his or her image as a silhouette and use it as an electronic video matte, layering one image source (e.g., CNN) over another (e.g., the landscape) on the large video screen. The result might be an image of a pastoral scene in which human shaped keyholes regularly appeared and opened up a patchy view of the world of a CNN broadcast, or vice versa.

As part of a place named after another place, *Rio Videowall* foregrounded the disparate spatial scales on which everyday human activities like shopping unfold. When I first read about this installation, I was impressed by its complexity as a piece of art and activism, particularly the way in which the video wall's presence implicated the space of the mall within local and global economic processes of capitalism. Its images of the lost landscape produced a *chorographic* sense of the mall as a place,

FIG. 46

Rio Videowall, designed by Dara Birnbaum for an Atlanta shopping mall, mixed live CNN broadcasts with video images of the land on which the mall was built. The collage effect was triggered by hidden cameras that captured images of passersby as silhouettes in which one or another of these two video sources appeared.

that is, a sense of the mall as located on a particular, unique point on the earth. Indeed it seemed to offer images of this destroyed landscape as the repressed other of the omnipresent mutterings of the "global" CNN newscast. It linked and likened the physical space of the mall to the generalized abstractions of TV's continual information flows and cycles, using the body of the consumer as the point of this articulation. The installation thus visually and architecturally positioned its consuming spectator as the threshold where different layers of spatial experience collide. In so doing it ironized the eternal present of TV news, diminishing the latter's pretensions to realness, liveness, and immediacy with the more "live," more "real-time," more "present-tense" image of the shopper in the mall.

Yet the piece's intense, kaleidoscopic use of multiple image sources did not just replicate commonsense geographical notions of global generality and local specificity. It also deconstructed them. In transforming the specificity of the lost landscape into a set of images on a screen, Birnbaum called the "truth" of this landscape into question. This lackluster plot of ground could be anywhere; how would one know whether these images really showed the "actual" site or some other "generic" urban patch of grass? Similarly, the fact that the video wall's "global" media network, CNN, was a local economic institution employing a large sector of Atlanta's professional class would serve as a reminder, as Birnbaum noted in her proposal, that "instantaneous, of the moment, broadcast information" always originates from somewhere.[20] The piece thus seemed to embody geographically oriented media theory, tracing the complexity of presence and absence, liveness and recording, locality and placelessness, memory and forgetting in the human activities of the everyday built environment. In this respect, as I read about the piece from afar, I felt that it was designed to reveal Rio's complexity as a *place* in the sense of the term proposed by Doreen Massey: not a romantic, timeless sense of communal, ecological belonging but rather a dynamic expression of general space-time relations on all scales as they appear in one particular physical site. I looked forward to visiting Atlanta and experiencing this work in person.

When I planned my trip, I was aware from reading Birnbaum's account of the planning stage that the force of *Rio Videowall*'s spatial critique had been somewhat diminished by the difficulties of partnerships between art and commerce, but I did not anticipate exactly what these complications would be. I already knew that tensions had arisen over commercial imagery; Birnbaum, as an artist, not unreasonably considered the entire video installation to be a piece of art rather than an element in Rio's larger commercial structure. The wall, as she envisioned it, would be "neither aggressive nor flashy, but elegant and restful, an oasis amid commerce." [21] Ackerman, on the other hand, held that the video wall was the property of the mall and could be used for displaying other images, such as commercials and sports broadcasts. After a bitter negotiation Birnbaum and Ackerman finally agreed that the installation would function the way that she had designed it for "24-hours... per six-day week during Rio's normal operating hours for seven years." [22]

But these tensions between art and commerce were accompanied by some less easily anticipated tensions, and these were perhaps less easily resolved. One rather vexed contradiction in particular lay in the basic conditions underlying the conceptualization of the piece, specifically, its site-specific deconstruction of the complex geographies of contemporary consumer culture. This was the fact that in order for the video to represent the complexity of consumerism's global-local matrices, the space needed to be populated by throngs of shoppers continually passing in front of the hidden cameras located throughout the space. The success of the video's *critique* of commerce depended, in other words, on the success of the commerce all around it. In the absence of shoppers the critique could not be performed and the screen became nothing more than video wallpaper.

The extent of the video wall's dependency on the survival of the thing it sought to undermine was forcefully conveyed during a visit I paid to Rio in 1993. As I discovered, the material history of the place had shaped the meaning, and the signifying power, of the video screen installed at its center in profound ways. However, it did so in a manner that neither Birnbaum nor Ackerman—nor I, unfamiliar with the geography of the city of Atlanta—could have foreseen. Around 11 A.M. on a sunny Saturday in March, a time when one might expect to encounter throngs of shoppers in an outdoor mall, the open atrium mall was almost completely empty. The video wall was blank and dark, surrounded by stacked plastic chairs and tables. It was not the centerpiece of the mall as much as it was the centerpiece of Hoops, the outdoor bar nearby; like most TV sets in bars, it was probably often used to screen sports. From the large speakers attached to the screen, the sound of Black Entertainment Television (BET) echoed throughout the plaza. The stores were, for the most part, deserted shells with "For Lease" signs in the windows. The only businesses were two take-out food places, a gym, a vitamin store, and the bar. Of these, all save the gym were closed. In short, Rio was crumbling. Despite its Mondrian-esque postmodern architecture, its perisphere, and its surreal procession

FIG. 47

In 1993 I visited Rio expecting to find the video wall dominating the place. I discovered instead that the screen (on the right) was being used by a sports bar and that the mall was slowly going out of business. The place, it seems, had come to dominate the video wall.

of plump brass frogs marching in military formation across the reflecting pool, the mall looked like a failed investment. If Rio was any indication, the dream of a gentrified midtown Atlanta was now a developer's nightmare. And indeed, shortly after my visit the mall company filed for bankruptcy. Birnbaum's attempt to expose the spatial forms of contemporary retailing had been undermined by the very forces it sought to bring to its spectator's awareness.

Yet from another perspective the mall was quite a "success," albeit a kind of success that Birnbaum had not anticipated in her design. Rio may have failed to attract yuppies to the area, but when Rio was purchased later that year by Walter Davis, an Atlanta entrepreneur, it became a black business and cultural center: an art gallery devoted to African American artists moved in, as did a dance studio that served as a performance space for Kwanzaa celebrations, local theater productions, community-oriented festivals, and United Negro College Fund benefits.[23] Hoops was bought by a local African American radio personality, Youngblood, and renamed Youngbloods. The bar then became the site of an extremely popular live remote radio broadcast on the station at which Youngblood worked. Hosted by Melissa Sumers, a disk jockey known as "Atlanta's Girlfriend," the broadcast drew hundreds of black women fans to the mall on Thursdays.[24] In all of this it is possible that the video wall might have taken on a rejuvenated role in the mall's public space. It certainly provided Youngbloods patrons with a source of entertainment. However, the mall's management company told me in an interview that it gradually stopped working, its circuitry deteriorating through exposure to the elements over the years.[25] Sumers's popularity conveys how much radio seems today to be a more extensive space of black local representation than video or television. The success of the mall as a place for community gathering, indeed, seemed to have nothing whatsoever to do with the video wall. None of the employees at the mall with whom I spoke in the final year of Rio particularly lamented its passing.

The video wall's irrelevance in relation to the cultural context of Rio after 1993 suggests that Birnbaum's concern for the sense of the "place" destroyed by the mall, although admirable, was in an important sense incomplete. For this concern was rooted in a pastoral ideal of the lost natural landscape, and this ideal only obscured the fact that the small green space destroyed by Rio existed because of a prior destruction: that of an inner-city black neighborhood ravaged by urban renewal. Moreover, one might even argue that Birnbaum's use of closed-circuit video to critique commercial culture overlooked certain aspects of inner-city racial politics. After all, the surveillance cameras she placed around the mall implicated the installation in a racialized visual discourse of crime and visibility. At the same time, these cameras, although they positioned mall visitors as subjects of retailing's anti-theft panopticon, also worked to remove racial specificity from the scene of representation, as their role in the installation was to transform shoppers into silhouettes. This transformation of the "real" subject of the camera's gaze into a digitized, featureless outline erased all signs of race and other forms of human specificity. It emptied out identity and installed a standardized, abstracted subjectivity in its place, making the consumer and his or her particularity into a disembodied trace flitting across a screen.

Perhaps because of its permanence within a particular social space, *Rio Videowall* encountered difficulties that Cox and TWCDC's public video action avoided by attempting a less ambitiously site- and *viewer*-specific intervention. Birnbaum's admirable attempt to involve the actual spectator so closely and directly did not take into account the historical specificity of that spectator. Its critique of commercial culture could not help but reduce the consumer to a one-dimensional, faceless thing—enacting, rather than revealing, his or her "reification." *Rio Videowall* used the playfulness of an interactive, real-time image to indict, in some sense, an imagined consumer.

Yet ultimately Birnbaum's piece escapes the charges we might want to bring against it in the court of political and aesthetic "correctness." Its history and the history of the mall, so different from what Ackerman and Birnbaum first envisioned, indicates the strength of *place* and its material processes as forces that operate on the screen. When I visited Rio, early in the conceptualization of the research that would eventually become this book, I expected to find that its monumental video screen had shaped the character of the location. I was prepared to write about it as a signifying force that overpowered its context, forcing the subject's attention on its images instead of real life. But I learned a lot more when I discovered that the video's context—indeed, the local economic context that Birnbaum sought on some level to critique—turned out to be far more overpowering than its images. This encounter with Rio in 1993 was the first time I felt the possibility that place-based, site-specific video installation, whether commercial or "oppositional," can be far more shaped *by* the space it inhabits than it is capable of shaping the place itself.

Indeed, although Birnbaum and Ackerman neglected urban spatial-racial issues in their construction of Rio as a video place, the mall seems to have had a role in ameliorating to some extent the devastating effects of racialized urban geographies of development. Rio's failure as a postmodern agora for white yuppies was an opportunity for black entrepreneurial and cultural spheres to develop there instead. Rio did not literally rebuild neighborhood ties—who knows whether the people who patronized its businesses came from the midtown district or from elsewhere?—but it did help to restore some of the cultural life of the neighborhood that was flattened by the urban renewal bulldozer in the 1970s. Yet at the same time, the material processes of place are too dynamic to allow us to maintain a very optimistic view of commercial places as sites of cultural sustainability. At the time of this writing Rio no longer plays a role in Atlanta's black public cultures. Bought by a national urban development company, it was demolished by its new owners in July 2000. In its place they plan to erect an apartment complex with some retail outlets—a grocery store, a dry cleaner's, a video store.[26] The new purchasers sought substantial tax credit for this development, requesting that the area be zoned a "mixed use residential/commercial enterprise zone"—a category of federal aid for inner-city development.[27] The fact that they did so is revealing because it communicates how much the new owners saw the site as *un*developed. Rio clearly was a site of enterprise already, in part because of the sponsorship of prominent African American Atlantans, like comedian Chris Tucker who had recently started a comedy club in the mall. The request was denied, but the owner's decision to raze the site only underscores how uncommunitarian corporate goals can be articulated via inner-city development policies in the United States.

Rio was designed as a pomo rococo heaven, a place perhaps existing *outside of* history; it became important for a brief time in black metropolitan culture, but in the end it could not escape the economic forces of capital embodied in urban development. *Rio Videowall* is thus perhaps most instructive as a sign of the mall's history; over time, as a permanent architectural feature, the video screen bore witness to the everyday processes and the economic geography of its location. Gradually it corroded and became a decrepit eyesore like the rusted and battered aluminum siding that encased the mall's grimly festive exterior in faded pastels. A representative of the mall's management company told me that junk dealers regularly offer the company cash for the video wall. The mall's dated architecture, its crumbling video wall, its tarnished frogs signal its location just to the side of the networks of global economic flows that, according to Manuel Castells, run through the "global city." Rio thus calls our attention to the way that a logic of uneven development guides contemporary urban capitalism.[28] It forces us to remember that Atlanta, like other global cities is, "globally connected and locally disconnected" (404). As a battered monument to postmodernity, *Rio Videowall* embodied the unstable relationship between places and flows in contemporary geographies of capital, and its history allows us to scrutinize the terms in which we envision this relationship manifested in everyday spaces. It is tempting to think about the immediate built environment as a sign of larger-scale "spatial dominants." Numerous critics have interpreted postmodern architectural forms, of which Rio might be seen as an everyday, unremarkable version, as reflections of the wider spatial "logics" of contemporary capitalism and its crises. The value of reading "failed" sites like Rio, I think, is the way they resist the idealism in this mode of reading, showing instead how spaces that seemed to step outside of history in their exhibitionist attempts to rewrite it always weather and become history themselves.

Castells argues that "architecture and design, because their forms either resist or interpret the abstract materiality of the dominant space of flows, could become essential devices of cultural innovation and intellectual autonomy in the informational society" (423). But *Rio Videowall* is an architectural artifact that complicates this schema of "resistant" or "interpretive" form. It does so not simply because it reveals the tensions involved in making political art in a partnership with business interests but because it reveals how difficult it is to sustain a vision of the built environment as a singular and unchanging reflection of the "spatial dominant." Depending on whether we focus on *Rio Videowall*'s "theory" of space and place or on its history as part of a particular geography, the artwork "interprets" the global city's space of flows for us in very different ways. Is the mall's position within the network logic of the global city more forcefully conveyed by the *concept* of *Rio Videowall* or by what happened to this concept when it hit history and "real life"? If Rio had succeeded in its goal of producing a revitalized midtown—if the material passage of time had somehow *not* disarmed the video's critique nor subjected it to unforeseen spatial processes—would it have been more or less incisive as a revealing forced perspective on the multiscale flows of images and capital in the global city? If Rio had been a success, would its video intervention have been more, or less, revolutionary than the short-term intervention of TWCDC?

These questions have no answers. But this is precisely what makes them useful tools for thinking about the television console as a spatial apparatus through which power circulates *locally* as well as "globally," particularly in public places. For they reveal that TV's discursive effects are neither absolute nor predictable on this level and that TV is as subject to change as the histories and places, bodies and dollars that constitute its environment. They also alert us to the value of video as a form of public art. Video installation in museums and galleries, as Margaret Morse has noted, is a kinetic art of the body that sets "the mediated built environment into play for purposes of reflection." [29] But when video installation enters public places of transit and exchange, it can activate spatial operations that expand to proportions wider than the primarily bodily experience Morse highlights. In retail, transit, and other mundane spaces it can engage the mediated politics of work and leisure in effective ways. Such locations do not conceal forms of commerce and massification as sites like museums and galleries often do, and within them, the screen can be a way of rewriting relations of spectatorship and everyday life on the microlevel, introducing an activist sense of *contact* between the mobile bodily circuits of public persons and abstract forces of social power — in ways both predictable and unpredictable, as we have seen. Each of the two public video installations I have examined here attempted to connect the phenomenological experience of the viewer with other places and social relationships outside the place of viewing and to ask him or her to think about the social conditions in which this relationship is produced.

This complicates the work of cultural critics, who must assess public art's didactic orientations toward the public sphere. These installations are hard to evaluate outside of their changing, localized, and embodied everyday contexts. In this respect they communicate the need for a complex notion of "site" among those who *write* about public video installations, as well as among those who construct them. As Miwon Kwon points out, new, "unhinged" definitions of *site* have emerged in public art, definitions that can include *metaphorical* spaces, like "ethnic history" or institutional practices, and that are not necessarily fixed in place: "While site-specific art once defied commodification by insisting on immobility, it now seems to espouse fluid mobility and nomadism for the same purpose. But curiously, the nomadic principle also defines capital and power in our times. Is the unhinging of site-specificity . . . a form of resistance to the ideological establishment of art or a capitulation to the logic of capitalist expansion?" [30] This is an excellent question, although its categorical "either/or" phrasing anticipates a yes or no answer when the contingency of site seems to insist against this possibility. Taken together, these two very different forms of public video suggest that the politics of place must shape the answers we give to such questions. Criticism, as well as art production, must be site-specific too. When W. J. T. Mitchell proposes that "Utopia and contradiction are not alternative functions of public art, but different ways of describing its actual marginality . . . while indicating its imagined centrality and possibility as a site for critical performance" he lays the groundwork for such a possibility.[31] For this suggests, I would argue, that the categories we use to approach and pigeonhole public art, like "resistance" or "capitulation" cannot be rendered in absolute terms but must always be seen as contingent upon the spatial politics of the particular places in which the art sits.

On a larger scale we must note that Mitchell's words might just as easily apply to nonartistic or activist appearances of television in public space as well. The TV screen embodies all the political contradictions that come with art in public spaces, as well as those more particularly associated with television. As a public medium governed by private logics, as a private medium that comes to stand in for the public it addresses, as a private, domesticated possession that regularly appears in, and alters, public places, television spans utopia and critique as it brings modes of spectatorship into the illegible terrain of the everyday. These video installations by TWCDC and by Birnbaum, involving TV's commercial logics in a dialogue with radical alternatives to consumerism, end this book by providing us with provocative and instructive inkblots not for thinking about how to *begin* making rapprochements between utopian and critical ideas about TV, social change, and public space but for recognizing and exploiting how much these rapprochements are already available in the spaces of everyday life. This means taking seriously the site-specific power relations that become visible in ambient television installations. Only then can we devise policies, programs, and practices that develop the ideas about sociality and collectivity that TV's presence in such places raises.

NOTES

Introduction: The Public Lives of TV

1 See Miwon Kwon, "One Place after Another: Notes on Site-Specificity," *October* 80 (spring 1997): 85–110. See also the special issue of *Documents* 4/5 (spring 1994), for a variety of perspectives on site-specificity.

2 For a history of this discourse see Lynn Spigel, *Make Room for TV: Television and the Family Ideal in Postwar America* (Chicago: University of Chicago Press, 1992). For its role in contemporary constructions of (inter)national community see David Morley and Kevin Robins, *Spaces of Identity: Global Media, Electronic Landscapes, and Cultural Boundaries* (New York: Routledge, 1995).

3 Two compelling accounts of the image architectures, and gendered discourses, in which this mobile modern spectator is formed are Beatriz Colomina, *Privacy and Publicity: Modern Architecture as Mass Media* (Cambridge, Mass.: MIT Press, 1994), and Anne Friedberg, *Window Shopping: Cinema and the Postmodern* (Berkeley: University of California Press, 1993).

4 See Adam Hochschild, "Taken Hostage at the Airport," *New York Times,* October 26, 1996, 25; Cheryl Jackson, "Firms Can't Wait to Make Their Pitch," *Tampa Tribune,* January 4, 1997, C1. See also Colin Campbell, "Changes Afoot in TV Babble at Hartsfield," *Atlanta Journal-Constitution,* April 3, 1997, 1B; Colin Campbell, "Why Monopoly on Cacophony?" *Atlanta Journal-Constitution,* March 18, 1997, 1C. These critics employ contradictory notions of privacy and publicity in their assessments of TV in public space. On the one hand, it would seem, television "privatizes" public space, but on the other, TV's role in public space is the *invasion of* privacy. If TV can be the agent of both privatization and its destruction, a wrecker of both public life *and* privacy, of both community *and* individuality, then clearly it is a highly elastic phenomenon! For an incisive use of the concept of privatized public space within the framework of political economy see Armand Mattelart, *Advertising International: the Privatization of Public Space,* trans. Michael Chanan (New York: Routledge, 1991).

5 Movies from *A Face in the Crowd* to *The Truman Show* are part of a long tradition of critical diatribes against media "effects," diatribes that might cynically be interpreted as a "safe" form of movie politics given that anti-TV rhetoric is prevalent both on the right and the left.

6 Michael Sorkin, introduction to *Variations on a Theme Park: The New American City and the End of Public Space,* ed. Michael Sorkin (New York: Hill and Wang, 1992). I have collected numerous other uses of this metaphor in architectural and urbanist discourse. Some of the more extended explorations of the comparison between new urban space and television may be found in the following: Kent McDonald, "The Commercial Strip: From Main Street to Television Road," *Landscape* 28, no. 2 (1985): 12–19; Ada Louise Huxtable, *The Unreal America: Architecture and Illusion* (New York: New Press, 1997); Neil Leach, *The Anaesthetics of Architecture* (Cambridge, Mass.: MIT Press, 1999). From more or less considered perspectives these authors criticize contemporary public space because it resembles television's illusionistic productions. But there are notable exceptions to this generally condemnatory discourse, although they are not necessarily in agreement with each other about architectural aesthetics. These include Beatriz Colomina's *Privacy and Publicity,* and Robert Venturi, *Iconography and Electronics: Upon a Generic Architecture—A View from the Drafting Room* (Cambridge, Mass.: MIT Press, 1996). Margaret Morse's essay "An Ontology of Everyday Distraction: The Freeway, the Mall, and Television" also offers a more complicated view, although it does rest, ultimately, on an equation of shopping malls with sameness and "derealization" that echoes the conservative architectural ideologies addressed here. See Margaret Morse, "An Ontology of Everyday Distraction: The Freeway, the Mall, and Television," in *Logics of Television,* ed. Patricia Mellencamp (Bloomington: Indiana University Press, 1990), 193–221.

7 "Totalizing" denunciations of television as an instrument of spatial desecration are, I think, superficial gambits rather than analytical pathways, not least because, as a recent book on written signs in antebellum New York demonstrates incisively, almost identical debates were waged around the question of posters and newspapers over a century ago (to say nothing of more recent debates over billboards and other co-optations of public space with advertising). David Henkins, *City Reading: Written Words and Public Spaces in Antebellum New York* (New York: Columbia University Press, 1998). Similarly, as Michele Bogart has shown, debates over the privatization of space via billboards throw the twentieth century's ongoing uncertainties about the distinction between advertising and art into sharp relief. See Michele H. Bogart, *Artists, Advertising, and the Borders of Art* (Chicago: University of Chicago Press, 1995), 89–103. The cautionary lesson contained in this long history of anxieties about the desecration of public space is that activist rhetorics defending the city and its inhabitants from advertising can sound surprisingly like conservative indictments of the urban visual culture's aesthetic eclecticism. Much of the current public protest against TV's public presence is currently pitched in these terms, but as I will suggest in chapter 3, the politics of out-of-home TV might be more effectively communicated by activist work that calls attention to the economic relations through which users of public places become audience commodities. Simply denouncing urban consumer spectacle in the name of the individual's rights to an advertising-free space does little to address the key structural role assigned to the viewer within the political economy of "out-of-home advertising."

8 Jonathan Meades, "Eating Out," *Sunday Times Magazine,* December 20, 1997, 33.

9 For different articulations of the idea that places like shopping malls are all the same,

and thus "nonplaces," see Marc Auge, *Non-Places: Toward an Anthropology of Super-Modernity,* trans. John Howe (New York: Verso, 1995); James Howard Kunstler, *The Geography of Nowhere* (New York: Touchstone, 1993). Morse, in "An Ontology of Everyday Distraction," offers the most nuanced account, one that takes materiality into account, when she proposes, "Nonspace is ground within which communication as a flow of values among and between two and three dimensions and between virtuality and actuality—indeed, an uncanny oscillation between life and death—can 'take place'" (196). For critiques of the idea of malls as identical nonspaces see Meaghan Morris's "Things to Do with Shopping Centres," in *Too Soon Too Late: History in Popular Culture* (Bloomington: Indiana University Press, 1998); Marianne Conroy, "Discount Dreams: Factory Outlet Malls, Consumption, and the Performance of Middle-Class Identity," *Social Text 54* 16, no. 1 (1998): 63–83; and Grady Clay, *Real Places: An Unconventional Guide to America's Generic Landscape* (Chicago: University of Chicago Press, 1994).

10 On the urban development ideals of Harborplace see David Harvey, *The Condition of Postmodernity* (Cambridge, Mass.: Blackwell, 1989), 88–93. For a good model of spatial reading that articulates relationships between urban planning and forms of labor and consumption within particular sites see John Urry, *Consuming Places* (New York: Routledge, 1995).

11 Morris, "Things to Do," 91.

12 Alice Kaplan and Kristen Ross, introduction to *Yale French Studies* 73 (1987): 4. See also Toby Miller, *Technologies of Truth: Cultural Citizenship and the Popular Media* (Minneapolis: University of Minnesota Press, 1998), 57.

13 Paul Gessell, "Parties and Protests Greet Ellen's Coming Out: April 30 Is L-Day across North America, and Ottawa Is No Exception," *Ottawa Citizen,* April 16, 1997, A1.

14 Joan Ryan, "As Gay as He Wants to Be: How Rodman's Drag Queen Style Plays in the Castro," *San Francisco Chronicle,* June 6, 1996, A1.

15 See "The Simpson Verdict," *Providence Journal-Bulletin,* October 4, 1995, 6A; Deneen L. Brown and Nancy Lewis, "Some Riveted, Others Revolted," *Washington Post,* January 12, 1995, A14.

16 Toby Miller and Alec McHoul, *Popular Culture and Everyday Life* (London: Sage, 1998), 26–27.

17 Neil Smith, "Contours of a Spatialized Politics: Homeless Vehicles and the Production of Geographic Scale," *Social Text* 33 (1992): 62.

18 Ibid., 66.

19 On the role of property in the public sphere see Jürgen Habermas, *The Structural Transformation of the Public Sphere: An Inquiry into a Category of Bourgeois Society,* trans. Thomas Burger (Cambridge, Mass: MIT Press, 1989). For an application of these ideas to public space see P. Howell, "Public Space and the Public Sphere: Political Theory and the Historical Geography of Modernity," *Environment and Planning D: Society and Space* 11 (1993): 303–322. On the uses of consumption as a form of minoritarian visibility in the public sphere, see Bruce Robbins, "Introduction: The Public as Phantom" in *The Phantom Public Sphere,* ed. Bruce Robbins (Minneapolis: University of Minnesota Press, 1993), vii–xxvii.

20 On the debate between cultural studies and political economy see Lawrence Gross-

berg, "Cultural Studies vs. Political Economy: Is Anyone Else Bored with This Debate?" *Critical Studies in Mass Communication* 12, no. 1 (1995): 72–81; Nicholas Garnham, "Political Economy and Cultural Studies: Reconciliation or Divorce?" *Critical
Studies in Mass Communication* 12, no. 1 (1995): 62–71, and "Reply to Grossberg and
Carey," *Critical Studies in Mass Communication* 12, no. 1 (1995): 95–100.

21 John Hartley, *The Politics of Pictures* (London: Routledge, 1992), 110.

22 Luce Giard, in *The Practice of Everyday Life, Vol 2: Eating and Cooking,* ed. Michel
de Certeau, Luce Giard, and Olivier Meyrol (Minneapolis: University of Minnesota
Press, 1998), xxiii.

23 In a well-known passage from *The Practice of Everyday Life* de Certeau writes that "a
strategy assumes a place that can be circumscribed as proper . . . and thus serve as the
basis for generating relations with an exterior distinct from it (competitors, adversaries, 'clienteles,' 'targets,' or objects of research). . . . [It is] a spatial or institutional
localization. . . . On the contrary, because it does not have a place, a tactic depends on
time — it is always on the watch for opportunities that must be seized 'on the wing.' "
Michel de Certeau, *Practice of Everyday Life* (Berkeley: University of California Press,
1984), xix.

24 Tony Bennett offers an extensive critique of the tactics/strategies binary in *Culture:
A Reformer's Science* (London: Sage, 1998).

25 Patricia Mellencamp, *High Anxiety: Catastrophe, Scandal, Age, and Comedy* (Bloomington: Indiana University Press, 1992), xi.

26 For a similar use of television as a way of avoiding social space see Herman Bausinger,
"Media, Technology, and Daily Life," *Media, Culture, and Society* 6, no. 4 (1984): 343–
351, a study treated extensively by Ien Ang, with Joke Hermes, in *Living Room Wars:
Rethinking Media Audiences for a Postmodern World* (New York: Routledge, 1996),
109–110.

27 "TV Screens Turn Blue at Don Muang," *Bangkok Post,* August 17, 1999, n.p.

28 There may be an epidemic underway: other reports of guerilla actions involving hard-
core porn on transit zone TV sets are starting to come in. In February of 1999, according to *Variety,* "travellers on the Cairo subway recently got an eyeful when the
closed-circuit TV sets on station platforms suddenly started showing porn films instead of the usual array of soap and soft-drink ads." Peter Warg, "Commuters Red
over Blue Flicks," *Variety,* February 22–28, 1999, 168.

29 This is reminiscent of the 1994 protests against the Commuter Channel in Boston, in
which a group calling themselves the "guerilla girls" plastered stickers denouncing
the network all over the MBTA stations.

30 On the space-altering qualities of TV liveness see Mark Williams, "History in a Flash:
Notes on the Myth of TV 'Liveness,' " in *Collecting Visible Evidence,* ed. Jane Gaines
and Michael Renov (Minneapolis: University of Minnesota Press, 1999), 292–312;
Mimi White, "Site Unseen: CNN's *War in the Gulf*," in *Seeing through the Media: The
Persian Gulf War,* ed. Lauren Rabinovitz and Susan Jeffords (New Brunswick, N.J.:
Rutgers University Press, 1994), 121–141; Samuel Weber, *Mass Mediauras: Form, Tech-
nics, Media* (Palo Alto, Calif.: Stanford University Press, 1996); Mary Ann Doane,
"Information, Crisis, Catastrophe," in *Logics of Television,* ed. Patricia Mellencamp
(Bloomington: Indiana University Press, 1991); and Daniel Dayan and Elihu Katz,

Media Events: The Live Broadcasting of History (Cambridge, Mass.: Harvard University Press, 1992).

31   Spigel, *Make Room for TV,* 138–140. On the economic value of these ideas, see William Boddy, *Fifties Television: The Industry and Its Critics* (Urbana: University of Illinois Press, 1990), 20–21.

32   Weber, *Mass Mediauras,* 117.

33   Crucial insights on the range of domestic uses of television across divergent cultural and national contexts may be found in the following: Bausinger, "Media, Technology, and Daily Life"; Nick Browne, "The Political Economy of the Television (Super) Text," in *Television: The Critical View,* ed. Horace Newcomb (New York: Oxford, 1987); Charlotte Brunsdon, "Satellite Dishes and the Landscapes of Taste," in *The Audience and Its Landscape,* ed. James Hay, Lawrence Grossberg, and Ellen Wartella (New York: Westview Press, 1996); Marie Gillespie, "Sacred Serials, Devotional Viewing, and Domestic Worship: A Case Study in the Interpretation of Two TV Versions of *The Mahabharata* in a Hindu Family in West London," in *To Be Continued: Soap Operas around the World,* ed. Robert C. Allen (New York: Routledge, 1995); Ann Gray, *Video Playtime: The Gendering of a Leisure Technology* (New York: Routledge, 1992); Mary Beth Haralovich, "Sitcoms and Suburbs," in *Private Screenings: Television and the Female Consumer,* ed. Lynn Spigel and Denise Mann (Minneapolis: University of Minnesota Press, 1992); Ondina Fachel Leal, "Popular Taste and Erudite Repertoire: The Place and Space of Television in Brazil," *Cultural Studies* 4, no. 1 (1990): 19–39; James Lull, *Inside Family Viewing: Ethnographic Research on Television Audiences* (New York: Routledge, 1990); Andrew P. Lyons, "The Television and the Shrine: Towards a Theoretical Model for the Study of Mass Communications in Nigeria," *Visual Anthropology* 3 (1990): 429–456; Tania Modleski, "The Search for Tomorrow in Today's Soap Operas," *Film Quarterly* 33, no. 1 (1979): 12–21; David Morley, *Family Television: Cultural Power and Domestic Leisure* (New York: Routledge, 1990); Andrea L. Press, *Women Watching Television: Gender, Class, and Generation in the American Television Experience* (Philadelphia: University of Pennsylvania Press, 1991); Roger Silverstone, *Television and Everyday Life* (New York: Routledge, 1994); Lynn Spigel, *Make Room for TV;* Raymond Williams, *Television: Technology and Cultural Form* (New York: Schocken Books, 1975); Barbie Zelizer, "From Home to Public Forum: Media Events and the Public Sphere," *Journal of Film and Video* 43, nos. 1/2 (1991): 69–79.

34   Bruno Latour, *We Have Never Been Modern* (Cambridge, Mass.: Harvard University Press, 1993), 117.

35   See, for example, Morley and Robins, *Spaces of Identity,* and the essays in Roger Silverstone and Eric Hirsch, eds., *Consuming Technologies: Media and Information in Domestic Spaces* (London: Routledge, 1992).

36   David Harvey, *Justice, Nature, and the Geography of Difference* (Cambridge, Mass.: Blackwell, 1996), 49.

37   Aihwa Ong, *Flexible Citizenship: The Cultural Logics of Transnationality* (Durham, N.C.: Duke University Press, 1999), 19.

38   Ibid., 50.

39   Samuel Weber attempts to unify these scales of analysis in a phenomenological con-

sideration of television's relation to place. However, he tends to ask primarily how television as a space-altering technology "takes place"; I ask, on the other hand, how "place" can at times "take" television. See Weber, *Mass Mediauras,* 108–128.

40 This important point is Jane Feuer's, in "The Concept of Live Television: Ontology as Ideology," in *Regarding Television: Critical Approaches—An Anthology,* ed. E. Ann Kaplan (Frederick, Md.: AFI/University Publications of America, 1983).

41 My thinking on this issue is informed by the important work of Kevin Robins and David Morley on the "Global-Local" nexus. See Morley and Robins, *Spaces of Identity.*

42 See, for example, ibid. In the American context see Victoria Johnson, "Citizen Welk: Bubbles, Blue Hair, and Middle America," in *The Revolution Wasn't Televised: Sixties Television and Social Conflict,* ed. Lynn Spigel and Michael Curtin (New York: Routledge, 1997), 265–286, and the essays in Mark Williams, ed., *Quarterly Review of Film and Video: Special Issue on Local Television* 16, nos. 3/4 (1999).

43 For an excellent account of the gender politics of global-local designations in critical cultural theory see Caren Kaplan, *Questions of Travel: Postmodern Discourses of Displacement* (Durham, N.C.: Duke University Press, 1996), esp. chap. 4.

44 J. Nicholas Entriken, *The Betweenness of Place* (Baltimore: Johns Hopkins University Press, 1991), 133.

45 Doreen Massey, *Space, Place and Gender* (Minneapolis: University of Minnesota Press, 1994), 5.

46 Harvey, *Geography of Difference,* 27.

47 Ibid.

48 Doreen Massey, "Power-Geometry and a Progressive Sense of Place," in *Mapping the Futures: Local Cultures, Global Change,* ed. Jon Bird et al. (New York: Routledge, 1993), 68.

49 Joshua Meyrowitz, *No Sense of Place: The Impact of Electronic Media on Social Behavior* (New York: Oxford University Press, 1985).

50 Entriken, *Betweenness of Place.* See also John Agnew, "Representing Space: Space, Scale, and Culture in Social Science," in *Place/Culture/Representation,* ed. James Duncan and David Ley (London: Routledge, 1993), 261–264.

51 The phrase "spatial stories" is lifted from a chapter title in de Certeau's *Practice of Everyday Life.* It seems appropriate given Entriken's proposal that narrative forms work to convey and preserve the betweenness of place, a practice perhaps exemplified in Raymond Williams's novels of Welsh village life and social change. For a reading of these novels as exemplars of the dialectics of place see Harvey, *Geography of Difference.*

52 Lawrence Grossberg, "The Cultural Studies' Crossroads Blues, or Doing Cultural Studies in Helms' Country," keynote address, Crossroads in Cultural Studies, Tampere, Finland, July 1996, MS page 3.

53 I shot thirty-five rolls of film over the course of this project. Most of the images were taken without a flash, using 800 or 1000 ASA film shot at the rather slow shutter speed of 1/60 of a second (to minimize the appearance of "scan lines" on the TV screen). Flashes tend to interfere with the natural lighting of a space, creating "hot spots" and, more important, obscuring the ways the screen itself serves as a source of illumination within an environment. It took me quite a while to arrive at this technique,

and many of the earliest pictures I took are too indistinct for publication (hence the drawings). My framing strategy was generally to capture as much of the space surrounding the screen as possible in each case. Occasionally I took a close-up as well as a long shot, although the majority of images selected for this book fall into the latter category because they convey more contextual information. In some cases the framing is a little odd and off-kilter because the image was taken "on the fly." As some readers may have discovered on their own, taking pictures in certain environments—like shopping malls—is not easy. Security guards often intervene, claiming that it is against store policy. (This does not mean that it is illegal.) The camera is sometimes best wielded covertly, often with a pretext such as photographing a friend. The bizarre framing of several images contained in the following chapters should also make clear the fact that although these photographs may be "documentary" (i.e., they are not staged or posed), they are certainly not pristine examples of an "objective" social-scientistic approach to the documentation of space. Ultimately, I am skeptical that this kind of documentation is ever possible.

54   A third nondomestic TV site much publicized after the war is theater television. For an account of theater TV's immediate postwar history see Douglas Gomery, "Failed Opportunities: The Integration of the U.S. Motion Picture and Television Industries," *Quarterly Review of Film Studies* 9, no. 3 (1984): 219–28, and "Theater Television: The Missing Link of Technological Change in the U.S. Motion Picture Industry," *Velvet Light Trap* 21 (1985): 54–61. For the history of its afterlife in sports exhibition see my essay, " 'Like an Earthquake': Theater Television, Boxing, and the Black Public Sphere," *Quarterly Review of Film and Video* 16, nos. 3/4 (1999): 307–23.

Chapter 1   TV, Class, and Social Control in the 1940s Neighborhood Tavern

1   See Lynn Spigel, *Make Room for TV,* 39–41.

2   Illustrations of this type were particularly prevalent in national newsmagazines. In addition to fig. 1 see the illustrations accompanying the following articles, "Television in the Tavern," *Newsweek,* June 16, 1947, 64; "Television's Audience Problem," *Business Week,* September 13, 1947, 70–71, 74–75.

3   This episode of *The Ed Wynn Show* aired on February 4, 1950, and is available from Shokus Video.

4   A note on the word *tavern:* According to American language historian Roy Copperud, the term became popular after prohibition as a way of avoiding the undesirable connotations of *saloon.* In the press it generally described a low-key, beer-serving, male-oriented, working-class neighborhood drinkery, offering its core of regulars a few amusements and perhaps some food. To a lesser extent the word also designated downtown bars frequented by businessmen; slippage between the two appears to stem from the fact that both catered to a regular, predominantly male, patronage and served primarily beer. Generally, though, *tavern* differentiated primarily neighborhood bars from other places where alcohol was consumed at the time. See Roy Copperud, *American Usage and Style: The Consensus* (New York: Van Nostrand Reinhold, 1980), 43; H. L. Mencken, *The American Language: An Enquiry into the Development of English in the United States. Supplement I* (New York: Knopf, 1945), 292,

267; "At the Knife and Fork," *New Yorker,* June 29, 1946, 16–17; Boyd E. Macrory, "The Tavern and the Community," *Quarterly Journal of Studies on Alcohol* 13, no. 4 (1952): 625.

5 "Television's Audience Problem," 70.

6 "Television in the Tavern," 64.

7 "TV — A Market in New York Now," *Sponsor,* March 1947, 49. Discussions of the need to reduce on-air references to bar viewers can be found in interdepartmental communication held in the TV Network Sales files, NBC Archive, State Historical Society of Wisconsin, Madison, Wis. In March of 1947 Chicago TV station WBKB reported that two thirds of its audience were customers of the 250 TV-equipped taverns in the city. Later that year, when there were seven thousand sets in the city, over half the audience watched in the eighteen hundred taverns with TV. In September *Business Week* reported that although only three thousand of the forty-three thousand sets in the New York metropolitan area were in bars, home and tavern audiences were roughly equivalent in size. See "Television's Audience Problem." See also "Barrooms with a View," *Time,* March 24, 1947, 63; "See It in Church," *Newsweek,* October 27, 1947, 82; "Chicago Now Has 11, 500 Video Sets," *Advertising Age,* January 19, 1948, 58.

8 I have come across display advertisements in the *Chicago Defender,* an African American weekly, that in 1948 promoted televised sports events as part of a lineup that might include jazz, comedy, and burlesque. The particular mention of sports acquires extra significance when one considers that Jackie Robinson, the first black major league baseball player, signed with the Dodgers the year before.

9 For two examples of the popular romanticization of the tavern see Earl Wilson, *I Am Gazing into My Eight Ball: Burning the Midnight Earl with New York's Famous Saloon Editor* (Garden City, N.Y.: Doubleday, Doran, 1945), and Patricia Bronson, *Vittles and Vice: An Extraordinary Guide to What's Cooking on Chicago's Near North Side* (Chicago: Henry Regnery, 1952).

10 "The New Medium . . . It's Now a Huge Going Concern," *Sponsor,* July 1948, 75.

11 "Sees Demand for Television Sets," *New York Times,* January 1, 1947, 43; "3-by-4-Foot Picture in U.S. Television Set," *New York Times,* March 27, 1948, 22; "Television in the Tavern," 64; Edward P. Morgan, "Fifty Mile Bleachers," *Colliers,* September 27, 1947, 30. An RCA projection system was the centerpiece in a New York bar, billed as "the first cocktail lounge devoted to television," that featured "special chairs equipped to hold drinks and sandwiches." "TV Cocktailery," *Variety,* April 6, 1949, 30.

12 Bernard Rosenberg, "New York Bar Signs," *Quarterly Journal of Studies on Alcohol* 8, no. 2 (1947): 351.

13 Macrory, "The Tavern and the Community," 634, 616.

14 On the saloon see Roy Rosenzweig, *Eight Hours for What We Will: Workers and Leisure in an Industrial City, 1870–1920* (New York: Cambridge University Press, 1983), 35–64, 93–126; Kathy Peiss, *Cheap Amusements: Working Women and Leisure in Turn of the Century New York* (Philadelphia: Temple University Press, 1986), 17–21; John M. Kingsdale, "The Poor Man's Club: Social Functions of the Urban Working Class Saloon," *American Quarterly* 25, no. 4 (1973): 472–89; Madelon Powers, "Decay from Within: The Inevitable Doom of the American Saloon," in *Drinking: Behavior and Belief in Modern History,* ed. Susanna Barrows and Robin Room (Berkeley: University

of California Press, 1991). For more on the tavern see David Gottlieb, "The Neighborhood Tavern and the Cocktail Lounge: A Study of Class Differences," *American Journal of Sociology* 62, no. 6 (1957): 559–562.

15 Rosenberg, "New York Bar Signs," 348.

16 Tavern patron, quoted in Macrory, "Tavern and the Community," 631.

17 Patron, quoted in ibid., 616.

18 Critical debate became unnecessary, Habermas argues, "when people went to the movies together, listened to the radio, or watched TV." Habermas, *Structural Transformation,* 163. For a critique of the reification of categories of public and private in bourgeois ideologies, a conceptual division that informs Habermas's theory of the public sphere, see Spigel, *Make Room for TV,* 100–101. See also Lora Romero, *Home Fronts* (Durham, N.C.: Duke University Press, 1997), as well as Cathy Davidson, ed., *No More Separate Spheres,* a special issue of *American Literature* 30, no. 3 (1998).

19 Kingsdale, "Poor Man's Club"; Rosenzweig, *Eight Hours,* 44, 58; Powers, "Decay from Within," 113; Gottlieb, "Neighborhood Tavern," 560; Macrory, "Tavern and the Community," 628.

20 Macrory, "Tavern and the Community," 630.

21 On the visual interior of the saloon see Rosenzweig, *Eight Hours;* see also Kingsdale, "Poor Man's Club," and Powers, "Decay from Within."

22 Rosenzweig, *Eight Hours,* 1–5, 222–228.

23 "Believe It or Not . . . You're in Show Business," *Beverage Media,* June 1947, 53.

24 Walter Benjamin, "The Work of Art in the Age of Mechanical Reproduction" in *Illuminations* (New York: Schocken Books, 1977), 236.

25 For contemporary versions of this lament see chap. 3. For a summary of anxieties about TV as intruder in domestic space see Spigel, *Make Room for TV,* 57.

26 Orrin Dunlap, *The Future of Television* (New York: Harper and Brothers, 1947), 56.

27 Morgan, "Fifty Mile Bleachers," 30; Sophie Ziencek, interviewed by author, Chicago, September 19, 1993.

28 Morgan, "Fifty Mile Bleachers," 30; Ziencek, interview; Joe Danno, interviewed by author, Chicago, October 19, 1993.

29 "Knife and Fork," 17.

30 Ibid.

31 Morgan, "Fifty Mile Bleachers," 30.

32 Spigel, *Make Room for TV,* 108.

33 "It's Like Working at the Mint," *Beverage Media,* June 1947, 59.

34 Advertisement, "Give them Better Television," *Beverage Media,* March 1947, 79.

35 See Macrory, "Tavern and the Community."

36 The "masculine domesticity" Lynn Spigel discerns in 1950s advice to men as participants in home life derives from the work of Margaret Marsh on the Progressive Era. (See *Make Room for TV,* 97.) The roots of this ideology in the tavern, as a stereotypically men-only space, seem to lie more specifically in the cultural history of the lodge and other institutions in nineteenth-century America. For more on this history see Dana Nelson, *National Manhood* (Durham, N.C.: Duke University Press, 1998).

37 On do-it-yourself see Steven M. Gelber, "Do It Yourself: Constructing, Repairing, and Maintaining Domestic Masculinity," *American Quarterly,* 49, no. 1 (1997): 66–112.

38 "Bar Bits," *Beverage Media,* June 1947, 68.

39 "It Comes Out Here," *Beverage Media,* June 1947, 60, 62.

40 "Jerseyites Prefer Their TV at Home," *Variety,* March 16, 1948, 27.

41 "Video 'Rescues' Youths," *Chicago Daily News,* September 17, 1948, 38.

42 Leo Bogart, *The Age of Television: A Study of Viewing Habits and the Impact of Television on American Life* (New York: Frederick Ungar, 1956), 87.

43 "Barroom Lament," *New York Times,* June 13, 1948, sec. XX, 6.

44 Ibid.

45 "Video Kayoes the Barroom Bore," *Chicago Daily News,* 17 September 1948: 32.

46 "Believe It or Not," 54.

47 "The Television Set," *Time,* December 15, 1947, 50.

48 Morgan, "Fifty Mile Bleachers," 30.

49 "Juke Box Television," *Broadcasting,* January 24, 1949, 36.

50 "Coin Operated Television," *New Orleans Times-Picayune,* December 17, 1948, sec. 4, 16. See also "Coin TV for Cafes," *Broadcasting,* July 25, 1949, 50.

51 See Spigel, *Make Room for TV,* 106–111.

52 "Legislation as Video Snag Gets Exhib Onceover," *Variety,* January 28, 1948, 5.

53 Morgan, "Fifty Mile Bleachers." See also "TV — A Market in New York Now," 48.

54 Morgan, "Fifty Mile Bleachers." See also *New York Times,* November 27, 1948, 23; "Philly Tavern Dealers Fight Tele Set Tax on Excess Fee Grounds," *Variety,* February 16, 1949, 33; "Phila. Tax," *Broadcasting,* January 3, 1949, 5; "Pa. Restaurants," *Broadcasting,* December 5, 1949, 64.

55 "Philly Tavern Dealers Fight," 33. The tax was eventually overturned by the state senate. See "TV Bar Tax Action," *Broadcasting,* April 25, 1949, 66.

56 For a description of the arguments on either side see "Main Event: TV vs. SRO," *Nation's Business,* March 1949, 46–48, 84.

57 "It's the Taverns That Still Worry Baseball Chiefs," *Variety,* June 16, 1948, 32. It should be noted that ballparks then, as now, made their profits on concessions, not tickets. The barroom may thus have posed a threat by providing sports fans with the "liquid," as well as the visual, pleasures of sports spectatorship.

58 "Baseball Chiefs," 32.

59 Al Schlossberg of the King's Palace, "quoted" in "Barrooms with a View," 63.

60 This belief is reiterated in terms of boxing in a *New Yorker* article that noticed that large groups of viewers in taverns acted like fans attending the event in person: "Along about the fourth round, some of the audience were carried away by the illusion that they were actually at the stadium. 'Hit him, Billy,' cried a partisan spectator. 'G'wan, you think he can hear you?' retorted a realist." "Knife and Fork," 17.

61 Paul Whiteman, "Video: Showbiz in the Parlor," *Variety,* July 28, 1948, 26.

62 Ben Duffy, "Who Needs a Haircut?" *Variety,* July 28, 1948, 29.

63 Rosenzweig, *Eight Hours,* 202.

64 Kingsdale, "Poor Man's Club," 485.

65 Raymond Calkins, quoted in Powers, "Decay from Within," 116. See also Rosenzweig, *Eight Hours,* 143–147.

66 Rosenzweig, *Eight Hours,* 106.

67 Some of these alternatives were for adults as well; the Salvation Army in New York's Bowery began a long fund-raising drive in 1947 to purchase a television for its Red Shield Club "so that men who are determined not to drink will not be lured into barrooms by television." "'Dry' Club Renews Video Appeal," *New York Times,* July 19, 1948, 12. See also "Angels Seeking Television's Aid," *New York Times,* June 21, 1948, 23; "Pub Crawlers," *Time,* August 2, 1948, 43.

68 "Video 'Rescues' Youths," 38. See also "Tele-Hangout," *Recreation,* February 1949, 494; "A Village Hires a Helper," *Recreation,* January 1948, 460; A. Gordon Nasby, "Television and the Church," *Christian Century,* February 2, 1949, 143; "Plan Parish Television," *New York Times,* October 2, 1947, 56; "Playground TV," *Broadcasting,* March 29, 1948, 24; "Chicago Pub Patrons Like Baseball on TV," *Broadcasting,* July 12, 1948, 68; "Church TV Center," *Broadcasting,* January 17, 1949, 70; "See It in Church," 24; "Chi Kids to See Ball Games as 'TV Guests,'" *Variety,* March 24, 1948, 31.

69 Nasby, "Television and the Church," 143.

70 "Village Hires a Helper," 460.

71 For a discussion of the larger debate on juvenile delinquency, parental oversight, and television see Lynn Spigel, "Seducing the Innocent," in *Ruthless Criticism: New Perspectives in U.S. Communications History,* ed. William Solomon and Robert W. McChesney (Minneapolis: University of Minnesota Press, 1993), 265–267.

72 Clarence R. Graham and William Hodapp, "Television's Town Hall," *Library Journal,* March 15, 1949, 410.

73 "Children, Parents Blamed in Library TV-Show Trouble," *Louisville Courier-Journal,* April 13, 1949, sec. 2, 1.

74 Ibid.

75 Michael O'Keefe, "Barroom Novelty," *New York Times,* July 4, 1948, sec. 2, 7.

76 "Barroom Video Curbed," *New York Times,* July 21, 1948, 25; Michael O'Keefe, "Concluding the Saga of Parkey Radigan," *New York Times,* August 8, 1948, Sec. 2, 7. See also "Pub Crawlers," 43. This practice of opening the tavern to children was unlikely to have been an isolated incident, although Parkey Radigan's "saga" was the most extensively documented. Some evidence suggests that the outrage child viewers provoked in the tavern was inconsistent, no doubt varying from region to region or even from town to town. In 1947, according to a brief report in *The Televiser,* a short-lived industry magazine, one Milwaukee tavern keeper closed his bar on Christmas Eve, when WTMJ ran a television version of its popular annual holiday broadcast, "then invited parents and their children in to watch the show." The article was careful to point out that "cloths were carefully placed over every bottle and only soft-drinks were served." "Case History," *Televiser,* January 1949, 10. The crackdown on Radigan may have been motivated by the publicity he received. Taverns, especially the back rooms of taverns, were routinely used for keeping children amused in urban neighborhoods. A Brooklyn tavern keeper named Harry Sweitzer, an ex-marine with a Ph.D., supported community youth activities so strongly that he "converted part of his tavern . . . to a small gymnasium for use by neighborhood kids." "Bar Bits," *Beverage Media,* April 1947, 55.

77 O'Keefe, "Concluding the Saga."

78 "See It in Church," 82; "Plan Parish Television," 56. See also "Playground TV," a WBKB press release that appeared in *Broadcasting* and seems to solicit manufacturer donations.

79 See also Lynn Spigel, "Seducing the Innocent," 279–280.

80 "Free Theater as Sales Hypo," *Variety,* February 23, 1949, 27.

81 "Make TV Work *for* You," *Beverage Media,* December 1950, 16 (emphasis in original).

82 Ibid.

83 Danno and Ziencek interviews.

84 See John R. Logan and Harvey L. Molotch, *Urban Fortunes: The Political Economy of Place* (Berkeley: University of California Press, 1987), for a good overview of these issues.

85 Kevin Lynch, *The Image of the City* (Cambridge, Mass.: MIT Press, 1960).

86 Kenneth French, *Jersey City, 1940–1960* (Dover, N.H.: Arcadia Press, 1997), 7.

87 The city lost several major industrial employers in the 1970s and 1980s. French notes that the closing of the Colgate company in 1988 "highlighted a shift in local employment from blue-collar to white-collar jobs." Ibid., 96. The population of the city decreased by almost 9 percent in the 1970s and is still decreasing today, although at a slower rate.

88 These and other details were recounted in an interview with Phil, the bartender and son-in-law of the owner, Frank Starr, now in his eighties.

89 For reasons directly related to media technologies and the communications economy, it is possible that the urban fortunes of this area of Jersey City may shift again, giving rise to yet another configuration of labor and leisure in the neighborhood and perhaps shaping the fate of Starr's Tavern and its patrons. In the summer of 2000, an article in the real estate section of the *New York Times* reported that the ACC building near Starr's is one of a number of decrepit factories in the Northeast recently purchased by "MetroNexis . . . one of two companies being backed by $1.25 billion from Morgan Stanley Real Estate Fund to build a global Internet communications network." It is very interesting to speculate on the patterns in urban development that will arise from the spread of Internet firms. According to the article, the infrastructural and architectural conditions that characterize former urban manufacturing plants like the ACC building—for example, their proximity to major transportation networks—are the features that make them attractive to Internet-based companies. This is because "old industrial and retail properties, formerly considered unrentable white elephants . . . have what the Internet companies need: sturdy floors and high ceilings to accommodate heavy, delicate equipment; abundant electric power . . . [and] proximity to the high-volume fiber cables . . . installed along established railroad lines." In this situation, material conditions frequently seen as anachronistic and devalued in an era of "postindustrial," mobile capitalism are reincorporated into the economic circuits of an information-based mode of capital accumulation. Of course, what the article does not address is the fact that these buildings were originally built on a scale that reflected the number of jobs they provided in the neighborhood. Though these firms' investment in urban districts may seem like an occasion for optimistic accounts of "revitalization," it is unlikely that the location

of Internet companies in former manufacturing districts will restore employment to postwar levels—even though the levels of capital investment in the site may be comparable. Indeed, the ACC building's sale presumably means that the workers employed in the light industries currently housed there will lose their jobs. See John Holusha, "Web Gives White Elephants a New Life," *New York Times* July 9, 2000, sec. 11: 1, 4.

90 Weber, *Mass Mediauras,* 122.

91 Press coverage of sports bars rises sharply at the end of the 1980s, although many reporters in this period dated the phenomenon to the 1970s. See, for example, Dan Logan, "Sports Bars Aim to Score Big with Giant TVs," *Los Angeles Times,* April 22, 1990, B20; David Haldane, "A Sports Bar for Players, Power Brokers," *Los Angeles Times,* October 2, 1986, pt. 9, 2. On the predicted decline of neighborhood bars in this period, see for example, Joe Mysak, "Jock Bars," *American Spectator,* May 1988, 37–38.

92 Lawrence A. Wenner, "In Search of the Sports Bar: Masculinity, Alcohol, Sports, and the Mediation of Public Space," in *Sport and Postmodern Times,* ed. Genevieve Rail (Albany: State University of New York, 1998), 323.

93 Mark Journey, "NFL Letters Threaten Sports Bars," *St. Petersburg Times,* September 18, 1990, 1; Jack Craig, "Patriots Toast of the Town? Some Bars Pirating Signals to Give Customers an Illegal Show," *Boston Globe,* September 27, 1991, 56.

94 Michael Granberry, "NFL Scrambling Plan Dims Picture for Sports Bars," *Los Angeles Times,* August 18, 1990, San Diego County ed.: B1.

95 The NFL Sunday Ticket Plan cost bars between $700 and $2500 a season, depending on their capacity. See Gordon Forbes, "NFL Taps Bars Game Day," *USA Today,* April 12, 1994, 1A, and "NFL TV Plan Focuses on Sports Bars," *USA Today,* April 12, 1994, 1C.

96 Rudy Martzke, "NFL Tackles Game Pirates," *USA Today,* September 28, 1994, 1A. Larry Stewart, "Bars Want to Take It, so Networks Could Dish It Out," *Los Angeles Times,* September 7, 1990, C3. Similar problems have periodically caused friction between sports-bar proprietors and the broadcast-rights holders for special sporting events. See Prentis Rogers, "HBO May Patrol Atlanta to find Bars Pirating Fight," *Atlanta Constitution,* November 21, 1991, E2; Paul Lomartire, "Satellite Feed in Sports Bars Offers Alternative but Raises Legal Issues," *Atlanta Journal-Constitution,* August 3, 1996, S29.

97 John W. Verity, "Move Over, Jimmy Johnson," *Business Week,* August 12, 1996, 86D. See also James Scarpa, "Draft Choice," *Restaurant Business,* August 10, 1996, 117–118; Joe Peterson, "All-Stars Sports Bar and Grill Aims for a Winning Combination," *Louisville Courier-Journal,* December 30, 1989, 21S; Steve Dale, "Sports Bars Are Up for All-Star Partying," *Chicago Tribune,* July 6, 1990, 2. *New York* reported in 1992 on the opening of a sports bar/strip club called *Scores.* See Meredith Berkman, "Shirts and Skins," *New York,* January 13, 1992, 15.

98 See chap. 5 for an analysis of this point-of-purchase TV venue.

99 Mary Gannon, "The Retailer and Television," *Television,* September 1947, 12.

Chapter 2 Gendered Fantasies of TV Shopping in the Postwar Department Store

1 Edith M. Stern, "Buy-Paths to Learning," *Readers Digest,* May 1938, 90, 92.

2 See Neil Harris, *Cultural Excursions: Marketing Appetites and Cultural Tastes in America* (Chicago: University of Chicago Press, 1990), 56–81.

3 Bud Gamble, "The Television Tour of 88 Department Stores," *Televiser* (fall 1945): 48. (This article was a postwar memoir of the prewar event.) On Bloomingdale's TV promotion activities in 1939, see I. A. Hirschmann, "Television: A New Dimension in Department Store Advertising," *Television* (spring 1944): 10, 38.

4 Gamble, "Television Tour," 48.

5 "Television Caravan," *Department Store Economist,* June 1947, 48. It is important to note that these early collaborations with stores were very advantageous to broadcasters. The first few postwar years were lean days for TV companies; their wartime government research contracts had ceased, receiver sales were slow in the transitional economy, and advertising revenues were scarce. On the department store activities that did exist during the war see James Schwoch, "Selling the Sight/Site of Sound: Broadcast Advertising and the Transition from Radio to Television," *Cinema Journal* 30, no. 1 (1990). Many of these proposed projects no doubt originated in the fact that stores were already extensively involved in radio. Ronald J. Arcenaux. "Attention Shoppers: WGBS and the History of Department Store Radio" (master's thesis, City University of New York, 1997). Department store companies applied for station licenses before the FCC freeze on frequency allocations. Other TV-related projects occurred in the department store in this period, also. In addition to selling TV receivers, stores hosted remote telecasts, celebrated the establishment of a new television station with in-store remotes and special promotions, and even, in the case of New York's Wanamaker's store, housed the flagship production studios of a television network. "Selling by Television," *Bulletin of the NRGDA,* February 1945, 68–72; "Linking Department Store Merchandising with Local Television Operation," DuMont Network promotional pamphlet, 1944 (National Museum of American History Archives Center, Smithsonian Institution, Washington, D.C.).

6 Frederick Kiesler, *Contemporary Art Applied to the Store and Its Display* (New York: Sir Isaac Pitman and Sons, 1930), 121.

7 For examples of how the introduction of lounges, escalators, and store exhibits in the department store articulated ideas about the female consumer during the first half of the century see Susan Porter Benson, *Counter Cultures: Saleswomen, Managers, and Customers in American Department Stores, 1890–1949* (Urbana: University of Illinois Press, 1986); Friedberg, *Window Shopping;* Harris, *Cultural Excursions;* William Leach, *Land of Desire: Merchants, Power, and the Rise of a New American Culture* (New York: Pantheon, 1993); Rachel Bowlby, *Just Looking: Consumer Culture in Dreiser, Gissing, and Zola* (New York: Methuen, 1985).

8 Friedberg, *Window Shopping,* 41.

9 E. B. Weiss, "Demonstrators, Mechanical Demonstrators, and Intra-Store Television," *Printer's Ink,* May 28, 1948, 53.

10 On the role of local institutions in shaping prenetwork television programming see Mark Williams. "From 'Remote' Possibilities to Entertaining 'Difference': A Regional

Study of the Rise of the Television Industry in Los Angeles, 1930–1952" (Ph.D. diss., University of Southern California, 1992).

11 For Du Mont's use of the show window metaphor see Trowbridge H. Stanley, "Display . . . the BASIS of Merchandising," *Display World,* May 1945, 24. For RCA's see "Selling by Television," 15. More general discussions of television as a show window appear in "Selling by Television," 68–72; Mary Gannon, "Television and the Department Store," *Television,* November 1945, 9; Jim Owens, "Report on Local Advertising," *Television,* November 1948, 9–12; I. A. Hirschmann, "Television in the Retail Field," *Journal of Marketing* 8, no. 1 (1943): 395–397; "The Merchandise Man's Victory Problems," *Bulletin of the National Retail and Dry Goods Association,* October 1945, 19–20. Comparisons between television and retail sales techniques were not limited to the window metaphor. One CBS engineer, writing in a retail journal, told display managers that television and the department store were so similar they should be considered "blood relations." And Louis Sposa of the DuMont network noted in 1947, "The department store demonstrator would probably be rather good on television. . . . She is accustomed to *showing,* not telling, the merits of her product, and that's teleselling technique" (emphasis in original). See James Leaman, "The Display Designer . . . and TELEVISION," *Display World,* April 1944, 42; Louis Sposa, *Television Primer of Production and Direction* (New York: McGraw-Hill, 1947), 155.

12 For a field constantly declaring its own innovation, market research's gendered categories of consumer behavior are surprisingly rigid and static. For example, Paco Underhill's cutting-edge retail bestseller of the 1990s, *Why We Buy: The Science of Shopping* (New York: Simon and Schuster, 1999), offers a gender-polarized schema of shopper activity in the store that is virtually identical to the one offered in a 1947 trade press article called "Some Aspects of Sex Differences in Relation to Marketing." R. S. Alexander, *Journal of Marketing* 12, no. 2 (1947): 159–172.

13 See Mimi White, *Tele-Advising: Therapeutic Discourse in American Television* (Chapel Hill: University of North Carolina Press, 1992), and Anne Friedberg, *Window Shopping,* for discussions of the gender politics of assorted forms of technologically mediated consumption.

14 Anne Friedberg offers a dazzling analysis of these connections in *Window Shopping.* See also Hansen, *Babel and Babylon: Spectatorship in American Silent Film* (Cambridge, Mass.: Harvard University Press, 1991). Charles Eckert, "The Carole Lombard in Macy's Window," in *Fabrications: Costume and the Female Body,* ed. Jane Gaines and Charlotte Herzog (New York: Routledge, 1990); Jane Gaines, "The Queen Christina Tie-ups: Convergence of Show Window and Screen," *Quarterly Review of Film and Video* 11, no. 1 (1989); Sarah Berry, "Screen Style: Consumer Fashion and Femininity in 1930s Hollywood" (Ph.D. diss., New York University, 1997).

15 See "Seeing Means Selling: Visual Principles Give the Plus Push to Store Merchandising," *Stores,* October 1949, 14–15, 34.

16 L. Mercer Francisco, "The Talking Picture: An Example of the Machine Method Applied to Selling," *Journal of Marketing* 9, no. 2 (1944): 119.

17 Quoted in Richard Longstreth, *City Center to Regional Mall: Architecture, the Automobile, and Retailing in Los Angeles, 1920–1950* (Cambridge, Mass.: MIT Press, 1997), 226. See also Harris, *Cultural Excursions,* 279.

18   According to *Business Week,* the assembly line as a way of moving goods throughout the store first appeared in this period. See "Disassembly Line for Stores: Thalhimers," *Business Week,* December 18, 1948, 78–80.

19   The concept of flow was first articulated in Raymond Williams, *Television.*

20   I base this assessment on my survey of every issue of three retail trade journals from 1936 to the mid-1950s: *Display World, Stores,* and *Department Store Economist* (formerly *Bulletin of the National Retail and Dry Goods Association [NRDGA]*).

21   Floyd A. Lewis, "Store Transactions Speeded by Modern Communications Systems," *Department Store Economist,* April 1948, 20.

22   Arthur C. Kaufman, "Experiment in Selling by Television," *Bulletin of the National Retail and Dry Goods Association,* January 1945, 16.

23   Longstreth, *City Center,* 141.

24   Spigel, *Make Room for TV,* 89, 111.

25   E. B. Weiss, "How to Sell to and through the *New* Department Store," *Printer's Ink,* November 28, 1947, 31, 72; E. B. Weiss, "Department Stores Are Becoming Chain Stores," *Printer's Ink,* December 5, 1947, 39–40; "Stores to Expand," *Business Week,* March 23, 1946, 80; "Department Stores Hurrying to Suburbs," *Business Week,* October 4, 1947, 25. For a regional history of these changes see Longstreth, *City Center.*

26   The receivers used were apparently the same ones featured in RCA's exhibit at the world's fair in 1939 and in the tour of eighty-eight stores that took place that year. RCA seems to have recycled these antiquated models one more time, in its 1947 Television Caravan tour, cosponsored with Allied Stores. See "250,000 See Store Video," *Radio Age,*" January 1946, 28–29; Kaufman, "Experiment." See also Hilda Jones, "Intra-Store Television as a Sales-Promotion Medium," *Journal of Retailing,* February 1948, 15–20; "Television Caravan," 48.

27   Advertisement, *Philadelphia Inquirer,* October 24, 1945, 24.

28   Kaufman, "Experiment," 16.

29   Friedberg, *Window Shopping,* 4.

30   Merle Curti, "The Changing Concept of Human Nature in the Literature of American Advertising," *Business History Review* 41 (winter 1967): 345.

31   Margaret Morse, "Ontology of Everyday Distraction."

32   Longstreth, *City Center,* 217.

33   E. B. Weiss, "New Concepts of Store Architecture Affect Store Promotion," *Printer's Ink,* March 26, 1948, 46–48; "Stores to Expand," 80; "Total Visibility at Bambergers," *Stores,* October 1949, 28; "For a More Efficient Big Volume Store," *Architectural Record,* February 1947, 92; Louis Parnes, "A New Construction Applied to Department Stores," *Department Store Economist,* May 1945, 38. The concept of flow seems highly overdetermined in retail discourses of the period. In 1948, for example, one retail writer used a flow metaphor to describe the relationship between the suppliers, stores, and customers: "the modern buyer's first goal is a *steady flow of merchandise* from the manufacturer, through the store, to the consumer" (emphasis in original). James C. Cumming, *Keys to Selling Department Stores* (New York: Fairchild Publishing, 1948), 13.

34   Parnes, "New Construction," 38. See also Lee Waldrip, "Display and Visual Merchandising," *Display World,* June 1948, 74.

35 "More Efficient Big Volume Store," 92.

36 "Selling by Television," 70, 72.

37 Gannon, "Television and the Department Store," 11.

38 Grace Neville, "Some Thoughts on Intra-Store Tele," *Televiser,* March–April 1947, 33.

39 Stanley, "Display," 24. See also Albert Bliss, "Psychology of Seeing," *Display World,* April 1946, 70; Waldrip, "Display and Visual Merchandising," 117.

40 For Cowee well-located product display could direct the shopper as she moved about the store and "capture an audience of potential purchasers." Howard R. Cowee, "Display—or Visual Merchandising?" *Journal of Retailing,* May 1945, 51. See also Al Bliss, "Getting, Stopping, and Selling . . . STORE TRAFFIC," *Display World,* January 1945, 78.

41 H. R. Cowee, "Display—or Visual Merchandising?" 51, Irving C. Eldredge, "What's to Be Sold Must First Be Seen," *Stores,* October 1949, 18. See also Stanley, "Display," 24; Weiss, "New Concepts," 46–48.

42 H. R. Cowee, "Display—or Visual Merchandising," 51.

43 Howard M. Cowee, "Research in Visual Merchandising," in *Display Manual,* ed. Howard P. Abrahams et al. (New York: Visual Merchandising Group of the National Retail and Dry Goods Association, 1951), 48.

44 E. B. Weiss, "That Proverbial Weak Link: The Sales Person," *Printer's Ink,* April 30, 1947, 42–46. See also E. B. Weiss, "Self-Service and Robot Selling," *Printer's Ink,* June 11, 1947, 42, "Demonstrators," and "New Concepts." For an early articulation of the staffing problems department stores faced at midcentury see Morris Thomas, "Department Store Problems," *Journal of Marketing* 8, no. 1 (1943): 21–24.

45 J. D. McLean, quoted in "Selling by Television," 70. McLean's speech is essentially the same as an article written by an employee of GE's TV station, WRGB, that was published in the TV trade journal the *Televiser* that same year. Although it is unclear which is the original, the fact that McLean's version is truncated suggests that his is not. See Helen T. Rhodes, "Television Programming for Department Stores," *Televiser* (spring 1945): 46–47.

46 Rhodes, "Television Programming," 46. This idea of television as a technology for organizing one's time, as well as one's vision, particularly in matters of domestic labor, was by no means confined to the store. It was, as Lynn Spigel has shown, a perennial trope in the broadcast industry's explanation of the benefits of daytime programming for an imagined homemaker hard at work and isolated in the home. See Spigel, *Make Room for TV,* 87.

47 See Eldredge, "What's to Be Sold," 18; Howard P. Abrahams, "How Visual Merchandising Has Grown," in *Display Manual,* ed. Howard P. Abrahams et al. (New York: Visual Merchandising Group of the National Retail and Dry Goods Association, 1951); Alexander, "Aspects of Sex Differences," 159–172. See also Irwin A. Shane, "Television for Retailers," *Televiser* (fall 1944): 34–35, 46.

48 Kaufman, "Experiment," 58.

49 "250,000 See Store Video," 28–29; Kaufman, "Experiment," 16–18, 56–58. Weiss, "Demonstrators," 52.

50 Weiss, "Demonstrators," 52.

51 Haralovich, "Sitcoms and Suburbs," 127.

52 Albert Bliss, "Visual Merchandising . . . Its Promises and Obligations," *Display World*, August 1944, 50. Bliss and other visual merchandisers mounted numerous attempts to institute what was virtually a "ratings system" for display. Organizations such as the Point of Purchase Advertising Institute and the Visual Merchandising Division of the Bliss Display Corporation began systematic studies of what Cowee called "display audience characteristics." In 1949 the National Association of Display Industries conducted a nationwide survey of interior and window displays that would, according to the journal *Stores*, "lay the groundwork for an index of display 'readership' and its relations to sales." Eldredge, "What's to Be Sold," 33.

53 Eldredge, "What's to Be Sold," 33. These constructions of women as efficient, information-driven consumers no doubt reflected changes in consumer industry relations in this period following the Lea-Overland Act in the 1930s, an act that called for stricter labeling and advertising laws. Yet retailers tended to see these changes in the presentation of merchandise information as an indication of the "truth" of consumer desire. See "Better Display Wanted by Women Customers," *Display World*, March 1947, 70; J. Kingsley Gould, "The Manufacturer's Viewpoint on Display and Point of Purchase," in *Display Manual*, ed. Howard P. Abrahams et al. (New York: Visual Merchandising Group of the National Retail and Dry Goods Association, 1951), 77.

54 See Benson, *Counter Cultures*.

55 W. L. Stensgaard, "The Shape of Things to Come," *Display World*, September 1944, 5. As Susan Porter Benson notes, the term *showmanship* was "an advertising department 'watchword' " of large retail emporia. Benson, *Counter Cultures*, 104.

56 Stensgaard, "Showmanship for Intra-store Television," *Display World*, December 1945, 61.

57 White, *Tele-Advising*, 99.

58 "Seeing Means Selling," 14.

59 Weiss, "Demonstrators," 52.

60 Hirschmann, "New Dimension," 10, 38. Didactic modes of address are popular in retailing today, in what the *New York Times*, in an article on the Discovery Channel's flagship store, dubbed "The Teach and Sell School of Retailing." "The Teach and Sell School of Retailing," *New York Times*, February 28, 1998, D1, D14.

61 Shopping shows were few in comparison with, say, sports programs. Yet discussions and comparisons of these shows were frequent in the broadcast trade press—less so, interestingly, in the retail papers, where they were generally viewed as novelties given the small audiences involved. Their prevalence may be explained by the fact that these shows' reliance on purely commercial presentations made them case studies to be scrutinized for ideas about TV advertising aesthetics. See Gannon, "Retailer and Television," 12; Mary Gannon, "Ten Men on a Horse," *Television*, July 1948; Owens, "Report on Local Advertising"; "The Fair Store," *Television*, February 1946, 32; "Backstage with Television," *Stores*, March 1948, 44; "Holmes Gives Preview of Video Shows," *New Orleans States*, November 16, 1948, 6; "Regular Television from Gimbel's Sales Floor," *Stores*, April 1949; "Series Success," *Broadcasting*, October 10, 1949, 46.

62 DuMont Network, "Linking Department Store Merchandising with Local Television Operation."

63 "Carlson Says Video Powerful, Subtle," *Broadcasting,* November 19, 1945, 101.

64 On catalogs and consumption in the home see Alexandra Keller, "Disseminations of Modernity: Representation and Consumer Desire in Early Mail Order Catalogs," in *Cinema and the Invention of Modern Life,* ed. Leo Charney and Vanessa Schwartz (Berkeley: University of California Press, 1995); on store magazines see Leach, *Land of Desire.*

65 Spigel, *Make Room for TV,* 22. As Spigel notes, Christine Frederick's 1929 marketing handbook, *Selling Mrs. Consumer,* was influential in this construction of domestic leisure and labor.

66 Spigel, *Make Room for TV,* 83.

67 Judy Dupuy, *Television Show Business* (Schenectady, N.Y.: General Electric Corporation, 1945), 73 (emphasis mine).

68 A Gimbel's sales manager, commenting on a show the store produced in 1948, offered a more masculinist explanation of why women might not be interested in domestic training programs: "Most women resent women experts. That is, they don't like being told how to do their own jobs by another woman, no matter how well-qualified the other woman may be." For this reason the store used a male MC named Jack Creamer to demonstrate home techniques to women, who, he claimed, were amused and entertained "when the 'male animal' invade[d] their domestic domain and show[ed] them how to get things done around the house." David Arons, "Television Becomes Sell-a-Vision at Gimbel's Philadelphia," *Television,* June 1948, 23.

69 Owens, "Report on Local Advertising," 10.

70 R. C. Kash, "Display . . . and TELEVISION," *Display World,* October 1944, 30.

71 Mary Gannon, "Television and the Department Store," 11. See also Jones, "Intra-Store Television," 17.

72 "Table Top Receivers Popularize Tele," *Department Store Economist,* September 1948, 113.

73 David Arons, "30 Day Experiment Doubles Sales," *Television,* May 1949, 21 (emphasis in original). See also "Regular Television from Gimbel's Sales Floor," 31. A similar show that aired a year earlier from Philadelphia's Lit Brothers store offers further support for the idea that in-store audiences were primary targets of store-sponsored shows' commercial messages. The show was cosponsored by Admiral, Philco, and RCA; as TV set manufacturers they were probably not interested in "preaching to the converted" home viewers. Gannon, "Ten Men," 40.

74 For a detailed historical account of the evolution of these ideologies, particularly their occult manifestation, see Jeffrey Sconce, *Haunted Media: Electronic Presence from Telegraphy to Television* (Durham, N.C.: Duke University Press, 2000).

75 "Fair Store," 32.

76 DuMont, a struggling network, used the first person, "tour of the store" format of the shopping show in what was likely an attempt to stimulate its local advertising revenues. *Broadcasting* reported in 1948 that a DuMont program for women was "set in a department store background" and included "21 portions of entertainment and 12 one-minute 'store bulletins' (news and service announcements) which may be replaced at individual outlets by commercials for local advertisers. This first network co-op [multiple sponsor] show of television will utilize the 'subjective camera tech-

nique' in which the camera takes the place of the woman shopper, making the home viewer feel as if she were in the store in person." "Dumont Daytime," *Broadcasting*, December 12, 1949. See also "TV Net Plans Daytime Programming," *Radio Daily*, November 25, 1949, 3.

77 "Fair Store," 32. This was not the first of the store's TV ventures. In 1945 it sponsored a program demonstrating beauty tips for teenagers, also on WBKB. See "Beauty Methods Demonstrated on TV Show by Chicago Store," *Broadcasting*, November 19, 1945, 28.

78 See Robert E. Lee, *Television: The Revolutionary Industry* (New York: Essential Books, 1944), 131.

79 Gannon, "Ten Men," 24.

80 This was a form of ratings that benefited the station as well because it generated sales data that could be used to attract other sponsors.

81 Morse, "Ontology of Everyday Distraction."

82 Spigel, *Make Room for TV*, 109.

83 For an account of this history of the transformation in the economic relations of department store retailing, see Barry Bluestone et al., *The Retail Revolution: Market Transformation, Investment, and Labor in the Modern Department Store* (New York: Auburn House, 1981).

Chapter 3 Out-of-Home Networks in the 1990s

1 Ira Steinowitz, Judith Graham, and Laurie Freeman, "IRI Rolls into Future with Video Carts," *Advertising Age*, May 2, 1988, 6.

2 On new "post-Fordist paradigms of consumption," see Urry, *Consuming Places*, 141–151.

3 Retail textbooks from the 1940s certainly anticipate this state of affairs; see Cumming, *Keys to Selling Department Stores*. But as Bluestone et al. note in *Retail Revolution*, this shift in brand relations occurred in later decades, once national brands had ascended in the retail economy.

4 See Gerald Berstell, "Point-of-Sale Research Reveals Spontaneous Buying Decisions," *Marketing News*, June 8, 1992, H-31, and "Study What People Do, Not What They Say," *Marketing News*, January 6, 1992, 7; Laura Castaneda, "There's More in Store," *Dallas Morning News*, January 16, 1996, 1D; Rebecca Piirto Heath, "POP Art," *Marketing Tools*, April 1997, 42–55; David Kay, "Go Where the Consumers Are and Talk to Them," *Marketing News*, January 6, 1997, 14; John T. Landry, "Positioning the Product: Know Where Your Rivals Are," *Harvard Business Review*, Nov.–Dec. 1996, 13.

5 Underhill, *Why We Buy*, 63.

6 See, for example, Julia Thrift, "What's in Store for Brands," *Marketing*, Feb. 27, 1997, 25–29. See also Castaneda, "More in Store"; Heath, POP Art.

7 Cited in Castaneda, "More in Store."

8 Please note that for consistency I refer to Turner's airport TV system as the Airport Network throughout, although before 1994 it was called the Airport Channel.

9 Fredric Jameson, *Postmodernism; or, the Cultural Logic of Late Capitalism* (London: Verso, 1991), 44.

10 Noting that "the words 'local' and 'global' offer points on view of networks that are by nature neither local nor global, but are more or less long and more or less connected," Bruno Latour proposes that "an Ariadne's thread . . . would allow us to pass with continuity from the local to the global, from the human to the nonhuman. It is the thread of practices and instruments, of documents and translations." The professional discourse of place-based media is not in any sense the totality of connections such as Latour describes, but it is certainly one strand of it. See Latour, *We Have Never Been Modern*, 122, 121.

11 The term *place-based media* seems to have been coined by *Advertising Age*, which used it throughout the 1990s to describe not only television but also print advertising and syndicated radio networks designed for particular places. However, in keeping with the larger purposes of this book I focus here on place-based *video* operations — which are, in any event, the most publicized place-based media ventures because so many of them are owned by, or partnered with, Turner Private Networks, a subsidiary of Turner (and, further up the chain, of Time-Warner). The field was reported to be growing at a 50 percent annual rate in 1994, when *Advertising Age* estimated its worth as $700 million. However, this year preceding the rise of the Internet seems to have been its peak moment. Keith J. Kelly, "Flops Fail to Derail Place-based," *Advertising Age*, August 8, 1994, 12.

12 The networks dipped exploratory toes into the field of out-of-home advertising in the 1980s and early 1990s, but — probably because of the emergence of the Internet as a more suitable outlet for their expansion and diversification — these activities have ceased or else remain only on a very small scale. See Scott Donaton, "Flaws Ax Checkout Channel," *Advertising Age*, February 22, 1993, 3; Eben Shapiro, "TV Commercials Chase Supermarket Shoppers," *New York Times*, May 25, 1992, 35.

13 Celia Lury and Alan Warde, "Investments in the Imaginary Consumer: Conjectures Regarding Power, Knowledge, and Advertising," in *Buy This Book: Studies in Advertising and Consumption*, ed. Mica Nava, Iain McRory, and Barry Richards (New York: Routledge, 1997), 89. See also Toby Miller, *Technologies of Truth: Cultural Citizenship and the Popular Media* (Minneapolis: University of Minnesota Press, 1998).

14 John Caldwell, *Televisuality: Style, Crisis, and Authority in American Television* (New Brunswick, N.J.: Rutgers University Press, 1994), 222.

15 For an account of this crisis, and particularly of the people-meter "solution," see Ien Ang, *Desperately Seeking the Audience* (New York: Routledge, 1991), 68–97.

16 Barry Layne, "NTA Study Finds 28 Million Viewers Out-of-Home," *Hollywood Reporter*, March 11, 1993. See also Steve McLellan, "Networks to Fund Test of Out-of-Home Viewing," *Broadcasting*, April 6, 1992, 42. Individual networks had previously examined out-of-home viewers for sports programming, attempting to account for viewers in bars. See Ceril Shagrin and Richard Montesano, "Television's Unmeasured Audience: Out-of Home Television Viewing," Transcript Proceedings, ARF Fourteenth Annual Electronic Media Research Workshop (New York: Advertising Research Foundation, 1995), 120–135. See also Shapiro, "TV Commercials," 35.

17 Quoted in Layne, "NTA Study."

18 Alison Fahey, "Turner's New Gamble," *Advertising Age*, April 22, 1991, 3–4.

19 Interview by Denise Gellene, "The Persuaders," *Los Angeles Times*, December 31, 1998,

C6. See also Wendy Tanaka, "Move Over Billboards, Advertising Industry Taking a Chance on Apples," *State Journal-Register* (Illinois), 1997, 20.

20 Quoted in Jackson, "Firms Can't Wait," C1. Explaining NBC's since-abandoned venture in place-based media, NBC-on-Site, a general manager at NBC explained that the network's "mission is to sell eyeballs to advertisers. . . . If eyeballs are in grocery stores, then it's a natural extension for our business." Quoted in David Barboza, "With Consumers Surfing Around TV Commercials at Home, Some Companies Take the Ads on the Road," *New York Times,* July 14, 1995, D4.

21 *CNN Airport Network* (brochure) (Atlanta: Turner Broadcasting System, 1994). See also Barboza, "With Consumers Surfing."

22 Whittle closed down this network in 1994. See "Whittle Cancels News Network for Doctors," *New York Times,* August 2, 1994, D3.

23 Colin Campbell, "Changes Afoot." See also Colin Campbell, "Why monopoly on cacophony?"

24 Quoted in John P. Cortez, "Media Pioneers Try to Corral On-the-Go Consumers," *Advertising Age,* August 17, 1992, 25.

25 Richard Mahler, "While You Wait: TV Marketers Hunt Captive Viewers," *Electronic Media,* December 30, 1993, 1.

26 Jane Hodges, "Parking Garages Supplying Newest Venue for TV Spots," *Advertising Age,* September 9, 1996, 35.

27 It is evident enough from this example that place-based media are not designed to target the individuals for whom the place in question is a workspace. Indeed, employees may be as much of a hindrance as an aid to the successful construction of an audience commodity. The Checkout Channel (an early Turner venture in place-based media) was perceived to have failed in part because observers noticed that the clerks forced to work in its presence tended to mute the volume of its constantly rotating appeals. "Turner Checks Out," *Advertising Age,* March 1, 1993, 16.

28 See Michael J. Weiss, *The Clustering of America* (New York: Harper and Row, 1988).

29 Julia Steenhuysen, "Whittle Rips 'Out-of-Step' Shops," *Advertising Age,* August 27, 1990, S-2. It should be noted here that Whittle's gender-neutral example belies the fact that the Special Reports network actually placed itself in physicians' offices oriented toward a very specific population: women with children. According to some rather dubious company figures reported in the *New York Times,* this market was "among the most infrequent television viewers." Thus, it argued, "The waiting rooms of pediatricians, obstetrician-gynecologists and family practitioners are the places to reach them." Randall Rothenberg, "Two Views on Whittle's TV Reports," *New York Times,* June 1, 1990, D3. On the environmental effects of this gendering of the waiting room see chap. 6.

30 David J. Moore. "Just What the Doctor Ordered," Transcript Proceedings, Electronic Media and Technologies IX: Ratings at a Crossroads (New York: Advertising Research Foundation, 1990), 304.

31 Cortez, "Media Pioneers," 25.

32 See Tania Modleski, "Search for Tomorrow," 12–21; Raymond Williams, *Television;* Paddy Scannell, "Radio Times," in *Television and Its Audience,* ed. Philip Drum-

mond and Rob Paterson (London: British Film Institute, 1988); and Browne, "Political Economy."

33 In the transit car, for instance, this sense of a solution to the problems of work-leisure relations is conveyed by the ads for vocational schools and retraining institutes that depict alternative options to one's current employment, reflecting the fact that it is on the journey to and from work where one feels most strongly the dread and despair of a hated job. In contrast, when one emerges into the station and rides the escalator from the depths, the walls lined with advertisements for entertainment products address this transition to leisure time, offering a menu of movies, TV shows, and CDS as a means of recuperating from the pressures of the workday.

34 Beth Corbett. "Place-Based Media Research: Doing it Right the First Time," Transcript Proceedings, ARF Fourteenth Annual Electronic Media Research Workshop (New York: Advertising Research Foundation, 1995), 147.

35 Shapiro, "TV Commercials," 35. On seasonal changes in the Airport Network see Tammi Wark, "Business Travel Today, *USA Today,*" December 26, 1996, 1B.

36 Ang, *Living Room Wars,* 73.

37 John J. McMenamin, "Airport Channel Methodology," *Advertising Age,* January 10, 1994, 23.

38 B. Corbett, "Place-Based Media Research," 143.

39 Joe Mandese, "Measuring Place-Based Media," *Advertising Age,* November 15, 1993, 33.

40 Ibid.

41 Robert Klara, "TV Commercials Follow Shoppers to the Food Court; but Will Diners Respond to Restaurant Ads?" *Restaurant Business,* March 20, 1996, 22.

42 Marla Matzer, "Mall TV: Turner It On," *Brandweek,* June 17, 1996, 20.

43 Arif Dirlik, "The Global in the Local," in *Global/Local: Cultural Production and the Transnational Imaginary,* ed. Rob Wilson and Wimal Dissanayake (Durham, N.C.: Duke University Press, 1996), 34.

44 For a thorough analysis of the surveillance techniques of market research on a global scale see Richard Maxwell, "Ethics and Identity in Global Market Research," *Cultural Studies* 10, no. 2 (1998): 218–236.

45 Quoted in Eric Schmuckler, "Niche Ability," *Brandweek,* April 29, 1996, 25–26.

46 Morley and Robins, *Spaces of Identity,* 16.

47 Ibid.

48 Richard Feldman. "Demonstrating the Real Advertising Value of Place-Based and Interactive Media," Transcript Proceedings, ARF Eleventh Annual Electronic Media Workshop (New York: Advertising Research Foundation, 1992), 95.

49 Ibid., 97.

50 Colin Campbell of the *Atlanta Journal-Constitution* quoted in Lee Hall, "CNN's Terminal Headache," *Electronic Media,* April 28, 1997, 28.

51 Colin Campbell, "Changes Afoot."

52 Ibid.

53 Of course, free enterprisers might argue that CNN had *purchased* this space from the airport in exchange for a share of its advertising revenues. Protesting the Airport Net-

work from such a perspective would be analogous to protesting the sale of ad space on airport walls, surely a spurious complaint. But such objections to the idea of CNN as an environmental intrusion would necessarily deny any difference between sound and image as environmental features of everyday life.

54 Jim Perkins, quoted in "Video Invasion: TVs Take Over Marketplace" (wire report), *Charleston Gazette,* April 9, 1997, 7a. See also Kevin Heubusch, "When Shoppers Pause, Companies Sell," *American Demographics,* March 1997, 34.

55 John J. McMenamin, "Travellers Appreciate News," *Atlanta Journal-Constitution,* March 26, 1997, 14A.

56 Hochschild, "Taken Hostage," 25.

57 The policy implications of amplified sound received international attention in 1969 when UNESCO, responding to complaints about Muzak, passed a resolution attacking "the intolerable infringement of individual freedom and the right of everyone to silence, because of the abusive use, in private and public places, of recorded or broadcast music." Quoted in Joseph Lanza, *Elevator Music: A Surreal History of Muzak, Easy Listening, and other Moodsong* (New York: St. Martin's Press, 1994), 153.

58 Morley and Robins, *Spaces of Identity,* 224.

59 Richard Wilk, quoted in Morley and Robins, *Spaces of Identity,* 227.

60 Dirlik, "Global in the Local," 39.

61 Latour, *We Have Never Been Modern,* 122.

62 Hartley, *Politics of Pictures,* 110.

Chapter 4 Shaping Public and Private Space with TV Screens

1 On the deregulation and policy issues related to Fowler's statement see Ellen Seiter, *Sold Separately: Parents and Children in Consumer Culture* (New Brunswick, N.J.: Rutgers University Press, 1995), and Heather Hendershot, *Saturday Morning Censors: Children's Television Regulation before the V-Chip* (Durham, N.C.: Duke University Press, 1998).

2 Lynn Spigel, *Make Room for TV,* 73–75.

3 Ibid, 93–94.

4 Janet Hoskins, *Biographical Objects: How Things Tell the Stories of People's Lives* (New York: Routledge, 1998). See also Nicholas Thomas, *Entangled Objects: Exchange, Material Culture, and Colonialism in the Pacific* (Cambridge, Mass.: Harvard University Press, 1991).

5 See Susan Strasser, *Never Done: A History of American Housework* (New York: Pantheon Books, 1982).

6 The wide range of discursive acts performed by television are documented in a number of excellent ethnographic accounts of viewing practices and behaviors. Such studies offer much rich material on the communicative functions of the screen as an object—regardless of what appears on the screen. See, e.g., Lila Abu-Lughod, "The Interpretation of Culture after Television," *Representations* 59 (1997): 107–133; Purnima Mankekar, "National Texts and Gendered Lives: An Ethnography of Television Viewers in a North Indian City," *American Ethnologist* 20, no. 3 (1993): 543–563; Gillespie, "Sacred Serials," 354–380; Lyons, "Television and the Shrine," 429–456.

7 For discussions of the decoration of the TV set as a form of local communication see Hartley, *Politics of Pictures;* Leal, "Popular Taste"; John Fiske, "Ethnosemiotics, Some Personal and Theoretical Reflections," *Cultural Studies* 4, no. 1 (1990): 85–99.

8 Spigel, *Make Room for TV,* 102–109.

9 Spigel's critique of the work of Joshua Meyrowitz is a very helpful discussion of the gender codes contributing to the spatial organization of public and private. See Spigel, *Make Room for TV,* 215.

10 Advertisements for wall and ceiling mounts designed to hold the screen above the heads of its viewers emphasize this antitheft purpose as much as physical safety and stability. The rhetoric of ICW International's merchandise catalog (the company sells nothing but mounting devices for TV and computer equipment) places the threat of theft on a par with natural disasters when it praises the Telemount 20 line's "ability . . . to resist the load of the TV/Monitor, plus dynamic forces such as earthquakes, persons interfering with the mount, etc." ICW International catalog, Boulder, Colo., 29. Because of the ever-present possibility of earthquakes, certain load and stress specifications for TV mounts are mandated by law in the state of California.

11 For the history of this idea see Lyn H. Lofland, *A World of Strangers: Order and Action in Urban Public Space* (New York: Basic Books, 1973).

12 See Spigel, *Make Room for TV,* 116. John Kasson, in *Amusing the Million: Coney Island at the Turn of the Century* (New York: Hill and Wang, 1978), offers an analysis of the social conditions underlying the emergence of this idea in American culture.

13 On the historical emergence of this paradigm of theater architecture in the modern era see Iain Mackintosh, *Architecture, Actor, and Audience* (London: Routledge, 1993), 10, 39–40. See also Susan Maslan, "Resisting Representation: Theater and Democracy in Revolutionary France," *Representations* 52 (fall 1995): 27–51, esp. 30.

14 See chap. 6 of Habermas, *Structural Transformation.*

15 This situation is discussed, in more abstract phenomenological terms, in Weber, *Mass Mediauras,* 124.

16 As several anthropologists have noted, it is a convention of domestic space as well. See, in particular, Lyons, "Television and the Shrine," 429–456.

17 Leal, "Popular Taste," 19–39.

18 On the cultural politics of personal inscriptions that are unreadable yet recognizable as statements see Grey Gundaker, *Signs of Diaspora/Diaspora of Signs* (New York: Oxford University Press, 1998), 77–78.

19 Marshall McLuhan and Quentin Fiore, *The Medium Is the Massage: An Inventory of Effects* (New York: Bantam, 1967).

20 Joseph Rykwert, "The Sitting Position: A Question of Method," in *Meaning in Architecture,* ed. Charles Jencks (New York: Braziller, 1970), 237.

21 See chap. 3. Anne Friedberg, in *Window Shopping,* offers a thorough examination of the metaphors of mobility associated with spectatorship. For a discussion of the ideologies attached to this idea in early television discourse see Spigel, *Make Room for TV,* 111–113.

22 "Large Hard Lines: Virgin Megastore," *Chain Store Age Special Issue: Retail Store of the Year,* February 1997, 26.

23 On the tactile pleasure of recorded music's materiality and its packaging see John

Corbett, *Extended Play: Sounding Off from John Cage to Doctor Funkenstein* (Durham, N.C.: Duke University Press, 1994).

24 According to a survey conducted by *Video Store* magazine, children's video sales constituted 65 percent of total video sales in 1996 (*Video Store* 19, no. 42, October 19, 1997), 16.

25 Samuel Delaney offers an excellent account of spectatorial and social relations in Times Square in this period in *Times Square Red, Times Square Blue* (New York: New York University Press, 1999).

26 Suzy Menkes, "Fashion's TV Frenzy," *New York Times,* April 2, 1995, A47.

27 Other televisual signs in Times Square use the Internet to produce an intimate spectatorial experience in the midst of a public mass. A Joe Boxer billboard won a prize from the Municipal Arts Society in 1997 for its innovative personal address — Net users can post a personal message to the company via its Web site, which is projected and displayed on the Times Square billboard. The "hail" here is freighted with the possibility of actually seeing oneself addressed via the huge letters, although the spectatorial relation offered here is more properly the frisson of identification with someone else, of inhabiting, if only via misrecognition, the private subjectivity of another.

28 The sign on top of this T V set changes quite regularly. Here its lettering is ambiguous: the festival it names translates as "parents' festival," but no such festival exists. However, the spoken word for *parent* sounds a lot like the name of the festival of Double Celebration (Shuang Qin Jie) honoring the founding of the republic of Taiwan. I am indebted to Zhang Zhen for her translation of these signs.

29 Mayfair Mei-hui Yang, introduction to *Spaces of Their Own: Women's Public Sphere in Transnational China,* ed. Mayfair Mei-hui Yang (Minneapolis: University of Minnesota, 1999), 7–8.

Chapter 5 Television at the Point of Purchase

1 See Nick Couldry, *The Place of Media Power: Pilgrims and Witnesses of the Media Age* (London: Routledge, 2000), 4–6.

2 Patricia Mellencamp, "TV Time and Catastrophe: Beyond the Pleasure Principle of Television," in *Logics of Television,* ed. Patricia Mellencamp (Bloomington: Indiana University Press, 1990), 262.

3 Underhill, *Why We Buy,* 62. On the NikeTown store as a kind of walk-in T V commercial see Tom Vanderbilt, *The Sneaker Book: An Anatomy of an Industry and an Icon* (New York: New Press, 1998), 154.

4 Underhill, *Why We Buy,* 45–52.

5 See Margaret Morse, "Sport on Television: Replay and Display," in *Regarding Television: Critical Approaches — An Anthology,* ed. E. Ann Kaplan (Frederick, Md.: American Film Institute/University Publications of America, 1983).

6 The mixture of aesthetics that constitutes point-of-purchase video makes it impossible to describe solely in the language of media bombardment or, for that matter, the "boudoir talk" of flanerie and other romances of the commodity. The phrase "boudoir talk" is Meaghan Morris's. See her "Things to Do with Shopping Centers"

and Daniel Miller's *Capitalism: An Ethnographic Approach* (New York: Berg, 1997) for two discussions of the overvaluation of the spectacular and the devaluation of the ordinary in critical approaches to consumer culture.

7   On the Discovery store see "Teach and Sell School."

8   See Ben Fine, "From Political Economy to Consumption," in *Acknowledging Consumption: A Review of New Studies,* ed. Daniel Miller (London: Routledge, 1995), for a review of different political economic approaches to the vicissitudes of consumption, particularly the theoretical problems faced by market-driven models (as well as Marxist difficulties with the plethora of desires represented in flows of supply and demand).

9   See Berstell, "Point-of-Sale Research" and "Study What People Do."

10 Heath, "POP Art," 55.

11 See Vanderbilt, *Sneaker Book;* "Teach and Sell School"; Laurie MacDonald, "Under Renovation: Entertainment-Oriented Shoe Retail Showcases," *Footwear News,* August 5, 1996, 8.

12 British retail and design journalist Julia Thrift defines the architecture of such own-brand flagship stores as "a context which immerses the customer in a brand's imagery, in an environment designed to reinforce every aspect of its core values." Store design, she notes, involves "turning what has previously been a range of products, a logo, and an ad strategy into an attention-grabbing, three-dimensional space, an opportunity for the customers to surround themselves with the brand." Thrift, "What's in Store," 26.

13 Ibid., 28.

14 Ibid.

15 Neil Harris, *Humbug: The Art of P. T. Barnum* (Boston: Little, Brown, 1973).

16 Like credit unions and co-ops, Costco and similar retail institutions are open only to members (to join one pays a small annual fee). Originally established as a benefit for labor union members and government employees, these stores represent a moment of collective consciousness in retailing and consumption worthy of more extensive historical and cultural analysis than this chapter allows.

17 For a discussion of the class politics of satellite dishes as signifiers of conspicuous television consumption in Britain see Brunsdon, "Satellite Dishes."

18 Underhill, *Why We Buy,* 22.

19 Conroy, "Discount Dreams," 71.

20 Ibid., 64. See also Ben Fine, "Political Economy," for a similar account of the specific factors shaping the rise of the supermarket in Britain.

21 Lisa Saxton, "Video Draws Sales — But Needs Support," *Supermarket News,* January 7, 1991, 40. See also Leah Rickard, "Video Struggles to Find a Place in Grocery," *Advertising Age,* May 2, 1994, s-14. Skepticism about the effectiveness of point-of-purchase advertising does exist in the academic circles devoted to the evaluation of marketing techniques. See, for example, Cathy Bond, "Effective Demands," *Marketing,* December 5, 1996, 34–38.

22 Leslie Gilbert, "Exotic Produce Shouldn't Be a Mystery," *Supermarket Business,* April 1988, 47.

23 Ibid.

24 See, for example, "Category Killer," *Discount Merchandiser,* June 1992, 44; "Category Killers," *Discount Store News,* December 4, 1995, 104.

25 Nathan Morton, president and CEO of computer superstore CompUSA, quoted in "Category killer," 44.

26 The semiotics of "warehouse" and "economy" retail designs are fascinating. As retail designer Milton Glaser points out, generic packaging costs as much to design and produce as brand-name packaging, but its black-and-white simplicity, in signaling an interest in reducing unnecessary expenses on the part of the manufacturer, harmonizes with the parsimonious sensibilities of the consumer. "Generic marketing is a response to a kind of calculating consumer able to read through the myth of ads and know that he or she does not require a fancier food." Milton Glaser, "I Listen to the Market," in *On Signs,* ed. Marshall Blonsky (Baltimore: Johns Hopkins University Press, 1985), 471.

27 Underhill, *Why We Buy,* 118.

28 My assessment of the merchandise categories generally promoted in the Bed Bath and Beyond chain's point-of-purchase video demonstrations is based on observations recorded during three site visits to different stores on the East Coast of the United States: Wynnewood, Penn.; New York City; and Potomac Mills Mall, near Washington, D.C. These observations are not automatically generalizable, but they do tally with the merchandising strategies recommended in the retail trade literature on point-of-purchase video. See Heath, "POP Art"; Pat Sloan, "Bozell Rewires Media Strategy," *Advertising Age,* December 16, 1991, 12.

29 White, *Tele-Advising,* 97.

30 "BBB Finds Home in Variety of Places," *Home Textiles Today,* 1996, 20.

31 See Jean-Christophe Agnew, "A House of Fiction: Domestic Interiors and the Commodity Aesthetic," in *Consuming Visions: Accumulation and Display of Goods in America, 1880–1920,* ed. Simon J. Bronner (New York: Norton, 1989).

32 Bluestone et al., *Retail Revolution,* 18.

33 E. B. Weiss predicted this trend in the late 1940s in his series of articles on the future of department store retailing for *Printer's Ink;* it is documented in full in Bluestone et al., *Retail Revolution.*

34 According to Underhill, catchment basins are designed not only so that women shoppers can feel "sheltered" from the vision of other shoppers but also because of what he calls, in characteristically direct and vulgar style, their "butt sensitivity" — an aversion to being brushed from behind by other shoppers. Underhill, *Why We Buy,* 118.

35 Beatriz Colomina, "The Split Wall: Domestic Voyeurism," in *Sexuality and Space,* ed. Beatriz Colomina (New York: Princeton Architectural Press, 1992), 82.

36 On the visual aesthetics that emerge within perfume marketing see Constance Classen, David Howes, and Anthony Synot, *Aroma: The Cultural History of Smell* (London: Routledge, 1994), 188.

37 Underhill, *Why We Buy,* 118–119.

38 For fuller details of scent marketing see Maxine Wilkie, "Scent of a Market," *American Demographics* 17 (August 1995): 40–43.

39 Vanderbilt, *Sneaker Book,* 4.

40 Ibid.

41 Joanne Gordon, "Footaction: Going the Distance," *Chain Store Age,* October 1997, 54–60; "Piece of the Action," *Sporting Goods Business,* April 14, 1997, 32–33. Most chains in this retail category have in-store video systems: Footaction, Athlete's Foot, Champs, Foot Locker.

42 The global labor politics of shoe production are the repressed other of the shoe store's display of racial imagery. These issues are out of the purview of this study, but useful overviews of the labor conditions of fashion manufacturing may be found in Vanderbilt's *Sneaker Book* and in *No Sweat: Fashion, Free Trade, and the Rights of Garment Workers,* ed. Andrew Ross (New York: Verso, 1997).

43 In a *Forbes* magazine article that succinctly epitomizes white anxieties about black economic activity, designer Tommy Hilfiger articulates one of the more virulently racist white "sayings" about black consumption. Hilfiger tells an interviewer, "Many of these people would rather have a Rolex than a home." Quoted in Joshua Levine, "Badass Sells," *Forbes,* April 21, 1997, 142–144. See Vanderbilt, *Sneaker Book,* chap. 4, for a full account of the fetishization of function in sneaker fashion.

44 Dylan Siegler, "Bad Boy Links with Shoe Retailer for CD," *Billboard,* August 1, 1998, 65, 69.

45 Tim Cincotta, quoted in ibid.

46 See Regina Austin, " 'A Nation of Thieves': Consumption, Commerce, and the Black Public Sphere," *Public Culture* 7 (1994): 226, esp. n. 2, for a number of different ways that black customers are treated with suspicion in retail establishments. When I worked at a chain bookstore in a racially mixed and economically depressed area of downtown San Francisco, my manager (a white man) often asked me (a white woman) to follow black customers around the store.

47 Quoted in Siegler, "Bad Boy," 65, 69.

48 Quoted in "More Jumbo Financing: Hibbet Eyes 500 Markets," *Sporting Goods Business,* August 10, 1998, 19.

49 Footaction marketing executive Tim Cincotta, quoted in "Star Gazing," *Sporting Goods Business,* April 14, 1997, 33.

50 Eric Lott, *Love and Theft: Blackface Minstrelsy and the American Working Class* (New York: Oxford University Press, 1995).

51 This phrase is an advertising account executive's attempt to summarize the look of a Fila commercial acknowledged in the industry as a breakthrough advertisement in its harnessing of "inner city" aesthetics. Peter de Pasquale, quoted in Levine, "Badass Sells," 142.

52 See Kevin Robins and Mark Hepworth, "Electronic Spaces: New Technologies and the Future of Cities," *Futures* (1988): 163–164, for a discussion of the dramatization of the point of sale.

Chapter 6 Television While You Wait

1 For discussions of television's temporal effects see, for example, Modleski, "Search for Tomorrow," 12–21; Browne, "Political Economy"; Scannell, "Radio Times"; Williams, *Television;* Spigel, *Make Room for TV;* and Morley, *Family Television.*

2 See Spigel, *Make Room for TV,* 74–75.

3 On the construction of the nation in print media as a fiction of copresence and simultaneity see Benedict Anderson, *Imagined Communities: Reflections on the Origin and Spread of Nationalism* (London: Verso, 1983). Key critical and theoretical discussions of liveness may be found in Feuer, "Concept of Live Television"; Dayan and Katz, *Media Events;* Mellencamp, "TV Time"; and Mary Ann Doane, "Information, Crisis, Catastrophe"; Monika Elsner, Thomas Muller, and Peter M. Spangenberg, "The Early History of German Television: The Slow Development of a Fast Form," *Historical Journal of Film, Television, and Radio* 10, no. 2 (1990): 193–218; Sasha Torres, "King TV," in *Living Color: Race and Television in the United States,* ed. Sasha Torres (Durham, N.C.: Duke University Press, 1999); Zelizer, "Home to Public Forum," 69–79; John Caldwell, *Televisuality: Style, Crisis, and Authority in American Television* (New Brunswick, N.J.: Rutgers University Press, 1994); Williams, "History in a Flash," 292–312. On issues of live TV broadcasting and public space see McCarthy, " 'Like an Earthquake.' "

4 Doane, "Information, Crisis, Catastrophe," 233.

5 See, e.g., Dafna Lemish, "The Rules of Viewing Television in Public Places," *Journal of Broadcasting* 26, no. 4 (1982): 758–781.

6 On the institutional and interpersonal sociology of time see Eviatar Zerubavel, *Hidden Rhythms: Schedules and Calendars in Social Life* (Chicago: University of Chicago Press, 1981); Clay, *Real Places;* Kevin Lynch, *What Time Is This Place?* (Cambridge, Mass.: MIT Press, 1972).

7 CNN Airport Network, "Working for Passengers," Promotional materials, 1994.

8 Barry Schwartz, *Queuing and Waiting: Studies in the Organization of Access and Delay* (Chicago: University of Chicago Press, 1975), 3.

9 Roy P. Fairfield, "Humanizing the Waiting Space," *Humanist* 37, no. 4 (1977): 43.

10 As Adam Philips notes, boredom is rarely discussed in psychoanalysis because psychoanalytic theory "tends to equate significance with intensity and so has rarely found a place, in theory, for all those less vehement, vaguer, often more subtle feelings and moves that most of our lives consist of." Adam Philips, *On Kissing, Tickling, and Being Bored: Psychoanalytic Essays on the Unexamined Life* (Cambridge, Mass.: Harvard University Press, 1993), 68.

11 Ibid., 78.

12 See Vincent Crapanzano, *Waiting: The Whites of South Africa* (New York: Random House, 1985), 44.

13 On the waiting room as a space of dwelling for homeless and mentally ill persons see Greg Lee Carter, "The Interactions between the Staff and the 'Denizens' of a Social Security Waiting Room: An Observational Analysis," *Sociological Viewpoints* 4, no. 1 (1988): 1–16.

14 Michel Foucault, *Discipline and Punish,* trans. Alan Sheridan (New York: Vintage Books, 1979), 293–308. Although he is working with quite different theoretical and empirical materials than Foucault, urbanist Charles B. Goodsells elaborates on the relations among waiting, architecture, and disciplinary operations of the state in "Welfare Waiting Rooms," *Urban Life* 12, no. 4 (January 1984): 467–477. The idea of the waiting room as self-improvement center is certainly apparent in the waiting room of

Celebration Health, the hospital serving Walt Disney's model community in Florida, which gives patients pagers and directs them to "specially designed education or fitness centers" while they wait for their appointments. See Robert Lowes, "Is Your Waiting Room a Practice Builder — or a Holding Pen?" *Medical Economics,* July 13, 1998, 132. On contemporary pedagogical practices in the waiting room see "Kaiser Expands Program to Expose Children to Books," *Medical Industry Today,* September 15, 1997, n.p.

15 See Cindy Patton's *Fatal Advice: How Safe-Sex Education Went Wrong* (Durham, N.C.: Duke University Press, 1996) for a discussion of the links between HIV prevention videos and surveillance, and of activist-produced videos designed to counter such tendencies. For an example of the public health perspective on clinic video screenings see L. O'Donnell et al., "The Effectiveness of Video-Based Interventions in Promoting Condom Acquisition among STD Clinic Patients," *Sexually Transmitted Diseases* 22, no. 2 (1995): 97–103.

16 "TV in the Waiting Room: There's More to Watch than Soap Operas," *Medical Economics,* July 13, 1998, 140.

17 Networks for medical settings arrived on the scene, along with many other highly targeted cable and satellite channels, in the early 1980s. See John Brecher. "Keeping the Patient in Stitches," *Newsweek,* August 1, 1983, 65.

18 "Advertising in the Doc's Office," *Phillips Business Information: Healthcare Pr & Marketing News* 6, no. 2 (1997). For a discussion of the ethical questions of waiting-room TV see Hochschild, "Taken Hostage," 25.

19 It is a testament to the anonymous public qualities of the space that not once was my presence questioned by the staff present in the reception area, despite the fact that I carried a camera and spent in one instance more than ninety minutes in one waiting room. Being a "participant observer" in an anonymous public setting is an interesting form of social experience. My research was conducted largely in silence, although on every occasion I left the building feeling as if I had had a great many interactions with other waiting people. However, these interactions were largely nonverbal, involving smiles, gestures, and other expressive ways of forging a sense of commonality within a place. For a detailed description of the sociological characteristics of public space see Erving Goffman, *Relations in Public: Microstudies of the Public Order* (New York: Harper and Row, 1972); Lofland, *World of Strangers.*

20 Moore, "What the Doctor Ordered," 303.

21 Ibid.

22 Schwartz, *Queuing and Waiting,* 14, 16.

23 "TV in the Waiting Room," 140.

24 See Jürgen Habermas, *Legitimation Crisis* (Boston: Beacon Press, 1975); James R. O'Connor, *The Fiscal Crisis of the State* (New York: St. Martin's Press, 1973).

25 Schwartz, *Queuing and Waiting,* 16. Schwartz's hypothesis is borne out in the spatial contexts of welfare reform in the late 1990s.

26 Doane, "Information, Crisis, Catastrophe," 237. See also Mellencamp, "TV Time."

27 Doane, "Information, Crisis, Catastrophe," 238. For more on Benjamin's theory of shock see pt. 1 of Hansen, *Babel and Babylon.*

28 In 1997 a trade publication reported that "a national poll of 1,014 Americans found

that about half spend 20 minutes or more in the waiting room." *Hospitals and Health Networks,* September 5, 1997, 26. It should be noted, however, that statistical data on waiting time are somewhat conflicting; moreover, such information is often proprietary, as research on this issue is conducted primarily by health-care organizations themselves. During one ninety-minute site visit I observed numerous people whose wait exceeded the entire duration of my time there. Now this kind of duration was due in part to the fact that the city was in the midst of a flu epidemic. However, the fact that waiting time could be dramatically increased during the relatively minor crisis of a seasonal, predictable epidemic does indicate a definite shortcoming in this "just in time" model. According to one source, HMOs are moving away from this model by hiring consultants to redesign waiting rooms. See Laura Billings, "Ladies in Waiting," *American Health for Women,* April 1998, 104.

29 This subscription information is provided on the company's website: http://www.accenthealth.com/subscribe

30 Mike Stobbe, "Health TV Company Announces Merger," *Tampa Tribune,* October 27, 1999, Business and Finance section, 1.

31 "TV in the Waiting Room," 141 (emphasis mine). According to this article, network officials claim that repetitiveness leads 4 percent of subscribing practices to remove the network each year.

32 Tom Selleck.

33 Prior to the installation of this satellite-based in-house TV system, Planet Hollywood TV screens played videotapes of movies. Jeff Jensen, "New TV Net Set for Planet Hollywood Restaurant Chain," *Advertising Age,* July 13, 1998, 18.

34 As Robert Pittman, CEO of the Six Flags park explained in *Advertising Age,* "This is the ultimate zap-proof TV. . . . No one can change the volume, no one can change the channel and they can't go to the bathroom because they'd lose their place in line." Quoted in Scott Donaton, "Six Flags Woos Nat'l Advertisers," *Advertising Age,* January 11, 1993, 13.

35 Cheryl Ursin. "Theme Restaurants Play to Diners' Appetite for Fun," *Restaurants USA,* August 1996, 25.

36 Scannell, "Radio Times."

37 Ibid., 28.

38 The link between reading and eating is particularly strong in the fast-food industry. A study by the McDonald's corporation found that 75 percent of customers read the menu board *after* ordering. An increased awareness of their customers' tendencies to look for things to read while eating is leading fast-food chains to incorporate more and more printed material in the designs of their tray liners and napkins. See Underhill, *Why We Buy,* 66–67.

39 Paul Farhi, "TV Channels Its Energy All Over Town," *Washington Post,* May 5, 1997, A1.

40 David Glynos, Interview with the author, 1998. David Glynos is the owner and manager of the Video Diner.

Chapter 7 Terminal Thoughts on Art, Activism, and Video for Public Places

1 Stuart Hall, "Cultural Studies: Two Paradigms," *Media, Culture, and Society* 2 (1980): 57–72.

2 For a strong critique of de Certeau's binary schema, one aligned with a Foucauldian agenda, see Bennett, *Culture*, 177–180.

3 de Certeau, *Practice of Everyday Life*, xix.

4 Harvey, *Geography of Difference*, 27.

5 Lucy Lippard, "Trojan Horses: Activist Art and Power," in *Art after Modernism: Rethinking Representation*, ed. Brian Wallis (New York: Godine, 1984), 342.

6 Andy Cox, e-mail interview with the author, December 1998. (All subsequent quotes from Cox are taken from this correspondence.)

7 On the political problematic delineated by the avant-garde in aesthetic theory and art institutions see Peter Burger, *Theory of the Avant Garde*, trans. Michael Shaw (Minneapolis: University of Minnesota Press, 1984). On situationism see Ken Knabb, *Situationist International Anthology* (Berkeley: Bureau of Public Secrets, 1981); Edward Ball, "The Great Sideshow of the Situationist International," *Yale French Studies* 73 (1984): 21–37; Astrid Vicas, "Reusing Culture: The Import of Détournement," *Yale Journal of Criticism* 11, no. 2 (1998): 381–406; Thomas McDonough, "Situationist Space," *October* 67 (winter 1994): 58–77.

8 Ball, "Great Sideshow," 24; Raoul Vaneigem, *The Revolution of Everyday Life*, trans. Donald Nicholson-Smith (London: Left Bank Books and Rebel Press, 1983).

9 Guy Debord, "Introduction to a Critique of Urban Geography," trans. Ken Knabb, *Situationist International Anthology*, ed. and trans. Ken Knabb (Berkeley: Bureau of Public Secrets, 1989), 5.

10 Ball, "Great Sideshow," 31.

11 Ibid., 90.

12 Krzysztof Wodiczko, *Critical Vehicles: Writings, Projects, Interviews* (Cambridge, Mass.: MIT Press, 1999), 27, 28.

13 Ibid., 164–165.

14 Exchange with Douglas Crimp in Krzysztof Wodiczko, Douglas Crimp, and Barbara Kruger, "Discussion," in *Dia Art Foundation Discussions in Contemporary Culture Number One*, ed. Hal Foster (Seattle: Bay Press, 1987), 48.

15 See Dara Birnbaum, "The Rio Experience: Video's New Architecture Meets Corporate Sponsorship," in *Illuminating Video: An Essential Guide to Video Art*, ed. Doug Hall and Sally Jo Fifer (San Francisco: Aperture, 1990); Regina Cornwell, "Art in the Agora," *Art in America*, February 1991, 134–137, 161.

16 Cornwell, "Art in the Agora," 137.

17 Charles Rutheiser, *Imagineering Atlanta: The Politics of Place in the City of Dreams* (New York: Verso, 1996), 224–225.

18 Robin Reidy, quoted in Birnbaum, "Rio Experience," 193.

19 Ibid., 192.

20 Ibid.

21 Cornwell, "Art in the Agora," 134.

22 Ibid, 137.

23 Rutheiser noted in 1997 that Rio "re-opened with a new collection of shops oriented to the surrounding African-American community" (194–195). News reports over the years indicate how much these shops promoted black cultural identity. See, e.g., Scott Walton, "People in the Arts: Ron Lee," *Atlanta Journal-Constitution*, August 7, 1994, N2; Paula Crouch Thrasher, "Children's Theater," *Atlanta Journal-Constitution*, September 30, 1995, 22L; Howard Pousner, "Festivalgoers Need No Schooling," *Atlanta Journal-Constitution*, October 25, 1993, C7; Mara Rose Williams, "Local UNCF's Art Auction Ranks High as Fund-Raiser," *Atlanta Journal-Constitution*, February 20, 1997, 7N.

24 Miriam Longino, "Disc Jockey's Brand of Spunk and Soul Endears Her to Fans Who Embrace Her as 'Everybody's Sister,' " *Atlanta Journal-Constitution*, April 2, 1997, 1B.

25 Matt Quillen, interview with the author, August 20, 1999.

26 Ibid.

27 City of Atlanta, City Council Minutes, City Ordinance 99-0-0-477, June 7, 1999. On Rio's recent sale see Sallye Salter, "Midtown Project Hits Snag on Tax Break," *Atlanta Journal-Constitution*, April 28, 1999, 2D. For critical perspectives on enterprise zones and their Clinton-era cousins, "empowerment zones," in urban policy making see Philip Kasinitz and Jan Rosenberg, "Why Enterprise Zones Will Not Work," *City Journal* 3, no. 4 (1993); Mitchell L. Moss, "Where's the Power in Empowerment Zones," *City Journal* 5, no. 2 (1995): 76–81; James S. Russell, "Can Architects Help Cities Recover Civic Greatness?" *Architectural Record*, August 1996, 32.

28 Manuel Castells, *The Information Age: Economy, Society, and Culture. Volume 1: The Rise of the Network Society* (Oxford: Blackwell, 1996), 386.

29 Margaret Morse, *Virtualities: Television, Media Art, and Cyberculture* (Bloomington: Indiana University Press, 1998), 161.

30 Kwon, "One Place after Another," 91.

31 W. J. T. Mitchell, "Introduction: Utopia and Critique," in *Art and the Public Sphere*, ed. W. J. T. Mitchell (Chicago: University of Chicago Press, 1992), 4.

WORKS CITED

Anonymous Press Articles and Trade Pamphlets

"3-by-4-Foot Picture in U.S. Television Set." *New York Times,* March 27, 1948, 22.

"250,000 See Store Video." *Radio Age,* January 1946, 29.

Advertisement. "Give Them Better Television." *Beverage Media,* March 1947, 79.

"Advertising in the Doc's Office." Phillips Business Information: *Healthcare Pr & Marketing News* 6, no. 2 (1997).

"Angels Seeking Television's Aid." *New York Times,* June 21, 1948, 23.

"At the Knife and Fork." *New Yorker,* June 29, 1946, 16–17.

"Backstage with Television." *Stores,* March 1948, 44.

"Bar Bits." *Beverage Media,* April 1947, 55.

"Bar Bits." *Beverage Media,* June 1947, 68.

"Barroom Lament." *New York Times,* June 13, 1948, sec. XX, 6.

"Barroom Video Curbed." *New York Times,* July 21, 1948, 25.

"Barrooms with a View." *Time,* March 24, 1947, 63–64.

"BBB Finds Home in Variety of Places." *Home Textiles Today,* 1996, 20.

"Beauty Methods Demonstrated on TV Show by Chicago Store." *Broadcasting,* November 19, 1945, 28.

"Believe It or Not . . . You're in Show Business." *Beverage Media,* June 1947, 53–54.

"Better Display Wanted by Women Customers." *Display World,* March 1947, 70.

"Carlson Says Video Powerful, Subtle." *Broadcasting,* November 19, 1945, 101.

"Case History." *Televiser,* January 1949, 9–10.

Catalog. Boulder, Colo.: ICW International, 1999.

"Category Killer." *Discount Merchandiser,* June 1992, 44.

"Category Killers." *Discount Store News,* December 4, 1995, 104.

"Chi Kids to See Ball Games as 'TV Guests.' " *Variety,* March 24, 1948, 31.

"Chicago Now Has 11,500 Video Sets." *Advertising Age,* January 19, 1948, 58.

"Chicago Pub Patrons Like Baseball on TV," *Broadcasting,* July 12, 1948, 68.

"Children, Parents Blamed in Library TV-Show Trouble." *Louisville Courier-Journal,* April 13, 1949, sec. 2, 1.

"Church TV Center." *Broadcasting,* January 17, 1949.

"Coin Operated Television." *New Orleans Times-Picayune,* December 17, 1948, sec. 4, 16.

"Coin TV for Cafes." *Broadcasting*, July 25, 1949.

"Department Stores Hurrying to Suburbs." *Business Week*, October 4, 1947, 25.

"Disassembly Line for Stores: Thalhimers." *Business Week*, December 18, 1948, 78–80.

"'Dry' Club Renews Video Appeal." *New York Times*, July 19, 1948, 12.

"Dumont Daytime." *Broadcasting*, December 12, 1949.

"The Fair Store." *Television*, February 1946, 32.

"For a More Efficient Big Volume Store." *Architectural Record*, February 1947.

"Free Theater as Sales Hypo." *Variety*, February 23, 1949, 27.

"Holmes Gives Preview of Video Shows." *New Orleans States*, November 16, 1948, 6.

"It Comes Out Here." *Beverage Media*, June 1947, 60, 62.

"It's Like Working at the Mint." *Beverage Media*, June 1947, 55, 59.

"It's the Taverns That Still Worry Baseball Chiefs." *Variety*, June 16, 1948, 32.

"Jerseyites Prefer Their TV at Home." *Variety*, March 16, 1948, 27.

"Juke Box Television." *Broadcasting*, January 24, 1949.

"Kaiser Expands Program to Expose Children to Books." *Medical Industry Today*, September 15, 1997, n.p.

"Large Hard Lines: Virgin Megastore." *Chain Store Age Special Issue: Retail Store of the Year*, February 1997, 26.

"Legislation as Video Snag Gets Exhib Onceover." *Variety*, January 28, 1948, 5.

"Linking Department Store Merchandising with Local Television Operation." DuMont Network Promotional Pamphlet. 1944. National Museum of American History Archives Center, Smithsonian Institution, Washington, D.C.

"Main Event: TV vs. SRO." *Nation's Business*, March 1949, 46–48, 84.

"Make TV Work *for* You." *Beverage Media*, December 1950, 16–17.

"The Merchandise Man's Victory Problems." *Bulletin of the National Retail and Dry Goods Association*, October 1945.

"Minutes." Atlanta: City Council, 1999.

"More Jumbo Financing: Hibbet Eyes 500 Markets." *Sporting Goods Business*, August 10, 1998, 19.

"The New Medium . . . It's Now a Huge Going Concern." *Sponsor*, July 1948, 75.

"Pa. Restaurants." *Broadcasting*, December 5, 1949.

"Phila. Tax." *Broadcasting*, January 3, 1949.

"Philly Tavern Dealers Fight Tele Set Tax on Excess Fee Grounds." *Variety*, February 16, 1949, 33.

"Piece of the Action." *Sporting Goods Business*, April 14, 1997, 32–33.

"Plan Parish Television." *New York Times*, October 2, 1947, 56.

"Playground TV." *Broadcasting*, March 29, 1948.

"Pub Crawlers." *Time*, August 2, 1948, 43.

"Regular Television from Gimbel's Sales Floor." *Stores*, April 1949.

"See It in Church." *Newsweek*, October 27, 1947, 82.

"Seeing Means Selling: Visual Principles Give the Plus Push to Store Merchandising." *Stores*, October 1949, 14–15, 34.

"Sees Demand for Television Sets." *New York Times*, January 1, 1947, 43.

"Selling by Television." *Bulletin of the NRGDA*, February 1945, 68–72.

"Series Success." *Broadcasting*, October 10, 1949, 46.

"The Simpson Verdict." *Providence Journal-Bulletin,* October 4, 1995, 6A.

"Star Gazing." *Sporting Goods Business,* April 14, 1997, 33.

"Stores to Expand." *Business Week,* March 23, 1946, 80–83.

"Survey." *Video Store* 19, no. 42 (1997): 16.

"Table Top Receivers Popularize Tele." *Department Store Economist,* September 1948, 113.

"The Teach and Sell School of Retailing." *New York Times,* February 28, 1998, D1, D14.

"Tele-Hangout." *Recreation,* February 1949, 494.

"Television Caravan." *Department Store Economist,* June 1947, 48.

"Television in the Tavern." *Newsweek,* June 16, 1947, 64.

"The Television Set." *Time,* December 15, 1947, 50.

"Television's Audience Problem." *Business Week,* September 13, 1947, 70.

"Total Visibility at Bambergers." *Stores,* October 1949, 28.

"Turner Checks Out." *Advertising Age,* March 1, 1993, 16.

"TV—a Market in New York Now." *Sponsor,* March 1947, 49.

"TV Bar Tax Action." *Broadcasting,* April 25, 1949, 66.

"TV Cocktailery." *Variety,* April 6, 1949, 30.

"TV in the Waiting Room: There's More to Watch Than Soap Operas." *Medical Economics,* July 13, 1998.

"TV Net Plans Daytime Programming." *Radio Daily,* November 25, 1949.

"TV Screens Turn Blue at Don Muang." *Bangkok Post,* August 17, 1999.

Untitled report. *Hospitals and Health Networks,* September 5, 1997, 26.

"Video 'Rescues' Youths." *Chicago Daily News,* September 17, 1948, 38.

"Video Invasion: TVs Take Over Marketplace." *Charleston Gazette,* April 9, 1997, 7a.

"Video Kayoes the Barroom Bore." *Chicago Daily News,* September 17, 1948, 32.

"A Village Hires a Helper." *Recreation,* January 1948, 460.

"Whittle Cancels News Network for Doctors." *New York Times,* August 2, 1994, D3.

"Working for Passengers." Research Study. Cable News Network, 1994.

Books, Articles, Theses

Abrahams, Howard P. "How Visual Merchandising Has Grown." In *Display Manual,* ed. Howard P. Abrahams et al., 7–11. New York: Visual Merchandising Group of the National Retail and Dry Goods Association, 1952.

Abu-Lughod, Lila. "The Interpretation of Culture after Television." *Representations* 59 (1997): 107–133.

Agnew, Jean-Christophe. "A House of Fiction: Domestic Interiors and the Commodity Aesthetic." In *Consuming Visions: Accumulation and Display of Goods in America, 1880–1920,* ed. Simon J. Bronner, 133–155. New York: Norton, 1989.

Agnew, John. "Representing Space: Space, Scale, and Culture in Social Science." In *Place/ Culture/Representation,* ed. James Duncan and David Ley, 251–271. London: Routledge, 1993.

Alexander, R. S. "Some Aspects of Sex Differences in Relation to Marketing." *Journal of Marketing* 12, no. 2 (1947): 159–172.

Anderson, Benedict. *Imagined Communities: Reflections on the Origin and Spread of Nationalism.* London: Verso, 1983.

Ang, Ien. *Desperately Seeking the Audience.* New York: Routledge, 1991.

———. *Living Room Wars: Rethinking Media Audiences for a Postmodern World.* New York: Routledge, 1996.

Arcenaux, Ronald J. "Attention Shoppers: WGBS and the History of Department Store Radio." Master's thesis, City University of New York, 1997.

Arons, David. "30 Day Experiment Doubles Sales." *Television,* May 1949.

———. "Television Becomes Sell-a-Vision at Gimbel's Philadelphia." *Television,* June 1948, 22–24, 42.

Auge, Marc. *Non-Places: Toward an Anthropology of Super-Modernity.* Trans. John Howe. New York: Verso, 1995.

Austin, Regina. "'A Nation of Thieves': Consumption, Commerce, and the Black Public Sphere." *Public Culture* 7 (1994): 225–248.

Ball, Edward. "The Great Sideshow of the Situationist International." *Yale French Studies* 73 (1984): 21–37.

Barboza, David. "With Consumers Surfing around TV Commercials at Home, Some Companies Take the Ads on the Road." *New York Times,* July 14, 1995, D4.

Bausinger, Herman. "Media, Technology, and Daily Life." *Media, Culture, and Society* 6, no. 4 (1984): 343–351.

Benjamin, Walter. "The Work of Art in the Age of Mechanical Reproduction." Trans. Harry Zorn. *Illuminations,* ed. Hannah Arendt, 217–52. New York: Schocken Books, 1977.

Bennett, Tony. *Culture: A Reformer's Science.* London: Sage, 1998.

Benson, Susan Porter. *Counter Cultures: Saleswomen, Managers, and Customers in American Department Stores, 1890–1949.* Urbana: University of Illinois Press, 1986.

Berkman, Meredith. "Shirts and Skins." *New York,* January 13, 1992, 15.

Berry, Sarah. "Screen Style: Consumer Fashion and Femininity in 1930s Hollywood." Ph.D. diss., New York University, 1997.

Berstell, Gerald. "Point-of-Sale Research Reveals Spontaneous Buying Decisions." *Marketing News,* June 8, 1992, H-31.

———. "Study What People Do, Not What They Say." *Marketing News,* January 6, 1992, 7.

Billings, Laura. "Ladies in Waiting." *American Health for Women,* April 1998, 104.

Birnbaum, Dara. "The Rio Experience: Video's New Architecture Meets Corporate Sponsorship." In *Illuminating Video: An Essential Guide to Video Art,* ed. Doug Hall and Sally Jo Fifer, 189–204. San Francisco: Aperture, 1990.

Bliss, Al. "Getting, Stopping, and Selling . . . Store Traffic." *Display World,* January 1945.

Bliss, Albert. "Psychology of Seeing." *Display World,* April 1946, 70.

———. "Visual Merchandising . . . Its Promises and Obligations." *Display World,* August 1944, 50.

Bluestone, Barry, et al. *The Retail Revolution: Market Transformation, Investment, and Labor in the Modern Department Store.* New York: Auburn House, 1981.

Boddy, William. *Fifties Television: The Industry and Its Critics.* Urbana: University of Illinois Press: 1990.

Bogart, Leo. *The Age of Television: A Study of Viewing Habits and the Impact of Television on American Life.* New York: Frederick Ungar, 1956.

Bogart, Michele H. *Artists, Advertising, and the Borders of Art.* Chicago: University of Chicago Press, 1995.

Bond, Cathy. "Effective Demands." *Marketing,* December 5, 1996, 34–38.

Bowlby, Rachel. *Just Looking: Consumer Culture in Dreiser, Gissing, and Zola.* New York: Methuen, 1985.

Brecher, John. "Keeping the Patient in Stitches." *Newsweek,* August 1, 1983, 65.

Bronson, Patricia. *Vittles and Vice: An Extraordinary Guide to What's Cooking on Chicago's Near North Side.* Chicago: Henry Regnery, 1952.

Brown, Deneen L., and Nancy Lewis. "Some Riveted, Others Revolted." *Washington Post,* January 12, 1995, A14.

Browne, Nick. "The Political Economy of the Television (Super) Text." In *Television: The Critical View,* ed. Horace Newcomb. 4th ed. New York: Oxford, 1987.

Brunsdon, Charlotte. "Satellite Dishes and the Landscapes of Taste." In *The Audience and Its Landscape,* ed. James Hay, Lawrence Grossberg, and Ellen Wartella, 342–357. New York: Westview Press, 1996.

Burger, Peter. *Theory of the Avant Garde.* Trans. Michael Shaw. Minneapolis: University of Minnesota Press, 1984.

Caldwell, John. *Televisuality: Style, Crisis, and Authority in American Television.* New Brunswick, N.J.: Rutgers University Press, 1994.

Campbell, Colin. "Changes Afoot in TV Babble at Hartsfield." *Atlanta Journal-Constitution,* April 3, 1997, 1B.

———. "Why Monopoly on Cacophony?" *Atlanta Journal-Constitution,* March 18, 1997, 1C.

Carter, Greg Lee. "The Interactions between the Staff and the 'Denizens' of a Social Security Waiting Room: An Observational Analysis." *Sociological Viewpoints* 4, no. 1 (1988): 1–16.

Castaneda, Laura. "There's More in Store." *Dallas Morning News,* January 16, 1996, 1D.

Castells, Manuel. *The Information Age: Economy, Society, and Culture. Volume 1: The Rise of the Network Society.* Oxford: Blackwell, 1996.

Certeau, Michel de. *The Practice of Everyday Life.* Berkeley: University of California Press, 1984.

Classen, Constance, David Howes, and Anthony Synot. *Aroma: The Cultural History of Smell.* London: Routledge, 1994.

Clay, Grady. *Real Places: An Unconventional Guide to America's Generic Landscape.* Chicago: University of Chicago Press, 1994.

Colomina, Beatriz. *Privacy and Publicity: Modern Architecture as Mass Media.* Cambridge, Mass.: MIT Press, 1994.

———. "The Split Wall: Domestic Voyeurism." In *Sexuality and Space,* ed. Beatriz Colomina, 73–130. New York: Princeton Architectural Press, 1992.

Conroy, Marianne. "Discount Dreams: Factory Outlet Malls, Consumption, and the Performance of Middle-Class Identity." *Social Text 54* 16, no. 1 (1998): 63–83.

Copperud, Roy. *American Usage and Style: The Consensus.* New York: Van Nostrand Reinhold, 1980.

Corbett, Beth. "Place-Based Media Research: Doing It Right the First Time." In proceedings of the ARF Fourteenth Annual Electronic Media Research Workshop, 138–153. New York: Advertising Research Foundation, 1995.

Corbett, John. *Extended Play: Sounding Off from John Cage to Doctor Funkenstein.* Durham, N.C.: Duke University Press, 1994.

Cornwell, Regina. "Art in the Agora." *Art in America,* February 1991, 134–137, 161.

Cortez, John P. "Media Pioneers Try to Corral On-the-Go Consumers." *Advertising Age,* August 17, 1992, 25.

Couldry, Nick. *The Place of Media Power: Pilgrims and Witnesses of the Media Age.* London: Routledge, 2000.

Cowee, Howard M. "Research in Visual Merchandising." In *Display Manual,* ed. Howard P. Abrahams et al., 40–51. New York: Visual Merchandising Group of the National Retail and Dry Goods Association, 1951.

Cowee, Howard M. "Display—or Visual Merchandising?" *Journal of Retailing,* May 1945.

Cox, Andy. Personal correspondence with author. December 1998.

Craig, Jack. "Patriots Toast of the Town? Some Bars Pirating Signals to Give Customers an Illegal Show." *Boston Globe,* September 27, 1991, 56.

Crapanzano, Vincent. *Waiting: The Whites of South Africa.* New York: Random House, 1985.

Cumming, James C. *Keys to Selling Department Stores.* New York: Fairchild Publishing, 1948.

Curti, Merle. "The Changing Concept of Human Nature in the Literature of American Advertising." *Business History Review* 41 (winter 1967): 339–345.

Dale, Steve. "Sports Bars Are Up for All-Star Partying." *Chicago Tribune,* July 6, 1990, 2.

Danno, Joe. Interview by author. Chicago, October 19, 1993.

Davidson, Cathy, ed. *No More Separate Spheres,* a special issue of *American Literature 70,* no. 3, 1998.

Dayan, Daniel, and Elihu Katz. *Media Events: The Live Broadcasting of History.* Cambridge, Mass.: Harvard University Press, 1992.

Debord, Guy. "Introduction to a Critique of Urban Geography." *Situationist International Anthology,* ed. and trans. Ken Knabb. Berkeley: Bureau of Public Secrets, 5–8. 1989.

Delaney, Samuel R. *Times Square Red, Times Square Blue.* New York: New York University Press, 1999.

Dirlik, Arif. "The Global in the Local." In *Global/Local: Cultural Production and the Transnational Imaginary,* ed. Rob Wilson and Wimal Dissanayake, 21–45. Durham, N.C.: Duke University Press, 1996.

Doane, Mary Ann. "Information, Crisis, Catastrophe." In *Logics of Television,* ed. Patricia Mellencamp. Bloomington: Indiana University Press, 1990.

Donaton, Scott. "Flaws Ax Checkout Channel." *Advertising Age,* February 22, 1993, 3.

———. "Six Flags Woos Nat'l Advertiser." *Advertising Age,* January 11, 1993, 13.

Duffy, Ben. "Who Needs a Haircut?" *Variety,* July 28, 1948, 29.

Dunlap, Orrin. *The Future of Television.* New York: Harper and Brothers, 1947.

Dupuy, Judy. *Television Show Business.* Schenectady, N.Y.: General Electric Corporation, 1945.

Eckert, Charles. "The Carole Lombard in Macy's Window." In *Fabrications: Costume and the Female Body,* ed. Jane Gaines and Charlotte Herzog. New York: Routledge, 1990.

Eldredge, Irving C. "What's to Be Sold Must First Be Seen." *Stores,* October 1949.

Elsner, Monika, Thomas Muller, and Peter M. Spangenberg. "The Early History of German Television: The Slow Development of a Fast Form." *Historical Journal of Film, Television, and Radio* 10, no. 2 (1990): 193–218.

Entrikin, J. Nicholas. *The Betweenness of Place: Towards a Geography of Modernity.* Baltimore: Johns Hopkins University Press, 1991.

Fahey, Alison. "Turner's New Gamble." *Advertising Age,* April 22, 1991, 3–4.

Fairfield, Roy P. "Humanizing the Waiting Space." *Humanist* 37, no. 4 (1977): 43.

Farhi, Paul. "TV Channels Its Energy All Over Town." *Washington Post,* May 5, 1997, A1.

Feldman, Richard. "Demonstrating the Real Advertising Value of Place-Based and Interactive Media." In proceedings of the ARF Eleventh Annual Electronic Media Workshop, 92–99. New York: Advertising Research Foundation, 1992.

Feuer, Jane. "The Concept of Live Television: Ontology as Ideology." In *Regarding Television: Critical Approaches — An Anthology,* ed. E. Ann Kaplan. Frederick, Md.: AFI/ University Publications of America, 1983.

Fine, Ben. "From Political Economy to Consumption." In *Acknowledging Consumption: A Review of New Studies,* ed. Daniel Miller, 127–163. London: Routledge, 1995.

Fiske, John. "Ethnosemiotics, Some Personal and Theoretical Reflections." *Cultural Studies* 4, no. 1 (1990): 85–99.

Forbes, Gordon. "NFL Taps Bars Game Day." *USA Today,* April 12, 1994, 1A.

———. "NFL TV Plan Focuses on Sports Bars." *USA Today,* April 12, 1994, 1C.

Foster, Hal, et al. "On Site Specificity." *Documents* 4/5 (spring 1994): 11–21.

Foucault, Michel. *Discipline and Punish.* Trans. Alan Sheridan. New York: Vintage Books, 1979.

Francisco, L. Mercer. "The Talking Picture: An Example of the Machine Method Applied to Selling." *Journal of Marketing* 9, no. 2 (1944): 119–123.

French, Kenneth. *Jersey City, 1940–1960.* Dover, N.H.: Arcadia Press, 1997.

Friedberg, Anne. *Window Shopping: Cinema and the Postmodern.* Berkeley: University of California Press, 1993.

Gaines, Jane. "The Queen Christina Tie-Ups: Convergence of Show Window and Screen." *Quarterly Review of Film and Video* 11, no. 1 (1989): 35–60.

Gamble, Bud. "The Television Tour of 88 Department Stores." *Televiser* (fall 1945): 48.

Gannon, Mary. "The Retailer and Television." *Television,* September 1947, 11–14, 40.

———. "Television and the Department Store." *Television,* November 1945, 7–15.

———. "Ten Men on a Horse." *Television,* July 1948: 22–25, 40.

Garnham, Nicholas. "Political Economy and Cultural Studies: Reconciliation or Divorce?" *Critical Studies in Mass Communication* 12, no. 1 (1995): 62–71.

———. "Reply to Grossberg and Carey." *Critical Studies in Mass Communication* 12, no. 1 (1995): 95–100.

Gelber, Steven M. "Do It Yourself: Constructing, Repairing, and Maintaining Domestic Masculinity." *American Quarterly* 49, no. 1 (1997): 66–112.

Gellene, Denise. "The Persuaders." *Los Angeles Times,* December 31, 1998, C6.

Gessell, Paul. "Parties and Protests Greet Ellen's Coming Out: April 30 Is L-Day across North America, and Ottawa Is No Exception." *Ottawa Citizen,* April 16, 1997, A1.

Giard, Luce. Preface to *The Practice of Everyday Life, Vol. 2: Eating and Cooking,* ed. Michel de Certeau, Luce Giard, and Olivier Meyrol. Minneapolis: University of Minnesota Press, 1998.

Gilbert, Leslie. "Exotic Produce Shouldn't Be a Mystery." *Supermarket Business,* April 1988, 47.

Gillespie, Marie. "Sacred Serials, Devotional Viewing, and Domestic Worship: A Case Study in the Interpretation of Two TV Versions of *The Mahabharata* in a Hindu Family in West London." In *To Be Continued: Soap Operas around the World,* ed. Robert C. Allen, 354–380. New York: Routledge, 1995.

Gimbel's. Advertisement. *Philadelphia Inquirer,* October 24, 1945, 24.

Glaser, Milton. "I Listen to the Market." In *On Signs,* ed. Marshall Blonsky, 467–474. Baltimore: Johns Hopkins University Press, 1985.

Glynos, David. Interview by author. New York, N.Y. February 1998.

Goffman, Erving. *Relations in Public: Microstudies of the Public Order.* New York: Harper and Row, 1972.

Gomery, Douglas. "Failed Opportunities: The Integration of the U.S. Motion Picture and Television Industries." *Quarterly Review of Film Studies* 9, no. 3 (1984): 219–28.

———. "Theater Television: The Missing Link of Technological Change in the U.S. Motion Picture Industry." *Velvet Light Trap* 21 (1985): 54–61.

Goodsells, Charles B. "Welfare Waiting Room." *Urban Life* 12, no. 4 (1984): 467–477.

Gordon, Joanne. "Footaction: Going the Distance." *Chain Store Age,* October 1997, 54–60.

Gottlieb, David. "The Neighborhood Tavern and the Cocktail Lounge: A Study of Class Differences." *American Journal of Sociology* 62, no. 6 (1957).

Gould, J. Kingsley. "The Manufacturer's Viewpoint on Display and Point of Purchase." In *Display Manual,* ed. Howard P. Abrahams et al., 73–79. New York: Visual Merchandising Group of the National Retail and Dry Goods Association, 1951.

Graham, Clarence R., and William Hodapp. "Television's Town Hall." *Library Journal,* March 15, 1949, 410.

Granberry, Michael. "NFL Scrambling Plan Dims Picture for Sports Bars." *Los Angeles Times,* August 18, 1990, San Diego County ed., B1.

Gray, Ann. *Video Playtime: The Gendering of a Leisure Technology.* New York: Routledge, 1992.

Grossberg, Lawrence. "Cultural Studies vs. Political Economy: Is Anyone Else Bored with This Debate?" *Critical Studies in Mass Communication* 12, no. 1 (1995): 72–81.

———. "The Cultural Studies' Crossroads Blues, or Doing Cultural Studies in Helms' Country." Keynote address, Crossroads in Cultural Studies Conference, Tampere, Finland, 1996.

Gundaker, Grey. *Signs of Diaspora/Diaspora of Signs.* New York: Oxford University Press, 1998.

Habermas, Jürgen. *Legitimation Crisis.* Boston: Beacon Press, 1975.

———. *The Structural Transformation of the Public Sphere: An Inquiry into a Category of Bourgeois Society.* Trans. Thomas Burger. Cambridge, Mass.: MIT Press, 1989.

Haldane, David. "A Sports Bar for Players, Power Brokers." *Los Angeles Times,* October 2, 1986, pt. 9, 2.

Hall, Lee. "CNN's Terminal Headache." *Electronic Media,* April 28, 1997, 28.

Hall, Stuart. "Cultural Studies: Two Paradigms." *Media, Culture, and Society* 2 (1980): 57–72.

Hanhardt, John. "Video in Fluxus." *Art and Text* 37 (1990): 86–91.

Hansen, Miriam. *Babel and Babylon: Spectatorship in American Silent Film.* Cambridge, Mass.: Harvard University Press, 1991.

Haralovich, Mary Beth. "Sitcoms and Suburbs." In *Private Screenings: Television and the Female Consumer,* ed. Lynn Spigel and Denise Mann. Minneapolis: University of Minnesota Press, 1992.

Harris, Neil. *Cultural Excursions: Marketing Appetites and Cultural Tastes in America.* Chicago: University of Chicago Press, 1990.

———. *Humbug: The Art of P. T. Barnum.* Boston: Little, Brown, 1973.

Harltey, John. *The Politics of Pictures.* London: Routledge, 1992.

Harvey, David. *The Condition of Postmodernity.* Cambridge, Mass.: Blackwell, 1989.

———. *Justice, Nature, and the Geography of Difference.* Cambridge, Mass.: Blackwell, 1996.

Heath, Rebecca Piirto. "POP Art." *Marketing Tools,* April 1997, 42–55.

Hendershot, Heather. *Saturday Morning Censors: Television Regulation before the V-Chip.* Durham, N.C.: Duke University Press, 1998.

Henkins, David. *City Reading: Written Words and Public Spaces in Antebellum New York.* New York: Columbia University Press, 1998.

Heubusch, Kevin. "When Shoppers Pause, Companies Sell." *American Demographics,* March 1997, 34.

Hirschmann, I. A. "Television: A New Dimension in Department Store Advertising." *Television* (spring 1944): 10, 38.

———. "Television in the Retail Field." *Journal of Marketing* 8, no. 1 (1943): 395–397.

Hochschild, Adam. "Taken Hostage at the Airport." *New York Times,* October 26, 1996, 25.

Hodges, Jane. "Parking Garages Supplying Newest Venue for TV Spots." *Advertising Age,* September 9, 1996, 35.

Holusha, John. "Web Gives White Elephants a New Life." *New York Times,* July 9, 2000, Real Estate sec.: 11–1, 11–4.

Hoskins, Janet. *Biographical Objects: How Things Tell the Stories of People's Lives.* New York: Routledge, 1998.

Howell, P. "Public Space and the Public Sphere: Political Theory and the Historical Geography of Modernity." *Environment and Planning D: Society and Space* 11 (1993): 303–322.

Huxtable, Ada Louise. *The Unreal America: Architecture and Illusion.* New York: New Press, 1997.

Jackson, Cheryl. "Firms Can't Wait to Make Their Pitch." *Tampa Tribune,* January 4, 1997, C1.

Jameson, Fredric. *Postmodernism; or, the Cultural Logic of Late Capitalism.* London: Verso, 1991.

Jensen, Jeff. "New TV Net Set for Planet Hollywood Restaurant Chain." *Advertising Age,* July 13, 1998, 18.

Johnson, Victoria. "Citizen Welk: Bubbles, Blue Hair, and Middle America." In *The Revo-*

lution Wasn't Televised: Sixties Television and Social Conflict, ed. Lynn Spigel and Michael Curtin, 265–286. New York: Routledge, 1997.

Jones, Hilda. "Intra-Store Television as a Sales-Promotion Medium." Journal of Retailing, February 1948, 15–20.

Journey, Mark. "NFL Letters Threaten Sports Bars." St. Petersburg Times, September 18, 1990, 1.

Kaplan, Alice, and Kristen Ross. "Introduction." Yale French Studies 73 (1987): 1–4.

Kaplan, Caren. Questions of Travel: Postmodern Discourses of Displacement. Durham, N.C.: Duke University Press, 1996.

Kash, R. C. "Display . . . And Television." Display World, October 1944.

Kasinitz, Philip, and Jan Rosenberg. "Why Enterprise Zones Will Not Work." City Journal 3, no. 4 (1993).

Kasson, John. Amusing the Million: Coney Island at the Turn of the Century. New York: Hill and Wang, 1978.

Kaufman, Arthur C. "Experiment in Selling by Television." Bulletin of the National Retail and Dry Goods Association, January 1945, 15–16, 56–58.

Kay, David. "Go Where the Consumers Are and Talk to Them." Marketing News, January 6, 1997, 14.

Keller, Alexandra. "Disseminations of Modernity: Representation and Consumer Desire in Early Mail Order Catalogs." In Cinema and the Invention of Modern Life, ed. Leo Charney and Vanessa Schwartz, 156–182. Berkeley: University of California Press, 1995.

Kelly, Keith J. "Flops Fail to Derail Place-Based." Advertising Age, August 8, 1994, 12.

Kiesler, Frederick. Contemporary Art Applied to the Store and Its Display. New York: Sir Isaac Pitman and Sons, 1930.

Kingsdale, John M. "The Poor Man's Club: Social Functions of the Urban Working Class Saloon." American Quarterly 25, no. 4 (1973): 472–89.

Klara, Robert. "TV Commercials Follow Shoppers to the Food Court; but Will Diners Respond to Restaurant Ads?" Restaurant Business, March 20, 1996, 22.

Knabb, Ken. Situationist International Anthology. Berkeley: Bureau of Public Secrets, 1981.

Kunstler, James Howard. The Geography of Nowhere. New York: Touchstone, 1993.

Kwon, Miwon. "One Place after Another: Notes on Site-Specificity." October 80 (spring 1997): 85–110.

Landry, John T. "Positioning the Product: Know Where Your Rivals Are." Harvard Business Review, Nov.–Dec. 1996, 13.

Lanza, Joseph. Elevator Music: A Surreal History of Muzak, Easy Listening, and Other Moodsong. New York: St. Martin's Press, 1994.

Latour, Bruno. We Have Never Been Modern. Trans. Catherine Porter. Cambridge, Mass.: Harvard University Press, 1993.

Layne, Barry. "NTA Study Finds 28 Million Viewers Out-of-Home." Hollywood Reporter, March 11, 1993, 1.

Leach, Neil. The Anaesthetics of Architecture. Cambridge, Mass.: MIT Press, 1999.

Leach, William. Land of Desire: Merchants, Power, and the Rise of a New American Culture. New York: Pantheon, 1993.

Leal, Ondina Fachel. "Popular Taste and Erudite Repertoire: The Place and Space of Television in Brazil." *Cultural Studies* 4, no. 1 (1990): 19–39.

Leaman, James. "The Display Designer . . . and TELEVISION." *Display World,* April 1944, 42, 67.

Lee, Robert E. *Television: The Revolutionary Industry.* New York: Essential Books, 1944.

Lemish, Dafna. "The Rules of Viewing Television in Public Places," *Journal of Broadcasting* 26, no. 4 (1982): 758–781.

Levine, Joshua. "Badass Sells." *Forbes,* April 21, 1997, 142–144.

Lewis, Floyd A. "Store Transactions Speeded by Modern Communications Systems." *Department Store Economist,* April 1948, 20.

Lippard, Lucy. "Trojan Horses: Activist Art and Power." In *Art after Modernism: Rethinking Representation,* ed. Brian Wallis, 341–358. New York: Godine, 1984.

Lofland, Lyn H. *A World of Strangers: Order and Action in Urban Public Space.* New York: Basic Books, 1973.

Logan, Dan. "Sports Bars Aim to Score Big with Giant TVs." *Los Angeles Times,* April 22, 1990, B20.

Logan, John R., and Harvey L. Molotch. *Urban Fortunes: The Political Economy of Place.* Berkeley: University of California Press, 1987.

Lomartire, Paul. "Satellite Feed in Sports Bars Offers Alternative but Raises Legal Issues." *Atlanta Journal-Constitution,* August 3, 1996, S29.

Longino, Miriam. "Disc Jockey's Brand of Spunk and Soul Endears Her to Fans Who Embrace Her as 'Everybody's Sister.'" *Atlanta Journal-Constitution,* April 2, 1997, 1B.

Longstreth, Richard. *City Center to Regional Mall: Architecture, the Automobile, and Retailing in Los Angeles, 1920–1950.* Cambridge, Mass.: MIT Press, 1997.

Lott, Eric. *Love and Theft: Blackface Minstrelsy and the American Working Class.* New York: Oxford University Press, 1995.

Lowes, Robert. "Is Your Waiting Room a Practice Builder—or a Holding Pen?" *Medical Economics,* July 13, 1998, 132.

Lull, James. *Inside Family Viewing: Ethnographic Research on Television Audiences.* New York: Routledge, 1990.

Lury, Celia, and Alan Warde. "Investments in the Imaginary Consumer: Conjectures Regarding Power, Knowledge, and Advertising." In *Buy This Book: Studies in Advertising and Consumption,* ed. Mica Nava, Iain McRory, and Barry Richards, 87–102. New York: Routledge, 1997.

Lynch, Kevin. *The Image of the City.* Cambridge, Mass.: MIT Press, 1960.

———. *What Time Is This Place?* Cambridge, Mass.: MIT Press, 1972.

Lyons, Andrew P. "The Television and the Shrine: Towards a Theoretical Model for the Study of Mass Communications in Nigeria." *Visual Anthropology* 3 (1990): 429–456.

MacDonald, Laurie. "Under Renovation: Entertainment-Oriented Shoe Retail Showcases." *Footwear News,* August 5, 1996, 8.

Mackintosh, Iain. *Architecture, Actor, and Audience.* London: Routledge, 1993.

Macrory, Boyd E. "The Tavern and the Community." *Quarterly Journal of Studies on Alcohol* 13, no. 4 (1952): 609–37.

Mahler, Richard. "While You Wait: TV Marketers Hunt Captive Viewers." *Electronic Media,* December 30, 1993, 1.

Mandese, Joe. "Measuring Place-Based Media." *Advertising Age,* November 15, 1993, 33.

Mankekar, Purnima. "National Texts and Gendered Lives: An Ethnography of Television Viewers in a North Indian City." *American Ethnologist* 20, no. 3 (1993): 543–563.

Martzke, Rudy. "NFL Tackles Game Pirates." *USA Today,* September 28, 1994, 1A.

Maslan, Susan. "Resisting Representation: Theater and Democracy in Revolutionary France." *Representations* 52 (fall 1995): 27–51.

Massey, Doreen. "Power-Geometry and a Progressive Sense of Place." In *Mapping the Futures: Local Cultures, Global Change,* ed. Jon Bird et al. New York: Routledge, 1993.

———. *Space, Place, and Gender.* Minneapolis: University of Minnesota Press, 1994.

Mattelart, Armand. *Advertising International: The Privatization of Public Space.* Trans. Michael Chanan. New York: Routledge, 1991.

Matzer, Marla. "Mall TV: Turner it On." *Brandweek,* June 17, 1996, 20.

Maxwell, Richard. "Ethics and Identity in Global Market Research." *Cultural Studies* 10, no. 2 (1998): 218–236.

McCarthy, Anna. " 'Like an Earthquake': Theater Television, Boxing, and the Black Public Sphere." *Quarterly Review of Film and Video* 16, nos. 3/4 (1999): 307–23.

McDonald, Kent. "The Commercial Strip: From Main Street to Television Road." *Landscape* 28, no. 2 (1985): 12–19.

McDonough, Thomas. "Situationist Space." *October* 67 (winter 1994): 58–77.

McLellan, Steve. "Networks to Fund Test of Out-of-Home Viewing." *Broadcasting,* April 6, 1992, 42.

McLuhan, Marshall, and Quentin Fiore. *The Medium Is the Massage: An Inventory of Effects.* New York: Bantam, 1967.

McMenamin, John J. "Airport Channel Methodology." *Advertising Age,* January 10, 1994, 23.

———. "Travellers Appreciate News." *Atlanta Journal-Constitution,* March 26, 1997, 14A.

Meades, Jonathan. "Eating Out." *Sunday Times Magazine,* December 20, 1997, 33.

Mellencamp, Patricia. *High Anxiety: Catastrophe, Scandal, Age, and Comedy.* Bloomington: Indiana University Press, 1992.

———. "TV Time and Catastrophe: Beyond the Pleasure Principle of Television." In *Logics of Television,* ed. Patricia Mellencamp, 242–266. Bloomington: Indiana University Press, 1990.

Mencken, H. L. *The American Language: An Enquiry into the Development of English in the United States Supplement I.* New York: Knopf, 1945.

Menkes, Suzy. "Fashion's TV Frenzy." *New York Times,* April 2, 1995, A47.

Meyrowitz, Joshua. *No Sense of Place: The Impact of Electronic Media on Social Behavior.* New York: Oxford University Press, 1985.

Miller, Daniel. *Capitalism: An Ethnographic Approach.* New York: Berg, 1997.

Miller, Toby. *Technologies of Truth: Cultural Citizenship and the Popular Media.* Minneapolis: University of Minnesota Press, 1998.

Miller, Toby, and Alec McHoul. *Popular Culture and Everyday Life.* London: Sage, 1998.

Mitchell, W. J. T. "Introduction: Utopia and Critique." In *Art and the Public Sphere,* ed. W. J. T. Mitchell. Chicago: University of Chicago Press, 1992.

Modleski, Tania. "The Search for Tomorrow in Today's Soap Operas." *Film Quarterly* 33, no. 1 (1979): 12–21.

Moore, David J. "Just What the Doctor Ordered." In *Electronic Media and Technologies IX: Ratings at a Crossroads.* New York: Advertising Research Foundation, 1990.

Morgan, Edward P. "Fifty Mile Bleachers." *Colliers,* September 27, 1947, 28–30.

Morley, David. *Family Television: Cultural Power and Domestic Leisure.* New York: Routledge, 1990.

Morley, David, and Kevin Robins. *Spaces of Identity: Global Media, Electronic Landscapes, and Cultural Boundaries.* New York: Routledge, 1995.

Morris, Meaghan. "Things to Do with Shopping Malls." In *Too Soon Too Late: History in Popular Culture.* Bloomington: Indiana University Press, 1998, 64–92.

Morse, Margaret. "An Ontology of Everyday Distraction: The Freeway, the Mall, and Television." In *Logics of Television,* ed. Patricia Mellencamp, 193–221. Bloomington: Indiana University Press, 1990.

———. "Sport on Television: Replay and Display." In *Regarding Television: Critical Approaches—An Anthology,* ed. E. Ann Kaplan. Frederick, Md.: American Film Institute/University Publications of America, 1983.

———. *Virtualities: Television, Media Art, and Cyberculture.* Bloomington: Indiana University Press, 1998.

Moss, Mitchell L. "Where's the Power in Empowerment Zones." *City Journal* 5, no. 2 (1995): 76–81.

Mysak, Joe. "Jock Bars." *American Spectator,* May 1988, 37–38.

Nasby, A. Gordon. "Television and the Church." *Christian Century,* February 2, 1949, 143.

Nelson, Dana. *National Manhood.* Durham, N.C.: Duke University Press, 1998.

Neville, Grace. "Some Thoughts on Intra-Store Tele." *Televiser,* March–April 1947, 33.

O'Connor, James R. *The Fiscal Crisis of the State.* New York: St. Martin's Press, 1973.

O'Donnell, L., et al. "The Effectiveness of Video-Based Interventions in Promoting Condom Acquisition among STD Clinic Patients." *Sexually Transmitted Diseases* 22, no. 2 (1995): 97–103.

O'Keefe, Michael. "Barroom Novelty." *New York Times,* July 4, 1948, sec. 2, 7.

———. "Concluding the Saga of Parkey Radigan." *New York Times,* August 8, 1948, sec. 2, 7.

Ong, Aihwa. *Flexible Citizenship: The Cultural Logics of Transnationality.* Durham, N.C.: Duke University Press, 1999.

Owens, Jim. "Report on Local Advertising." *Television,* November 1948.

Parnes, Louis. "A New Construction Applied to Department Stores." *Department Store Economist,* May 1945.

Patton, Cindy. *Fatal Advice: How Safe-Sex Education Went Wrong.* Durham, N.C.: Duke University Press, 1996.

Peiss, Kathy. *Cheap Amusements: Working Women and Leisure in Turn of the Century New York.* Philadelphia: Temple University Press, 1986.

Peterson, Joe. "All-Stars Sports Bar and Grill Aims for a Winning Combination." *Courier-Journal* (Louisville, Ky.), December 30, 1989, 21S.

Philips, Adam. *On Kissing, Tickling, and Being Bored: Psychoanalytic Essays on the Unexamined Life.* Cambridge, Mass.: Harvard University Press, 1993.

Pousner, Howard. "Festivalgoers Need No Schooling." *Atlanta Journal-Constitution,* October 25, 1993, C7.

Powers, Madelon. "Decay from Within: The Inevitable Doom of the American Saloon." In *Drinking: Behavior and Belief in Modern History,* ed. Susanna Barrows and Robin Room. Berkeley: University of California Press, 1991.

Press, Andrea L. *Women Watching Television: Gender, Class, and Generation in the American Television Experience.* Philadelphia: University of Pennsylvania Press, 1991.

Quillen, Matt. Phone interview by author. September 1999.

Rhodes, Helen T. "Television Programming for Department Stores." *Televiser* (spring 1945): 46–47.

Rickard, Leah. "Video Struggles to Find a Place in Grocery." *Advertising Age,* May 2, 1994, s-14.

Robbins, Bruce. "Introduction: The Public as Phantom." In *The Phantom Public Sphere,* ed. Bruce Robbins. Minneapolis: University of Minnesota Press, 1993.

Robins, Kevin, and Mark Hepworth. "Electronic Spaces: New Technologies and the Future of Cities." *Futures,* April 1988, 155–76.

Rogers, Prentis. "HBO May Patrol Atlanta to Find Bars Pirating Fight." *Atlanta Constitution,* November 21, 1991, E2.

Romero, Lora. *Home Fronts.* Durham, N.C.: Duke University Press, 1997.

Rosenberg, Bernard. "New York Bar Signs." *Quarterly Journal of Studies on Alcohol* 8, no. 2 (1947): 348–52.

Rosenzweig, Roy. *Eight Hours for What We Will: Workers and Leisure in an Industrial City, 1870–1920.* New York: Cambridge University Press, 1983.

Ross, Andrew, ed. *No Sweat: Fashion, Free Trade, and the Rights of Garment Workers.* New York: Verso, 1997.

Rothenberg, Randall. "Two Views on Whittle's TV Reports." *New York Times,* June 1, 1990, D3.

Russell, James S. "Can Architects Help Cities Recover Civic Greatness?" *Architectural Record,* August 1996, 32.

Rutheiser, Charles. *Imagineering Atlanta: The Politics of Place in the City of Dreams.* New York: Verso, 1996.

Ryan, Joan. "As Gay as He Wants to Be: How Rodman's Drag Queen Style Plays in the Castro." *San Francisco Chronicle,* June 6, 1996, A1.

Rykwert, Joseph. "The Sitting Position: A Question of Method." In *Meaning in Architecture,* ed. Charles Jencks. New York: Braziller, 1970.

Salter, Sallye. "Midtown Project Hits Snag on Tax Break." *Atlanta Journal-Constitution,* April 28, 1999, 2D.

Saxton, Lisa. "Video Draws Sales—But Needs Support." *Supermarket News,* January 7, 1991, 40.

Scannell, Paddy. "Radio Times." In *Television and Its Audience,* ed. Philip Drummond and Rob Paterson, 135–166. London: British Film Institute, 1988.

Scarpa, James. "Draft Choice." *Restaurant Business,* August 10, 1996, 117–118.

Schmuckler, Eric. "Niche Ability." *Brandweek,* April 29, 1996, 25–26.

Schwartz, Barry. *Queuing and Waiting: Studies in the Organization of Access and Delay.* Chicago: University of Chicago Press, 1975.

Schwoch, James. "Selling the Sight/Site of Sound: Broadcast Advertising and the Transition from Radio to Television." *Cinema Journal* 30, no. 1 (1990), 55–66.

Sconce, Jeffrey. *Haunted Media: Electronic Presence from Telegraphy to Television*. Durham, N.C.: Duke University Press, 2000.

Seiter, Ellen. *Sold Separately: Parents and Children in Consumer Culture*. New Brunswick, N.J.: Rutgers University Press, 1995.

Shagrin, Ceril, and Richard Montesano. "Television's Unmeasured Audience: Out-of Home Television Viewing." In proceedings of the ARF Fourteenth Annual Electronic Media Research Workshop. New York: Advertising Research Foundation, 1995, 120–135.

Shane, Irvin A. "Television for Retailers." *Televiser* (fall 1944): 34–35, 46.

Shapiro, Eben. "TV Commercials Chase Supermarket Shoppers." *New York Times*, May 25, 1992, 35.

Siegler, Dylan. "Bad Boy Links with Shoe Retailer for CD." *Billboard*, August 1, 1998, 65, 69.

Silverstone, Roger. *Television and Everyday Life*. New York: Routledge, 1994.

Silverstone, Roger, and Eric Hirsch, eds. *Consuming Technologies: Media and Information in Domestic Spaces*. London: Routledge, 1992.

Sloan, Pat. "Bozell Rewires Media Strategy." *Advertising Age*, December 16, 1991, 12.

Smith, Neil. "Contours of a Spatialized Politics: Homeless Vehicles and the Production of Geographic Scale." *Social Text* 33 (1992): 55–81.

Sorkin, Michael. Introduction to *Variations on a Theme Park: The New American City and the End of Public Space*, ed. Michael Sorkin, xi–xv. New York: Hill and Wang, 1992.

Spigel, Lynn. *Make Room for TV: Television and the Family Ideal in Postwar America*. Chicago: University of Chicago Press, 1992.

———. "Seducing the Innocent." In *Ruthless Criticism: New Perspectives in U.S. Communications History*, ed. William Solomon and Robert W. McChesney. Minneapolis: University of Minnesota Press, 1993.

Sposa, Louis. *Television Primer of Production and Direction*. New York: McGraw-Hill, 1947.

Stanley, Trowbridge H. "Display . . . the BASIS of Merchandising." *Display World*, May 1945, 24.

Steenhuysen, Julia. "Whittle Rips 'Out-of-Step' Shops." *Advertising Age*, August 27, 1990, S-2.

Steinowitz, Ira, Judith Graham, and Laurie Freeman. "IRI Rolls into Future with Video Carts." *Advertising Age*, May 2, 1988, 6.

Stensgaard, W. L. "The Shape of Things to Come." *Display World*, September 1944.

———. "Showmanship for Intra-Store Television." *Display World*, December 1945.

Stern, Edith M. "Buy-Paths to Learning." *Reader's Digest*, May 1938.

Stewart, Larry. "Bars Want to Take It, so Networks Could Dish It Out." *Los Angeles Times*, September 7, 1990, C3.

Strasser, Susan. *Never Done: A History of American Housework*. New York: Pantheon Books, 1982.

Tanaka, Wendy. "Move Over Billboards, Advertising Industry Taking a Chance on Apples." *State Journal-Register* (Illinois), 1997, 20.

Thomas, Morris. "Department Store Problems." *Journal of Marketing* 8, no. 1 (1943): 21–24.

Thomas, Nicholas. *Entangled Objects: Exchange, Material Culture, and Colonialism in the Pacific*. Cambridge, Mass.: Harvard University Press, 1991.

Thrasher, Paula Crouch. "Children's Theater." *Atlanta Journal-Constitution*, September 30, 1995, 22L.

Thrift, Julia. "What's in Store for Brands." *Marketing*, February 27, 1997, 25–29.

Torres, Sasha. "King TV." In *Living Color: Race and Television in the United States*, ed. Sasha Torres. Durham, N.C.: Duke University Press, 1999.

Underhill, Paco. *Why We Buy: The Science of Shopping*. New York: Simon and Schuster, 1999.

Urry, John. *Consuming Places*. New York: Routledge, 1995.

Ursin, Cheryl. "Theme Restaurants Play to Diners' Appetite for Fun." *Restaurants USA*, August 1996, 25.

Vanderbilt, Tom. *The Sneaker Book: An Anatomy of an Industry and an Icon*. New York: New Press, 1998.

Vaneigem, Raoul. *The Revolution of Everyday Life*. Trans. Donald Nicholson-Smith. London: Left Bank Books and Rebel Press, 1983.

Venturi, Robert. *Iconography and Electronics: Upon a Generic Architecture—A View from the Drafting Room*. Cambridge, Mass.: MIT Press, 1996.

Verity, John W. "Move Over, Jimmy Johnson." *Business Week*, August 12, 1996, 86D.

Vicas, Astrid. "Reusing Culture: The Import of Détournement." *Yale Journal of Criticism* 11, no. 2 (1998): 381–406.

Waldrip, Lee. "Display and Visual Merchandising." *Display World*, June 1948.

Walton, Scott. "People in the Arts: Ron Lee." *Atlanta Journal-Constitution*, August 7, 1994, N2.

Warg, Peter. "Commuters Red over Blue Flicks." *Variety*, February 22–28, 1999, 168.

Wark, Tammi. "Business Travel Today." *USA Today*, December 26, 1996, 1B.

Weber, Samuel. *Mass Mediauras: Form, Technics, Media*. Palo Alto, Calif.: Stanford University Press, 1996.

Weiss, E. B. "Demonstrators, Mechanical Demonstrators, and Intra-Store Television." *Printer's Ink*, May 28, 1948, 46, 50, 92–93.

———. "Department Stores Are Becoming Chain Stores." *Printer's Ink*, December 5, 1947, 39–40, 62, 66, 68.

———. "How to Sell to and through the New Department Store." *Printer's Ink*, November 28, 1947, 31–34, 72, 76, 78.

———. "New Concepts of Store Architecture Affect Store Promotion." *Printer's Ink*, March 26, 1948, 42, 46, 48–49, 52.

———. "Self-Service and Robot Selling." *Printer's Ink*, June 11, 1947, 42–43, 72.

———. "That Proverbial Weak Link: The Sales Person." *Printer's Ink*, April 30, 1947, 42–46.

Weiss, Michael J. *The Clustering of America*. New York: Harper and Row, 1988.

Wenner, Lawrence A. "In Search of the Sports Bar: Masculinity, Alcohol, Sports, and the Mediation of Public Space." In *Sport and Postmodern Times*, ed. Genevieve Rail, 301–332. Albany: State University of New York, 1998.

White, Mimi. "Site Unseen: CNN's *War in the Gulf*." In *Seeing through the Media: The*

Persian Gulf War, ed. Lauren Rabinovitz and Susan Jeffords, 121–141. New Brunswick, N.J.: Rutgers University Press, 1994.

———. *Tele-Advising: Therapeutic Discourse in American Television.* Chapel Hill: University of North Carolina Press, 1992.

Whiteman, Paul. "Video: Showbiz in the Parlor." *Variety,* July 28, 1948, 26.

Wilkie, Maxine. "Scent of a Market." *American Demographics* 17 (August 1995): 40–43.

Williams, Mara Rose. "Local UNCF's Art Auction Ranks High as Fund-Raiser." *Atlanta Journal-Constitution,* February 20, 1997, 7N.

Williams, Mark. "From 'Remote' Possibilities to Entertaining 'Difference': A Regional Study of the Rise of the Television Industry in Los Angeles, 1930–1952." Ph.D. diss., University of Southern California, 1992.

———. "History in a Flash: Notes on the Myth of TV 'Liveness.' " In *Collecting Visible Evidence,* ed. Jane Gaines and Michael Renov, 292–312. Minneapolis: University of Minnesota Press, 1999.

———, ed. *Quarterly Review of Film and Video: Special Issue on Local Television* 16, nos. 3/4 (1999).

Williams, Raymond. *Television: Technology and Cultural Form.* New York: Schocken Books, 1975.

Wilson, Earl. *I Am Gazing into My Eight Ball: Burning the Midnight Earl with New York's Famous Saloon Editor.* Garden City, N.Y.: Doubleday, Doran, 1945.

Wodiczko, Krzysztof. *Critical Vehicles: Writings, Projects, Interviews.* Cambridge, Mass.: MIT Press, 1999.

Wodiczko, Krzysztof, Douglas Crimp, and Barbara Kruger. "Discussion." In *Dia Art Foundation Discussions in Contemporary Culture Number One,* ed. Hal Foster, 46–53. Seattle: Bay Press, 1987.

Yang, Mayfair Mei-hui. Introduction to *Spaces of Their Own: Women's Public Sphere in Transnational China,* ed. Mayfair Mei-hui Yang. Minneapolis: University of Minnesota, 1999.

Zelizer, Barbie. "From Home to Public Forum: Media Events and the Public Sphere." *Journal of Film and Video* 43, nos. 1/2 (1991): 69–79.

Zerubavel, Eviatar. *Hidden Rhythms: Schedules and Calendars in Social Life.* Chicago: University of Chicago Press, 1981.

Ziencek, Sophie. Interview by author. Chicago, September 19, 1993.

Anna McCarthy is Assistant Professor of Cinema Studies at New York University.

Library of Congress Cataloging-in-Publication Data

McCarthy, Anna.

Ambient television : visual culture and public space / Anna McCarthy.

p. cm. — (Console-ing passions)

Includes bibliographical references and index.

ISBN 0-8223-2683-3 (alk. paper) — ISBN 0-8223-2692-2 (pbk. : alk. paper)

1. Television broadcasting—Social aspects. I. Title. II. Series.

PN1992.6 .M377   2001

302.23′45—dc21   00-045183